A VALUABLE CONTRIBUTION

A VALUABLE CONTRIBUTION

THE LIFE STORY OF **BILL SINCLAIR** MA MBE

COLIN ROBBIE

First published in the United Kingdom in 2020 by
The Cloister House Press

Hardback
ISBN 978-1-913460-07-5
Paperback
ISBN 978-1-913460-06-8

In memory of

Ann Robbie (née Sinclair) and Bob Robbie

I still can't quite believe you're no longer around

To

Alex and Callum

'For posterity,' as Grandma would have said. Lest we forget

A person's value should not be measured in monetary terms or material possessions, but rather by the contribution and positive influence they have on the lives of others

Anonymous

CONTENTS

ABBREVIATIONS

02E	2nd Echelon
AAG	Assistant Adjutant General
AG	Adjutant General
APO	Army Post Office
ATS	Auxiliary Territorial Service
Brig	Brigadier
DAAG	Deputy Assistant Adjutant General
GHQ	General Headquarters
HQ	Headquarters
LRDG	Long Range Desert Group
NAAFI	Navy, Army and Air Force Institutes
NCO	Non-commissioned Officer
OCTU	Officer Cadet Training Unit
OTC	Officer Training Corps
PPA	Popski's Private Army
PT	Physical Training
PW	Prisoner of War
RAF	Royal Air Force
Rfts	Reinforcements
RSM	Regimental Sergeant Major
SAS	Special Air Service
UNWCC	United Nations War Crimes Committee
US	United States
WAAF	Women's Auxiliary Air Force

EARLY YEARS

William George Syme Sinclair was the youngest of seven siblings living at 14 Bristro Street, Leith. He was just fifteen years old and having lost both his parents to illness William was raised by an older brother and his wife. This led to something of an unhappy childhood for William, but football was the one notable exception. He was a talented player and turned out for several local clubs as he honed his skills and sought comfort and a sense of belonging with friends and teammates.

The *Edinburgh Citizen and Portobello Advertiser* of 9th February 1912 ran with the following review of Wemyss Athletic centre half and captain: W.G.S. Sinclair.

> In Midlothian circles, a better known and more popular player it would be difficult to find. Following an early training in the Boy's Brigade, Sinclair played for Alva Rangers, a second-class juvenile team which made quite a name for itself at that time. Amongst his club mates then were [T.] Aitken and G. Wood, (who are presently playing with him in the Prestonpans combination), Phillips and Yorston (Penicuik), and Logan, now of Bradford City. After serving a season with Dalry Albert in first-class juvenile circles, during which period he was selected to represent Edinburgh against Fifeshire, he joined the junior ranks — Dalkeith Thistle, Bonnyrigg Rose and Wemyss Athletic in turn benefitting by his services.

> As a centre-half, he is in the first flight amongst Midlothian Juniors, being strong in breaking-up tactics. That he still remains a junior is entirely his own fault, as he has had offers from Hearts,

Saints, Leith and several Fifeshire clubs. He has played at different times trial games for the clubs mentioned, but for business reasons prefers meantime to retain his junior status. Since joining Wemyss Athletic the club has become famous all over junior Scotland, and not a little of that is due to the superb play and generalship of Sinclair.

William became a warehouseman at Crabbies[1] before the Great War of 1914 took him into military service with the Royal Scots. By the time William was abroad fighting for King and Country, he'd met and married Elizabeth Knight Wilson McKenzie. In contrast to her husband, Elizabeth's childhood had been happy and simple. The McKenzies originated from Caithness, but Elizabeth's father worked at sea and travelled south before settling in Leith and starting a family of his own. Elizabeth was one of ten children born between 1880 and 1902. The family first lived in Bothwell Street off Easter Road before flitting a few miles to Gorgie Road.

Leith, with its papermills and distinctive redolence was where William Sinclair and Elizabeth McKenzie first met. They married on 21st November 1913 and took up residence back toward Easter Road. In 1914, the newly-weds were dealt a bitter blow when William was conscripted and sent abroad to fight. He despaired at having to leave his beloved wife, but duty called. During a period of leave for William in late 1915, Elizabeth fell pregnant, but the Royal Scots returned William to the frontline. It was a last goodbye to Leith and his much-loved wife.

The baby, William George McKenzie Sinclair (hereafter referred to as Bill) was born at the family home, 78 Iona Street, Leith on 16th July 1916. Just fourteen months later, his mother received the news she dreaded. Her husband had been killed in action near the Frezenberg Ridge at the third

---

[1] Producers of ginger wine and blended whisky

Battle of Ypres (Passchendaele), on 21ˢᵗ September 1917, aged twenty-seven.[2] William never met his son Bill.

Elizabeth moved back to her father's house in Gorgie Road. Her mother had passed away in 1914 but Ruth and Lily, two of Elizabeth's nine siblings, still lived with their father, who by that time, had crippling rheumatism. Elizabeth was able to help care for her father, and her sisters helped Elizabeth with the baby. Her father passed away in 1919.

Gorgie Road was the focal point for McKenzie gatherings and there was an open door for members of the family needing a temporary stopgap. Those first two decades of the twentieth century saw the McKenzie's spread out across the globe as far as South Africa and Canada, but home for Elizabeth's five brothers and four sisters would always be Edinburgh. Elizabeth remained ready to receive guests and provide good food and a warm atmosphere, and it was an environment in which her son flourished. Bill's Uncle Dan moved in for a short while before emigrating to South Africa, and Auntie Lily married and left soon after. Bill's Uncle George, known as Dod, had followed in his father's footsteps, serving as a merchant seaman with the Royal Navy. He married and divorced in a short period of time. During the marriage, his wife had an illegitimate child, George, for whom Uncle Dod took responsibility. However, with time away at sea, it was Elizabeth who raised him alongside her own son. Cousin George was four years older than Bill.

From 1921 to 1925, Bill attended Dalry Primary School where he enjoyed playing simple outdoor games such as Peevers, Girds and Hessie. Peevers involved chalking out a grid with numbers, then kicking a flat stone

---

[2] Lance Corporal W.G.S. Sinclair 351393, 'B' Company. 9th Battalion. Royal Scots is commemorated at Tyne Cot Memorial, Belgium: Panel 11 to 14 and 162. He is also listed in the Scottish National War Memorial Roll of Honour, held at Edinburgh Castle

or an empty boot polish tin, into the required square before hopping around it. Girds were large wooden, or metal, rings topped with a cleek to propel the ring along. In Hessie, the whole team had to be captured, and if one penetrated the den before this happened, all existing prisoners were released and the whole business started again. However, Bill preferred ball games. In the early 1920s he developed a passion for football, which would last a lifetime. Street games of football, known as fitba, were played with a rubber ball, or more often, a newspaper rolled up and bound with string.

Elizabeth showed Bill photographs and told him tales of his father's footballing abilities: Wemyss Athletic in 1912-13, Broxburn FC the following year, and spells at Airdrieonians and Leith FC.

As a youngster, Bill joined Tynecastle Rovers. He dreamed of being a footballer in the same vein as his father. Elizabeth, however, had more academic aspirations for her son. She had left school at the age of twelve to become a cleaner and was determined Bill should grasp the opportunity to do well at school. In the 1920s, Leith was expanding. Fields were being replaced by a plethora of shops, tenements, factory works and opposite 53 Gorgie Road — a cinema.

The better off entered the new cinema via the front door, paying 6 pence or 9 pence, which bought a tip-up seat at the back. Bill and his friends had to queue up in a passage at the side door, and for 2 pence or 3 pence the lads sat at the front on long, hard benches. The silent films were visually dramatic and the mood was enhanced by a pianist who played along to the films' changing themes: fast and racy to accompany a chase, sentimental Victorian melodies for love scenes and happy endings. Bill loved going to the pictures and would do so whenever he could afford it. Meanwhile, Elizabeth was becoming concerned that Gorgie Road no longer provided the kind of life she wanted for her family.

By 1926, Auntie Ruth had married her sweetheart Willie McAdam and moved to County Durham. She remained a frequent visitor to Gorgie Road and held Bill in high regard all of her life, as he did her. Uncle Dod, Uncle Bert, Auntie Meg, Auntie Lily and Uncle Jim all visited at various times, and when family gathered, there were frequent picnics to Dalmeny Woods, Cramond and the Pentlands — a place that would later hold special significance for Bill.

Elizabeth was still not sure about the long-term suitability of Gorgie Road as a home for her young family. Her brothers and sisters advised her to sell the property, insisting she keep all of the proceeds.[3] Elizabeth sold the McKenzie family home in 1928 for the sum of £250, just after the first electric tram arrived in the road. Her new home was 48 Cowan Road, just a mile south, but more residential and not too much further for Bill to travel to school. Elizabeth had successfully applied to The Heriot's Foundation, a fee-paying school which, at the discretion of the governors, offered succour and full fee remission to the sons and daughters of widows.

Bill's beginnings at Heriot's were not particularly noteworthy, but he worked his way up through the class and completed his Highers with aplomb, earning the dux medal in History during his final school year. At Heriot's he also joined the Officer Training Corps (OTC). He enjoyed the camaraderie of the corps, but it also fulfilled his desire for structure and discipline. He attained Certificate 'A' in November 1932.[4] Bill had high standards and worked aggressively to achieve them. His personal characteristics and academic results endeared him to the teaching staff at Heriot's and brought him to the attention of Headmaster, William Gentle.

Also at Heriot's, Bill discovered another ball game that would be a

---

[3] Elizabeth's siblings offered her the property as she was the only McKenzie to have lost someone to the First World War. The McKenzie boys all returned safe and sound
[4] Bill would attain Certificate 'B' in 1936

significant feature, and source of frustration, in his life — golf. In the past, he had caddied for Uncle Dod, plodding around the nine-hole course at Saughton. With the club moving in 1929 and becoming Carrick Knowe, Bill took up the sport for himself. He enjoyed playing and became proficient, despite a tendency to hit the ball too firmly in his youth. Childhood friends who would remain so for life joined in, and Ian Hunter, Dougie McVey, Billy Tait and others, took up the burgeoning sport. Bill went on to play for the school and won the class competition of 1929.

In 1933, Heriot's school golf club had one of its most successful seasons. A good victory over Stewart's was followed by sound wins against the Royal High School and Watson's. In the latter game, Heriot's won the foursomes by three games to two and the singles by six and a half to three and a half, which at the time represented their best victory. Against the Heriot's Former Pupil's Golf Club, they retained the Wallace Cup and completed the fixture with the Master's match at Baberton. In the boys vs. staff game, Bill beat Mr Munro one to nil. Overall the boys ran out the winners eleven to four.

Bill later became a member of the Edinburgh Thistle Club, playing over the city's Braid Hills course. He also began a thirty-year association with the golf club at Lothianburn. He played there innumerable times, obtaining ever better scores despite — and perhaps owing to — the vicious crosswinds that were a feature of the course. With only four clubs and a couple of balls, Bill continued to improve and eventually became a scratch golfer.[5]

In 1934, with the support of his mother, Bill applied to the University of Edinburgh. Headmaster, William Gentle wrote the following commendation to support Bill's application.

I hereby certify that William G.M. Sinclair has been a pupil of

---

[5] Golfer with a handicap of zero

this school from 1925 until the present time. Throughout his course he has proved himself a pupil of marked ability and each year has taken a prominent place in the prize list. In 1933 he was awarded the Group Leaving Certificate of the Scottish Education Department with passes in English, Higher Mathematics, Higher Science, Higher French and Lower Latin and this year he is a candidate for Higher Latin, Mathematical Analysis and Additional Geometry. In class work he has again shown himself to be one of the best of our pupils, and in History in particular has done exceptionally good work.

William Sinclair is highly industrious, of pleasing personality and of excellent character. I anticipate for him a highly successful career at the University, and it is with the fullest confidence I recommend his application for a University Bursary for favourable consideration.

Of the 878 candidates from 496 schools applying for a Kitchener Scholarship, 155 awards were made. Bill was one of them and is listed in the Kitchener Record of Scholars from that year.

'Wemyss Athletic Football Club 1912-13'
William George Syme Sinclair (seated centre holding ball)
T. Aitken and G. Wood are seated to the left and right of William respectively

William George Syme Sinclair (back row, second player from right)

William George Syme Sinclair
(back row, right), 1915

Elizabeth K.W. Mckenzie Sinclair
with son, Bill Sinclair, 1916

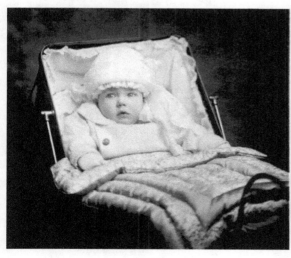

'1917'
Bill Sinclair

'Good luck, Uncle Dan, 1918'
Bill Sinclair

'Tyncastle Rovers FC'
Bill Sinclair (front row, right)

Willie McAdam (front) with wife
Auntie Ruth, Uncle Dod,
Bill Sinclair (back)

'School trip to Clermont Ferrand'
Bill Sinclair

Bill Sinclair (front row, left)
Billy Tait (back row, left)

*'Millport 1933, in the days
when I tried to knock every ball to
the edge of the earth'*
Bill Sinclair

'Varsity OTC Camp, 1937'
Bill Sinclair (back row, second from right)
Jack McKenzie (no relation: back row, second from left)

OTC camp
Bill Sinclair (far left)

In 1914, some three miles north east of the Sinclair household at Gorgie Road, John Blair Verth and his wife, Elizabeth Catherine Verth (née Moncur) were starting out as a married couple. Like William George Syme Sinclair, John was in the Royal Scots at the time of the First World War. John, an accomplished piper, met his wife to be, Elizabeth Catherine Moncur, before the conflict. They married on 4th September 1914 and lived at 4 Northumberland Place.

John was a picture frame gilder and later a sorting clerk and telegraphist at the General Post Office. For a time, he was also piper to the Countess de la Warr. Elizabeth was a seamstress. They had two children; Elizabeth McGillivary Verth (hereafter referred to as Lisbeth), born on 6th October 1915, and her brother John (known as Jack), born four years later on 12th November 1919.

Lisbeth attended Leith Walk Primary School. She was a bright child with a passion and a talent for the piano, encouraged by her mother from an early age. In view of this, in July 1929, the Edinburgh Education Authority awarded Lisbeth a Secondary Bursary. This was tenable at any recognised secondary school in the city. After some deliberation, the family chose Broughton School on McDonald Road. Lisbeth performed well at Broughton, gaining the Scottish Leaving Certificate in 1932 and receiving a commendation from Headmaster, W.L. Parson.

> Elizabeth Verth has now completed with great credit the full secondary certificate course and has gained the Scottish Leaving Certificate. Her conduct has been exemplary. I can commend her with great confidence.

Lisbeth was further assisted by a commendation from the minister, George Christie, at St Andrew's Church, George Street, Edinburgh, where she had been part of the congregation.

> I have great pleasure and every confidence in recommending

> Miss Elizabeth Verth, 4 Northumberland Place, as I have known her all her life. She comes from a most self-respecting and worthy family, and she sustains the very best they can show. She has been successful at school, is industrious and intelligent, with a bright and happy nature. She is most willing and eager in her duties. She has a pleasing address, is frank and yet refined in manner. She ought to give every satisfaction in office-work. She also has musical abilities and training of no ordinary standard.

The Caledonian Insurance Company offered Lisbeth a secretarial position in its Investment Department. Her compensation was 15 shillings per week.

Some five years later, in 1937, Lisbeth met a young man named Bill Sinclair.

John Blair Verth, 1915

John Blair Verth and wife
Elizabeth Catherine Verth (right)
with daughter, Lisbeth Verth

Catherine Bayne Verth (Auntie Kate), twin
sister of John, is seated on the left, 1916

'From Flo and Meg Moncur, 4th March 1918'
Lisbeth Verth

'Arbroath 1935'
Lisbeth Verth

Lisbeth Verth and brother,
John (Jack) Verth

Lisbeth Verth (back right)

Bill Sinclair and Lisbeth Verth were introduced over a partition in the Investment Department at the Caledonian Insurance Company, and first stepped out together on 18th November 1937. That first outing saw the nervous couple seek the relative safety of the pictures before hiking through the snow to Liberton and along the road to Fairmilehead, blissfully unaware of anyone but themselves. And so, began a relationship that soon flourished.

When Lisbeth was away on holiday or spending weekends with friends, the couple wrote to each other. The chaps at work pulled Bill's leg about it.

'If only you moved on a football pitch as quickly as you do getting up to scour the post every morning Bill,' Charlie Sullivan scoffed.

Teasing was not confined to the office. Lisbeth's mother and her brother Jack also made jokes about Bill's miserable demeanour when Lisbeth was not around.

Bill still had studies to contend with and they provided a much-needed distraction for the love-struck young man. He graduated in 1938 with an Ordinary Degree of Master of Arts (MA).

In 1938, Bill applied to study for his Teachers General Certificate at Moray House and was accepted. He continued playing sport and was awarded the Full Blue colours for golf in the 1938 to 1939 session. This entitled Bill to wear an Oxford Blue scarf and blazer with the date in silver lettering on the blazer and initials on the scarf.

Like his father before him, Bill was a talented football player and was becoming noticed. A review in the *People's Journal* read:

> W.G. Sinclair who has been transferred from Edinburgh University to Southern Amateurs, is about the best left back in Lothian Amateur circles.

Bill's life could not have been any better. He was enjoying his studies, relishing football, excelling at golf and falling in love. He longed to be with Lisbeth forever and asked her to marry him.

For reasons Bill could not comprehend Lisbeth refused his proposal. It was a devastating blow to the young man and resulted in a period of separation for the couple. Heartbroken, Bill threw himself into his studies. He missed Lisbeth dreadfully, but resisted the temptation to stay in contact. The proximity of the pair at work made things extremely difficult and caused time in the office to tick by slowly.

After what felt like an eternity, but in reality was only a matter of months, Lisbeth approached Bill and asked if they could try again. He was nervous of being hurt, but Lisbeth assured him she had simply felt pressured, and wasn't ready to commit at the time of his marriage proposal. She now realised that she could not imagine being separated from Bill forever. The relationship blossomed second time around and each became more serious in their intentions toward the other. They discussed marriage again and considered 1941 as a possibility for their wedding. Things were looking up for the couple.

On 30th March 1939, Lisbeth received the diploma she had been studying for, the coveted Licentiate of the Royal Academy of Music (LRAM) or as Bill sometimes called it, the 'Lisbeth Recently Annoyed Me' diploma. It was hung the same day in Northumberland Place.

Bill had a new football team. His transfer to Polkemmet had been confirmed. Polkemmet Juniors Football Club was formed for the 1938 to 1939 season and Bill joined the club in its second year, as it would give him the chance to play in front of larger crowds. For games such as the Scottish Cup, there could be up to three thousand spectators watching and Bill relished their roar. Later in life, he would look back on those days with great fondness. One match firmly stuck in his mind. The away game took place on October 28th 1939 at Winchburgh. Polkemmet won 6–2 with the following match report published in the *People's Journal*.

Winchburgh Juniors were beaten by a much better side when

they met Polkemmet Juniors at Winchburgh, although had Stirling scored from a penalty award in the first half a better result might have been returned. Muir returned to the Harthill side and scored three goals, Murray, Sinclair and Gallacher having the other Polkemmet points. Chalmers and Wallace accounted for the Winchburgh goals in the second half.

For that game Bill's wages were 11 shillings and 6 pence, and after deducting expenses, he'd netted a goal and 10 shillings profit. Bill went on to win an East of Scotland Cup medal with Polkemmet having transferred over from the defunct Dalkeith Juniors as an inside-left of decided promise.

Life would have been perfect for the couple if it hadn't been for the threat of war in Europe and uncertainty around what that might mean for Bill, and so they resolved to prove their commitment to each other and were engaged to be married on 1st September 1939. They dreamed of living in a wee house with a cosy warm fire and a gaggle of children.

In order to achieve their dreams, Bill would need to find gainful employment. By this time, he'd successfully completed four terms at Moray House and went out in search of a suitable teaching position.

Lisbeth Verth

'30th September 1938'
Bill Sinclair

Bill Sinclair

Bill Sinclair

In the early part of 1939, Adolf Hitler made plans to invade Poland and set a date of 1st September for the offensive. To mitigate the risk of being undermined, the Führer held secret talks with the Russians in August on the possible division of Poland. Diplomatic attempts to prevent the invasion of Poland failed and German hostilities began as planned.

In response to the invasion, Britain declared war on Germany on 3rd September. Prime Minister Neville Chamberlain confirmed this in a radio broadcast across the Empire.

On 17th September, with Germany already having made significant western advances into Poland, Russia began their invasion from the east. By 19th September, more than half of Poland was under Russian control and by the end of the month, Germany and Russia had agreed how to divide the country between them.

Hitler had been working on a European peace proposal, but Chamberlain subsequently rejected this on 12th October. The same day brought with it the first deportation of Austrian and Czech Jews to Poland. Four days later, the first bombing raid by the Luftwaffe over British skies took place along the Firth of Forth in an attempt to destroy the Forth Bridge. The attack failed and saw the first successful Spitfire downing of an enemy aircraft in the war.

At the end of November, Russia invaded Finland after its refusal to relinquish territory. The so-called Winter War followed, during which, the smaller Finnish Army inflicted significant damage on their invaders. The brave Finn's were helped by smart defensive tactics and bitterly cold temperatures.

By the beginning of December 1939, Royal Air Force (RAF) reconnaissance flights, were evolving into successful bombing raids against German warships. On 14th December this air-assault activity was matched by the first major naval battle of the conflict at River Plate.

The day after declaring war on Germany, the British Expeditionary Force under General Lord Gort had moved to France, but during those first few months they only engaged in minor skirmishes. The relative quiet led to the coining of the term, Phoney War. As New Year chimed in, this would not be the case for much longer.

YOUNG TEACHER

In January 1940, the RAF was patrolling the North Sea, and British Army numbers had swelled to more than a million. The country felt the first effects of food shortages as the government restricted butter, sugar and bacon. Paper was rationed from February and meat from March. Imports of food and other supplies were crucial, and so Allied shipping was protected.

The Suez Canal was a key component of British supply lines and provided a shorter sea route from its Empire. Middle East oilfields were also crucial in sustaining the Allied war effort. On 12th February 1940, Australians and New Zealanders began arriving in Suez to support the build-up of Allied forces. The General Officer Commanding Middle East was Archibald Wavell. His task was to build up Delta and Western Desert defences, without provoking the Italians, whose troops in the region outnumbered the British five to one. Wavell utilised the Long Range Desert Group (LRDG) for observation and intelligence gathering, deep into the desert behind Italian lines. These elite men quickly gained notoriety and status owing to the survival skills they had honed in the desert. LRDG information and action was extremely valuable to General Headquarters (GHQ) in the Middle East.

Like Allied forces, Nazi Germany also needed to secure supplies for the war effort but did not have the resources to serve its voracious appetite. Hitler had sought to agree a deal with Russia to provide raw materials as early as 1939 and the two countries finalised an agreement in February 1940. Italy and Germany would also create a pact, the so-called Pact of Steel, agreeing to a military and political alliance which gave rise to the birth of the Axis powers. This later expanded to become the Tripartite Pact, with Japan being the third constituent part.

Finland and Russia continued their Winter War into the early part of 1940. The Finns were suffering under a renewed Russian offensive. Their subsequent defeat resulted in the Moscow Peace Treaty, signed on 12th March. The treaty had Finland relinquishing border territory and what amounted to almost one-third of its economy. Despite Finland's concessions, the Soviets suffered significant losses in the Winter War. This poor military performance gave Hitler the impression that a German invasion of the Soviet Union could be successful, irrespective of the trade agreement forged between them, but this invasion would not be attempted until 1941.

In March 1940, Germany launched raids on Scapa Flow, the British naval base in the Orkney Islands. Scapa Flow had been used successfully in the First World War, but its defences had fallen into disrepair and the base was penetrated with combined U-boat and air attacks in late 1939. On 16th March 1940, a further attack resulted in the first British civilian death in an air raid of the Second World War.

*****

Bill wrote to Lisbeth on 2nd January 1940 feeling more than a little despondent. He'd left her that morning bound for Invergowrie. For the next three months, the small village on the north west bank of the Firth of Tay would be his home, at least during the working week.

On the train out to Invergowrie, casting his gaze across the river to Newport-on-Tay and Wormit, Bill was astonished to see lumps of ice floating in the river. As the train passed the rail-crossing and the stumps of the original Tay bridge, he turned to look in the opposite direction, towards Dundee itself. The train continued to hug the Firth of Tay, passing the bandstand at Magdalen Green. Bill stared beyond to the channels of streets stretching up and away to the Perth Road. Strawberry Bank, Windsor Street and Minto

Place all came and went, before Magdalen Green faded from view and the train continued west.

At Invergowrie, Bill had arranged to meet a Mr Murray from the Education Board to learn more about the teaching role he was about to begin and he hoped the official could help him locate somewhere reasonable to stay. On arrival, Bill had to locate Mr Murray's house. He sought help from a young lad he met in the village who was familiar with the house and happily gave directions, but they were too complicated and so Bill handed over a penny for the lad to accompany him.

Mr Murray was not at home when Bill arrived, but he was invited in by Mrs Murray. Besides a welcome cup of tea, she suggested he call on Miss Blyth at Cora-Linn across the road. She had a room available and could take him in until the end of March.

Cora-Linn was a large stone house, containing two flats, where an English nurse named Miss McCartney was already staying. Like so many others in January 1940, her future was uncertain and she was on twenty-four-hour notice for call-up. The house was near the shore and Bill was lucky enough to be offered a bedroom with a gas fire and view of the Tay. He also had shared use of the lounge, and Miss Blyth confirmed that there was an electric light, plenty of hot water and a wireless that Bill was free to take as his own for the duration of his stay. Miss Blyth seemed like a pleasant woman and Bill confirmed that he'd take the room at the reduced rate of 25 shillings per week, owing to the fact that he would only be there Monday to Friday.

As Mr Murray had still not arrived, Bill took a walk around the village and back to the train station he'd arrived at. For future reference, he enquired about the various options of travel in to Dundee. From Invergowrie, it was 6 pence for a return bus ticket to the centre, or 6½ pence on the train. Bill decided he would use the tram in future because it was cheaper still. Continuing on his walk, he came to a frozen pond where children were skating and playing hockey. He watched for a short time, but soon became cold so carried on walking. Arriving back at the Murray household, Bill felt more comfortable with what lay ahead. Invergowrie was bitterly cold at that moment, but he imagined it would be very pleasant in the summer months. Mr Murray finally arrived home, and after a short chat everything was settled and Bill agreed to begin at the school without further delay.

The village school where Bill took up his temporary post had two hundred pupils, including an advanced division accommodating children up to the age of fourteen. There were five other teachers; four women and one man. The headmaster (another Mr Murray known as Old Murray) was also taking classes due to staff shortages. Local children and evacuees were stuffed into every available school space, and spilt out into two local churches.

It was a baptism of fire for Bill. He was teaching children of different ages from four different schools using different books. Teaching English to a class of twenty-nine pupils with eight copies of *The Merchant of Venice* between them was difficult. Bill wished he was anywhere else in those first few days. The other young male teacher was named Bingham and was from Glasgow, and between the two of them, they made the best of it. Understanding the distress of many of the pupils in their charge, the teaching staff tried to entertain as much as educate, putting on parties and short plays to bring some enjoyment to an otherwise chaotic and difficult situation.

Bill arranged to meet the headmaster with the aim of fixing the timetable and bringing a little more order to the school day. Old Murray approved and Bill organised the timetable to provide himself with a free period on Friday afternoons. This enabled him to get away a whole hour and a half earlier on the 2.45pm train to Edinburgh. Arriving at Waverly Station he would make his way to the pillar box outside Lisbeth's workplace and wait for his fiancée to appear. And so, began a new routine.

It was a bad winter. Bill was waking up to nine inches of snow, drifting to depths of seven feet in places. Even Old Murray had never seen it so bad and he'd lived in the wilds of Inverness and Perthshire. Despite the weather, Bill was now settling in to his first teaching position. Besides teaching Maths and English, he took football for the boys and began arranging matches with other schools. Football was always an enjoyable distraction, whether playing or watching. At school break-time, Bill encouraged all the children to play basketball and football, including the girls. He would sometimes participate and recalled the girls beating the boys when he was standing in as centre-half on their team.

'Ach, nae wunder!' complained one boy.

'Grin and bear it lad,' came the advice, with a smile.

Bill also travelled further afield to watch football matches. One Saturday in February with no fixture back in Edinburgh, he ventured to Dundee in search of a game. On the tram to Lochee, he asked a fellow traveller where to get off for Glenesk Park. They got on the blether[6] and the chap asked where Bill's gas mask was. He hadn't brought it and was told there was no chance of getting in to watch the football without it. Not wanting to turn back, Bill continued on to Glenesk Park. Stepping off the tram, he entered a local newsagent, turned on his charm and persuaded the shopkeeper's wife to loan him her gas mask carrier. They stuffed it with cardboard to add weight and a few minutes later Bill walked past the policemen and into the match with an air of complete innocence. He duly returned the gas mask carrier in good shape later that afternoon.

During those early days in Invergowrie, familiar faces were disappearing from daily life because of the call-up. Bill knew his time would come; it was just a matter of when. Lisbeth's brother, Jack Verth, had undergone

---

[6] A lengthy chat or gossip

his medical on the same day that Bill's friend Sandy Fraser had received a call-up. Sandy was to report to Chatham Barracks. Bill wondered whether this would be his recruit destination. When would it be? What would he have to do?

'Stop fretting Sinclair,' he scolded himself out loud.

Until orders were received, he resolved to focus on matters at hand and that meant doing what he could for the children at Invergowrie.

As nice a place as Invergowrie was, other than writing to Lisbeth and taking walks out when the weather permitted it, there was not much to do and trips to the cinema provided a welcome distraction. Bill's love of film had not diminished since those outings to the pictures on Gorgie Road. Miss Blyth told Bill to take his budgie (gas mask) to the pictures in Dundee, as they wouldn't let him in without it. Bill thought she was exaggerating but sure enough, when he arrived, everybody had their gas mask with them.

Bill and Bingham continued to put on small weekly shows with the school children and on one occasion, the minister asked them to arrange a repeat performance in aid of Black Watch and Church of Scotland huts in France. Both accepted with pleasure and began planning the special performance. Part of this would be a Victorian Quartet composed of three scene shifters and Bill. They would sing *Sweet Adeline* and *Nellie Dean* wearing curly moustaches and top hats to complete the look. There was also to be a band comprising piano, saxophone, violin, mouth organs and kazoos, one of which Bill was to be play. Jack Brown would play the piano, who at sixteen years old was one of the youngest cinema organists in the country. The performances were planned for the 22nd and 23rd March 1940, which were the first days of the school Easter holidays. There would be plenty of time to prepare and rehearse, providing everyone mucked in.

Though he knew it was coming, it was still a shock when Bill received notification from the King, that he was to go for his army medical in Dundee on Monday 11th March 1940. The first doctor said Bill's eyes were the best he'd tested since the war began, though Bill suspected he said that to everyone.

Eyesight: grade 1

Nervous system: 1

Chest: 1 (expansion 5 inches)

Hearing: 1

Teeth: defective upper, but grade 1

'You are going to marry a perfect specimen of manhood my dear,' Bill wrote later to Lisbeth. 'Sum total: grade 1.'

During the medical, Bill told them he was a secondary school teacher. He hoped it might influence where he was sent.

'Doesn't make any difference,' was the reply.

'Too bad,' retorted Bill.

Next, he was interviewed by a major from the Seaforth Highlanders, and presented his Officer Cadet Training Unit (OCTU) 'B' certificate. The major studied it and asked Bill if he was a non-commissioned officer (NCO).

'Sergeant,' he replied.

The major told Bill it would be up to the commanding officer to put him in for a commission. Bill asked about getting a commission in the Gunners.

'With your maths and MA, it should be all right. That's an Infantry B, but I think you stand as much chance there as in the Infantry.'

Bill wasn't supposed to get any choice in the matter, but the major said he would put him down for the Gunners if that was what he wanted.

The last doctor said that if Bill was a quarter-inch taller he'd be recommending him for the Guards.

'Gerrout,' barked Bill.

The doctor laughed.

'You're better off in the Gunners. Three months serving and then you'll get a commission with all the credentials you have.'

As a result, the officer put down not only Royal Artillery but Royal Artillery Field which meant the great big chaps away at the back — thank goodness. In his letter to Lisbeth, Bill wrote:

> I thought it better to take the chance of not getting a commission but of getting somewhere safer seeing he offered it to me. If you have to run, you get a big start! Better to be married late than never! All the other lads were getting Black Watch.

Bill counted himself lucky. He asked where he would be sent and was told it would probably be Arbroath. At any rate, it would be somewhere in Scotland, and this was comforting news. The following day, Bill considered his choice, but still concluded he'd made the right decision. Better the Artillery than the Infantry, and with hard work, perhaps he could get a couple of stripes soon enough. Whatever happened, Bill was sure it wouldn't be long before he would have to leave Invergowrie, and after such a short period of teaching there.

In that time, Bill had formed a good working relationship with Old Murray, the headmaster, and spent some of his evenings with him checking test papers and adjusting timetables. They also walked together and Bill found his elder to be very good company. Walking out west toward Longforgan or north toward Liff, Old Murray would entertain Bill with stories from his past and tales of teaching mishaps. They discussed varsity, past and present, teaching methods and how the character of teachers and their approach to the profession were evolving. Old Murray saw potential in Bill and even at such a young age, thought he was headmaster material.

Despite the war, Bill enjoyed life as a teacher and tried not to worry — at least most of the time. Classroom space continued to be a problem, and gardening and outdoor Physical Training (PT) lessons were restricted by the bad weather. One particular day, there was not a single space in school or either church in which Bill could teach, so he took the class for a walk along Tayside, throwing stones at the lumps of ice formed by the bitter cold. The children had a great time.

Throughout March, Bill and Bingham carried on with rehearsals for the concert, despite one or two objections to their use of the church organ, upon which several pieces depended.

'If we can't get it,' remarked Bill to Bingham, 'I'm going to chuck the whole thing up. I've had my fun out of it so I won't mind. In fact, it'll solve some problems for me.'

He was referring to the fact that the concerts were due to take place on a Friday and Saturday, which meant he would not get to see Lisbeth until the Sunday unless she could come to a show. He would also miss playing in the football match away at Ormiston.

To distract his friend, Bingham persuaded Bill to help him in the woodwork shed making walls and scenery for the concert, and in the afternoon, they travelled to Lochee (with gas masks) and saw Lochee Harp vs. Inverurie Locos in a fourth-round Scottish Juniors match. Lochee won 3–2. Bill felt both sides were pretty useless and that Polkemmet could beat the pair of them together.

'Lochee will be a sacrifice for someone in the fifth round for sure,' he quipped and Bingham laughed out loud.

During the working week, Lisbeth continued to write with news from Northumberland Place, telling Bill how she was spending her time. She wrote fondly of her best friend Ann Bathgate amongst others. Bill enjoyed reading about people he could picture in his mind's eye. How Bill wished he could be with Lisbeth all the time, planning their marriage and the rest of their lives. But that was a distant prospect.

Number 4 Northumberland Place, where Lisbeth lived with her parents, was situated at the east end of Northumberland Street and formed part of the New Town of Edinburgh designed by James Craig. It was a tenement building, constructed of large blocks in a spectrum of colours from warm sandy yellow to cool grey and black. Lighting in the communal stairway of Northumberland Place was provided by gas lamp. There were two families on each floor: the Drakes and the Galloways were on the first floor and the Verths and the Bairds on the second floor. The Verths' flat was quite large with good-sized rooms. The hub of the house was the kitchen where the windows faced south and they cooked on an old range. Across the hall was the parlour. The family didn't use this room much, unless someone wanted to play the piano or listen to 78s on the wind-up gramophone. There were three bedrooms; one faced south and the other two looked north towards the River Forth and the hills of Fife. There were also two sizeable box rooms and a coal store.

In the hallway, stood the Grandfather Clock, which had been handed down to Lisbeth's father, John, him being the eldest son. There was no bath-room in the house, just the lavatory with a wash-hand basin. Baths were taken at Auntie Kate's in Montgomery Street. Lisbeth's father, Kate's twin, took his bath there every Friday.

On Saturday 23rd March, Lisbeth managed to get the morning off work, so that she would arrive in time for the second show that day. Bill was thrilled. Miss Blyth had agreed to let Lisbeth use her room at Cora-Linn, and she would bunk in with Miss McCartney. She was eager to see the girl who corresponded so frequently with her lodger. Miss Blyth thought she must be special, given that Bill would often be seen running from Cora-Linn in the early evening hoping to catch someone going into Dundee who could post another letter for him.

An excited Bill wrote to Lisbeth to confirm he would meet her on the platform, and that she needn't bring a ration book or anything else. Miss Blyth was to take care of everything.

Snow White and the Seven Dwarfs was a real hit, with the infants just about blowing their teeth out trying to whistle *Heigh Ho*. The audience was in hysterics and Jack Brown's organ playing created just the right atmosphere. Despite rationing, there was a great feast of sandwiches, sausage-rolls, cakes and tea followed by trifles and jellies. Distracted by all the delicious food, nobody noticed the scene shifters stealthily changing the set and putting on their Victorian costumes. They did a wonderful turn, despite Bill's moustache slipping sideways and falling to the floor, which caused great hilarity among the audience. The most important thing for Bill, was that Lisbeth was there. All the characters and places he'd written about in those first three months of 1940, she could see and experience for herself. Bill proudly introduced everyone to his fiancée and Miss Blyth was a perfect host. Lisbeth was just as she'd imagined her to be.

Those two days together were special. As Bill kissed Lisbeth and waved her off from Dundee on the Sunday, neither knew that in ten days' time, Bill would be heading north on the first stage of a very long trip. His next letter to Lisbeth was addressed from 'C' Company, 8th Gordons, Skene Square School, Aberdeen.

NEW RECRUIT

In April 1940, both Germany and Great Britain were looking at the strategic importance of neutral Norway. Control of the Nordics would provide a base for operations in the North Sea, and both sides had an interest in securing supplies of iron ore, which were transported by rail from Sweden to the Norwegian port of Narvik. Germany got there first and soon gained control over Denmark and Norway. The Allies retreated.

On 10th May, Germany invaded the Netherlands, Belgium and Luxembourg. The same day, owing to the deteriorating situation in Norway, Prime Minister Chamberlain resigned and Winston Churchill took over, although Chamberlain continued to serve in the Cabinet. Churchill gave his first address to Parliament on 13th May 1940.[7] This was the first of his three *Battle of France* speeches, during which he offered the following words.

> We have before us an ordeal of the most grievous kind. We have before us many, many long months of struggle and of suffering. You ask, what is our policy? I can say: It is to wage war, by sea, land and air, with all our might and with all the strength that God can give us; to wage war against a monstrous tyranny, never surpassed in the dark, lamentable catalogue of human crime. That is our policy. You ask, what is our aim? I can answer in one word: It is victory, victory at all costs, victory in spite of all terror, victory, however long and hard the road may be; for without victory, there is no survival.

Despite their withdrawal from Norway, the British had in fact inflicted

---

[7] 'Blood, toil, tears and sweat' speech

a good deal of damage on the German Navy. This curtailed German naval activity in the English Channel area and would be critical to the survival of Allied troops at the end of May 1940 as they evacuated Dunkirk.

With Hitler's army heading west with speed, British and French troops took up defensive positions between Brussels and the advancing Germans. The Allies were confident the enemy could not breach the Maginot Line. In fact, the Germans avoided it, instead crashing through the supposedly impenetrable Ardennes Forest. Road and rail infrastructure from that point on, aided the pace of their advance, enabling the transport of large volumes of men, equipment and supplies to serve the ever-expanding front line.

On 17th May, Germany took control of Brussels and all Dutch resistance ended. With Belgium, Holland and Luxembourg now under Hitler's control, the German Army turned north west, forcing the Allies back towards the coast. The British Expeditionary Force in France was surrounded with their backs against the Channel. Authorisation to evacuate was given in the last week of May.

*****

Bill had purchased a small diary from Boots the Chemist in Dundee at the beginning of the year in anticipation of what was to come, but didn't make an entry until Wednesday 3rd April 1940 — the day he joined the army. He noted that the train pulled out of Invergowrie station at 8.57am. Dinner was taken at 12.05pm and after various lengthy stops, the train arrived at its destination of Aberdeen at 6.30pm.

Reporting to the Gordon Highlanders barracks, Bill braced himself for the tough tasks that would lay ahead. The reality was in stark contrast to expectation. The new recruits received no instruction and no uniform. They remained in their civvies and were simply encouraged to explore. Bill used the opportunity to write to Lisbeth. Keen to ensure that their correspondence would continue uninterrupted, he located the post office to find out what time to post letters so they reached Lisbeth the next morning, but was told the service was unreliable.

Bill was also keen to maintain his weekly involvement in football. Unfortunately, the battalion team had already been picked. He put his name down anyway, and was on the reserve list if injury prevented someone from playing. And if he couldn't play, then he would go to Pittodrie and watch Aberdeen vs. Arbroath in the next home match. This would be affordable now as the army had already paid Bill for the first time: 10 shillings. He had joined a machine gun battalion, and within ten weeks would learn to handle everything from a rifle to an anti-tank gun.

Before long, kit was issued: three shirts, three pairs of socks, two towels, shaving brush, razor, scarf and eating utensils — all in a kit bag. Beds were allocated, comprising three planks of wood on two low trestles, with a mattress (palliasse), a pillow and four blankets. The new recruits had to fill the mattress and pillow with straw before making their beds. As he tested his for comfort, Bill thought about the comfortable bed, the gas fire and the view over the Tay he'd just left behind. The lads reported for supper at 9pm. Cold meat, potatoes and turnips were served on a single plate washed down with warm tea. Pudding quickly followed with the same knife, fork and spoon used for everything.

Despite the rather basic sleeping arrangements, Bill had a good first night. It was no Cora-Linn, but he felt fresh the next morning and ready for what lay ahead. Beds were made in the same way as the OTC, and so this was a familiar task which Bill completed before having a wash, shave and some breakfast. It was a relaxed atmosphere that first morning. Bill lounged around before receiving his great coat and two pairs of boots. He was chuffed with the coat. It was a beauty — double-breasted and brand new. Less appealing was the balmoral bonnet that had to be worn, though having put it on, Bill glimpsed his reflection in the window and thought it quite suited him.

During the afternoon, Bill spent hours giving information: former addresses, occupations and details of his time in the OTC. This gave way to a relaxed and informative lecture from a corporal and a sergeant on battalion orders. After these formalities, the men were asked about their involvement in sport and Bill told them of his footballing exploits in the Midlothian Juniors. He also signed up for badminton and hockey hoping to get some kind of game if he couldn't play football. After that, there was a lecture given by the padre on saving — money and souls! Thereafter it was just mucking around before a gaggle of lads headed *en masse* to the pictures. The Kingsway cinema was an art deco building located on the corner of King Street and Frederick Street, the latter providing a separate entrance for the cheaper seats. Chatting and laughing, the lads piled in to watch *Follow the Fleet* with Fred Astaire and Ginger Rogers.

By day four, things were settling down and Bill was finding his feet, which was no doubt the reason for easing the lads into it in those first few days. The recruits were gaining knowledge about their new environment. Each company had a sports afternoon and on Fridays they went to the baths for an hour. The grub was good, rather plain, but substantial, with a three-course meal every day. Bill hoped to get back to Edinburgh whenever possible, and learnt that recruits were to get two free rail warrants per year and at other times enjoyed a thirty percent discount on the fare — around 15 shillings. Bill would get one free weekend every month and seven days holiday every three months. Following training, he expected to be off to Constantinople, or somewhere in Turkey, in October.

That evening there was another visit to the pictures, but this time it was the Palace Theatre. Like the Kingsway, it was an art deco cinema just a short walk from Union Street in Bridge Place. That night's showing was

The Stars Look Down and the atmosphere and chatter was much the same as it had been the night before. The lads were finding their feet and forming friendships, becoming familiar with each other and dispensing with formality. It was a departure from the day's other main event; witnessing an incendiary bomb display and how to put the same out. Bill later wrote to Lisbeth explaining the procedure and hoped that none landed near Cowan Road or Northumberland Place.

'They make a right mess,' he noted.

Despite being surrounded by a good bunch of lads, Bill felt somewhat lonely in those first few days. He missed Lisbeth, and the comforts of Cora-Linn seemed distant. He began to form friendships though, and was already on good terms with Lance Corporal Bill Young, who was in charge of their room.

With the first four days under their belt, the recruits began to fall into their new routine. Our Bill was not an early riser, so the 6am wake-up call was unwelcome, but manageable. There was a bed, kit and room inspection, a run around the barracks, then a wash and shave before breakfast at 7.30am. After breakfast, shoes, boots and brasses were cleaned and the rest of the day was spent drilling and parading. From 3.50pm the lads were free. Tea was served at 4.30pm and they could leave the barracks at 5pm (2pm on Saturdays). Supper was at 7pm. Weekends involved the same routine though everything started an hour later on Sundays, and there was a visit to church. The company would be on duty one night in four, but not before training was complete.

The barracks itself was in the Rosemount area of Aberdeen where Bill had stayed on a previous holiday with his mother. How long the lads would be at Skene Square nobody knew for sure, but the word was, they would remain there for a month or two, before travelling to camp. In the meantime, Bill would try his best to make a good impression, and was appointed official right marker for the squad during drills.

Their PT instructor was Jock Thomson, the former Everton and Scottish left-half who had retired from football in 1938.

> Jock was a six-foot tall, ferocious tackler with an eye for attacking ventures up the field. Signed in March 1930 from Dundee, the left-half was drafted in an attempt to try and steer the Blues away from relegation. However, it proved to be a case of too little, too late, as Everton were relegated to the Second Division that season after finishing bottom of the league. Despite the disappointing start to life at Goodison, Thomson went on to star in all of Everton's successes up until the outbreak of World War II. Everton bounced straight back up to the top flight the very next season — a campaign during which Thomson missed just one game. The season after, in 1931/32, the Toffees stormed to the Division One title and Thomson again played a key role in the success. He also left Goodison with an FA Cup winners medal after being part of the side that overcame Manchester City 3–0 in the 1933 final at Wembley.
>
> The Fife-born wing-half made only one international appearance in Scotland's 5–2 win over Wales — a game which was played shortly after Everton's 1932 title win. He retired from playing in 1938 after five goals in 296 appearances for the club and later had a brief spell as manager of Manchester City.[8]

If only the army offered more money and a more reasonable place to stay (near Edinburgh) it could be quite a good life, concluded Bill. It was the end of week one. He and Lisbeth were planning to meet up despite the cost. She would decamp to Aberdeen for a whole week in May, if Bill could find suitable lodgings.

---

[8] Everton Football Club, *Players: Jock Thomson*

The 9th April brought with it Bill's first lesson on the machine gun at Aberdeen. He'd had previous experience with the OTC, so was a little further ahead in knowledge and application than most of the lads. There was also news that within days they would travel to Newcastle for machine gun training. The training was normally three weeks in duration, but because the lads had little experience the sergeant estimated six weeks. This would knock Lisbeth's holiday plans around, but until Bill knew for sure there was not much that could be done. He soon came to realise that the army adjusted plans *ad infinitum*. Bill mentioned the training in his letter to Lisbeth that day. He also repeated a rumour that was doing the rounds at the barracks: the Nazis had invaded Denmark, and Norway had declared war on Germany.

'If the other neutrals do the same, the war will be over in six months,' he wrote.

But the reality of war was beginning to have a real impact on people around Bill. His lance corporal's brother had recently been torpedoed and drowned off the coast of Belgium. Bill was nervous for Lisbeth in Edinburgh and warned her to be careful if she had to walk home from visiting friends during blackouts.

On 10th April, Bill received news that the machine gun training would be split across four sites, twenty-five men to each site: Newcastle, Chester, Aldershot and Gosport. He immediately put in for a pass to take his civvies home and see relatives before leaving Aberdeen. Bill wrote to Lisbeth.

'I'll travel by 3.15pm Aberdeen — at Caley[9] 7.30pm Friday. Leave Waverly 4.30pm Sunday. If anything is altered, I'll let you know.'

But the very next day he had to cancel his plans. The commanding officer refused his request. The only way they could meet now was *en route*

---

[9] The 'Caley' was the Caledonian Station at the West End of Princes Street, Edinburgh. It was demolished in 1969-70

to machine gun training. Bill would have to pass through Edinburgh regardless of which site he was travelling to and hoped Lisbeth could make it to the station to grab a few precious minutes on the platform, before he continued on his journey. He would send a wire to Northumberland Place to let Lisbeth know what time to arrive and which platform to head for.

In the meantime, the amount of equipment piled onto the lads was growing: gas cape, gas eye-pieces, anti-gas ointment, rifle and bayonet, belts, straps and a tin hat.

'We'll be like packed ponies,' Bill wrote.

On Friday 12th April, Bill wrote to Lisbeth again. None of the soldiers would be told their destination until they were on the train. All Bill knew was the day of departure, Sunday 14th April.

'All army movements are secret,' barked the commanding officer. 'You can let your people know where you are once you get there!'

Bill did not see Lisbeth at Edinburgh. Along with many other lads on the train, he had strained at the window and scoured the platform, but to no avail. The train pulled off with some lads happy at having glimpsed, fleetingly, their loved ones. For others, including Bill, there was disappointment.

He arrived in Chester on Monday 15th April at 5.30am. He knew Chester was a Roman city of some standing and that there was a castle. More than that, he had no clue. The lads found themselves in some stables; this would be home for the night. Bill grimaced at the sleeping arrangements as he'd only managed an hour's kip the previous night, but there were no other options.

Chester Castle was a welcome sight the following day. Inside, the facilities were a distinct improvement on the stables. A big fireplace, lockers, iron mattresses, a wireless in every room, curtains on the windows. There was also a great billiard room; 8 pence per hour for the table — billiards or snooker. This was more like it!

The officer in charge seemed like a decent chap and talked to the group before seeing each lad individually. He asked Bill if he would take a commission, to which Bill replied 'yes,' if he could. The officer also mentioned that each platoon officer was given a certain amount of training as an ordinary PBI (Poor B------ Infantryman). In his opinion a machine gun regiment was as good if not better than the Royal Artillery and he advised Bill to give it some thought. For the time being, he would receive an update on Bill each week. If nothing untoward was reported, Bill would be put up to the commanding officer and he would get every third weekend off. Things were looking up.

Discipline at the castle was pretty relaxed and the food was good. Porridge, two boiled eggs, bread, butter and marmalade for breakfast; beefsteak pie (more pie than one could eat), peas and turnip for dinner with fruit and custard for afters. The lads were allowed out until midnight every day. On Wednesdays and Saturdays, training finished at 12.30pm and on Sundays they could get out as soon as they pleased. There was no requirement for puttees[10] — the lads could opt for shoes, rather than boots, if they wished. All of this was quite a departure from the strict routine and discipline of Aberdeen. Bill had also managed to get a game of football and hoped to become a regular.

On 16th April, Bill was selected for training in No. 1 squad, which was for candidates up for a commission. Only the best men were selected when vacancies became available. Bill's hopes for early selection were boosted on learning he was the only one with any experience of machine gun work. He also volunteered to do some clerical tasks to help process a large number of conscripts soon to be arriving and arranged to meet his mother and

---

[10] Long wool wraps covering the lower leg from the ankle to the knee

Auntie Meg in London on his weekend off. He would tell them that he and Lisbeth were now planning to marry within the year.

Bill had enjoyed some fine weather since joining the army and loading lorries bound for The Dale barracks at Chester Castle was hot, sweaty work. The warmth of the sun, even in April, reminded him of the time he and Lisbeth had spent walking in the Pentland hills the previous year. It had been so tranquil, just the two of them, hiking through valleys, jumping streams and climbing fences, before lying down together to rest and soak up the sun's rays.

'East, west, home's best, wherever you are dear, whatever you're doing, I'll think of you and what you mean to me.'

Bill snapped back to the present on hearing a shout of 'that's the last,' and two bangs on the side of the truck, confirming the driver was free to go.

Bill switched his thoughts to the forthcoming London trip. He would have to have some inoculations on that Friday, but Sergeant Lockley confirmed he would be fit to travel. If everything went to plan, Bill would be in London from 6.40pm on Friday to 4.50pm on Sunday. Bill and his mother would stay with Auntie Meg and her husband Jim at 57 Perrymead Street, Fulham.

The trip didn't get off to the best of beginnings. There was a delay with the inoculations and Bill missed his train. Instead, he caught the 3.15pm to Crewe and wrote to Lisbeth from there whilst waiting for the connection to Euston. Despite one arm stiffening up from the typhoid injection, Bill was looking forward to the weekend. When he finally arrived at Euston, Mother and Auntie Meg were waiting. They journeyed to Fulham by bus, had supper and went up to bed around midnight.

The following morning Uncle Jim was working, so Bill went with his mother and Auntie Meg to see the sights. They took in Westminster Abbey, the Houses of Parliament, Downing Street, the Cenotaph, Horse Guards

Parade; and the Caledonian Insurance Company! Lunch was taken in Piccadilly before seeing Carlton Terrace, St. James's Palace, Buckingham Palace, Green Park and Hyde Park.

The following morning, Bill and his mother walked down to the Thames and Bill decided this would be the perfect time to talk to her about Lisbeth.

'I'm thrilled Bill,' said his mother.

She would do all that she could to help them, whether in the form of a deposit for a house, or for furnishings; whatever the married couple wanted. A date for the wedding had not been set but Bill was hoping it might coincide with some leave at the end of September. In a letter to Lisbeth from London, he mentioned that they should talk about it during her trip. Lisbeth now planned to visit Bill in Chester, during May.

Life continued at Chester Castle for another month in much the same way as that first fortnight. The typical routine of drill, arming (rifle), machine gun practice on the thirty yard range, and elementary gun drill was not too arduous. Watching on was Sergeant Lockley. He was a decent man and Bill liked him immensely. It transpired he was in the same battle at Passchendaele in which Bill's father died. For his part, Lockley received the Military Medal. This connection strengthened the bond between sergeant and private and Lockley saw real potential in Bill. Amongst other things, he was impressing him with his machine gun skills, firing at thirty yards, traversing. Bill still hoped for a commission.

'Don't worry Jock,' Lockley said, 'you're a dead cert. for it.'

Besides machine gun skills, Bill had impressed with his footballing abilities and a hat trick in a Gordons vs. Cheshires game had not gone unnoticed. Chester, at the time a Third Division side, expressed an interest in him.

'It could be worth 10 to 15 shillings per game,' Bill wrote. But at the time, he was more excited about Lisbeth's imminent visit than a commission or playing for Chester. Everything was set for 11th May.

On 10th May, Bill received news that they were confined to barracks until further notice. Hitler had invaded Holland and Belgium. As it was, Bill's containment only lasted for two days, so the rest of the week with Lisbeth was unconstrained. They talked about marriage and headed out toward Wales for walks, although on the Wednesday, poor weather forced them into the pictures at short notice. The Regal in Chester provided a safe haven from the pouring rain and *Sherlock Holmes* was very enjoyable. It was a wonderful few days and things felt almost normal, but it was back to work the following Sunday after waving Lisbeth off at Chester Station.

The next morning, the brigadier gave a lecture and reckoned on the war only lasting a further five months. Peeling potatoes that evening, Bill reflected on this. The Germans had reached Arras and Amiens in France. They appeared to be going strong, but if they'd overreached themselves, their infantry might not be able to follow up with the same pace. If this happened, their motorised divisions would become isolated and vulnerable. Regardless, air raids were expected soon and Bill wrote to Lisbeth to ensure she was prepared.

'Make sure of your bucket of sand or dry earth,' he advised.

German advances resulted in noticeable activity at Chester. Bill's training duration was shortened and a move to Aldershot for officer cadet training was imminent. An OTC list was sent, and Lockley was to get everyone through inoculations, vaccinations and dental checks, so those affected could proceed to OCTU at a moment's notice. Chester racecourse was being covered with camouflaged tents, and they were setting up searchlights and anti-aircraft batteries all over the football pitches. Lisbeth asked Bill for more advice on dealing with an incendiary and he responded as follows.

If an incendiary bomb should burst inside the house, shovel

three-quarters of the sand on to the ground about one yard from the bomb. Then first deal with the flames round about the bomb. You can control them with water but <u>don't</u> throw water on the bomb itself. It will burst all over the place if you do. Once you have controlled the flames round about the bomb, shovel the sand from the <u>floor</u> on to the bomb, scoop it all up on your shovel and deposit in a bucket which should still contain a quarter of the sand at the foot, if you have followed this rambling lecture, darling.

And remember, if you get a gas warning, do not remove your mask until you get the <u>gas</u> all clear, as mustard gas and lewisite are persistent and hang about for days — even months in wee cubby holes.

'Our boys haven't returned from Liverpool yet,' Bill added in the same letter. 'There were nine hundred wounded arrived, all bombed from the air I believe. It seems that we shall have to build more aeroplanes.'

Bill no longer felt like a new lad in the army. Weeks of training and education was turning raw recruits into soldiers.

OFFICER CADET TRAINING

Despite one in seven soldiers failing to make it out of Dunkirk and leaving vast swathes of equipment and armour behind, Operation Dynamo — the evacuation of Dunkirk — was deemed a success. Churchill referred to it as 'a miracle of deliverance, achieved by valour.' Losses aside, the mass evacuation enabled the Allies to regroup for what lay ahead. Churchill made this future intent clear in his 4th June address — the second of his Battle of France speeches.[11]

> We shall go on to the end, we shall fight in France, we shall fight on the seas and oceans, we shall fight with growing confidence and growing strength in the air, we shall defend our Island, whatever the cost may be, we shall fight on the beaches, we shall fight on the landing grounds, we shall fight in the fields and in the streets, we shall fight in the hills; we shall never surrender, and even if, which I do not for a moment believe, this Island or a large part of it were subjugated and starving, then our Empire beyond the seas, armed and guarded by the British fleet, would carry on the struggle, until, in God's good time, the New World, with all its power and might, steps forth to the rescue and the liberation of the old.

To complicate matters, on 10th June 1940, Italy declared war on Britain and France. Merchant ships had already ceased using the Mediterranean in anticipation. The next day, Egypt cut diplomatic relations with Italy and the RAF began attacking Italian air bases in Africa.

After the British Expeditionary Force evacuation at Dunkirk, the

---

[11] 'We shall fight on the beaches' speech

Germans turned south to take Paris. Despite valiant resistance from the remaining French forces and the 51st Highland Division (cut-off and unable to join the Dunkirk evacuation) the Germans entered Paris on 14th June. The French sought an armistice and in response to these events, Churchill gave the third Battle of France speech on 18th June.[12] His address to the House of Commons concluded with a rallying call.

> Hitler knows that he will have to break us in this Island or lose the war. If we can stand up to him, all Europe may be free and the life of the world may move forward into broad, sunlit uplands. But if we fail, then the whole world, including the United States, including all that we have known and cared for, will sink into the abyss of a new Dark Age made more sinister, and perhaps more protracted, by the lights of perverted science. Let us therefore brace ourselves to our duties, and so bear ourselves that, if the British Empire and its Commonwealth last for a thousand years, men will still say, 'This was their finest hour.'

On the same day as Churchill's address, Mussolini met Hitler to discuss French government terms. They signed the Franco-German armistice on 22nd June. To humiliate the French, Hitler forced them to meet in the same railway carriage in which Germany had formally surrendered in the First World War. Germany now controlled the Channel and the Atlantic coasts. To placate the French and dissuade them from continuing the fight, Hitler agreed that forty percent of the country could remain under the control of the French government.

General de Gaulle — who was relatively unknown — had travelled back to Britain with Churchill after the prime minister's last visit to France. On 18th June, de Gaulle broadcast a message from Britain in which he appealed

---

[12] 'This was their finest hour' speech

to his countrymen to continue the fight against Germany. He formed a Provisional French National Committee to continue the war and, by the end of June, the British Government recognised General de Gaulle as leader of the Free French.

With the fall of the French government, British naval supremacy in the Mediterranean was under threat, a situation compounded by Italy's declaration of war. To prevent the remaining French fleet falling into the hands of the Germans, Churchill authorised its destruction. Operation Catapult necessitated a difficult, but justifiable decision in the eyes of the British Government.

In July 1940, one of the single most important conflicts of the Second World War began — the Battle of Britain — a fight for air supremacy to stave off a German invasion. Hitler's plan for the invasion (Operation Sea Lion) depended on German air superiority, but the Luftwaffe did not prepare well for the conflict which started on 10th July. By contrast, the Hurricanes and Spitfires of the RAF were organised and the British radar defence system warned of incoming threats.

U-boats supported the German air offensive, extending their campaign in the Atlantic to stem supplies entering Britain. To avoid the aggressors, the Allies routed Atlantic convoys north of Ireland.

*****

On the morning of 30th May 1940, the men moved from Chester Castle to a new depot called The Dale. It was bounded by the railway and canal to the west and the Liverpool road to the east and north. Even the building of innumerable huts all around the barracks, could not spoil the pristine look of the new facility.[13] They slept on the floor in one of the huts on the first night to make room for the Cheshires returning from Belgium. There was

---

[13] Cheshire Regiment, 1939, *The Old 22nd*, p.19

no electricity and therefore no wireless, but the huts were warm enough. There were two fires in each, but given the time of year they were not required. Kit was stored in capacious wooden lockers.

The Dale was high above the town. From the dining hall Bill could look across the valley to the Welsh hills beyond. There were around one thousand troops at the barracks and Bill took his place in No. 1 squad.

As news filtered through on Hitler's progress, the atmosphere in the barracks became increasingly tense. A German invasion of mainland Britain was looking possible. Bill was pensive, but ready to do his duty, whatever it may be and whatever it may mean. He wrote to Lisbeth:

'If anything happens to me before I see you again, darling, remember that it was because I loved you so much and that I was glad it was so.'

Lads returning from overseas told stories of the British Army taking heavy casualties. Bill noted:

'One battalion of Gordons was smashed out of existence, and the 2nd & 4th Cheshires were badly hit.'

According to Lockley, the men would transfer to Aldershot soon enough — three weeks at most. 'Don't worry about it boys. Remember, the darkest hour is just before the dawn. The sun will shine again for all of us.'

Bill wasn't convinced, but his mood was lifted by a letter from Bingham with the latest news from Invergowrie. He responded immediately, and also wrote letters to Lance Corporal Bill Young up in Aberdeen and to Lisbeth's Auntie Kate in Edinburgh. Writing would continue to be a positive distraction for Bill; however, the intensity of training in early June limited his time. The training schedule meant Bill was standing to from 9.30pm to 10.30pm in full kit. After some sleep he was standing to again from 3.30am to 4.30am. After that, there was time for a wash, shave and a cup of tea, before a full day of parade, only breaking for breakfast and lunch. The lads were allowed out from tea-time until 9pm and then the whole thing started again.

Away from this daily routine, Bill was becoming more proficient with the machine gun. The training carried on apace and Lockley moulded the lads into a cohesive, disciplined and loyal bunch. In battle, the men would need to work as a team.

> Individuals, however highly trained, must learn to sink themselves in the common interest and act in concert with others. Mental alertness, attention, and intelligent anticipation, whilst keeping one's mind at the immediate disposal of his commander, are all mandatory requirements.[14]

Ablutions were taken care of in brand new facilities. There were multiple white sinks positioned in front of large sash windows, allowing the men to look out across the parade ground as they washed and shaved. The shower cubicles were brand new and full height with controls at shoulder level for hot and cold water. The cookhouse too was new, tiled and fitted out with the most modern equipment. The cooks produced dishes to gladden a soldier's heart and food was kept warm on a hotplate before being served. For breakfast a hot dish — bacon, eggs or maybe sausages with plenty of tea, bread and margarine. Dinner was a meat dish with plenty of vegetables and a good pudding. Often, there was a savoury dish for tea too, and to round the day off, a substantial supper. With a solid routine for physical training and the correct food intake, it was estimated the average soldier would gain around twelve pounds in weight over a twenty-week period.[15]

During Bill's time in Chester, Lisbeth continued to write with news from home. Polkemmet Juniors were not doing so well and were missing the men no longer available to play. The first week of June saw them lose against Whitburn. Gillies missed a penalty! 5–0 was an awful hammering.

Meanwhile, Chester FC had asked Bill to play for them, but he'd decided

---

[14] Cheshire Regiment, 1939, *The Old 22nd,* p. 29
[15] Ibid., pp. 37–43

against it. The season was practically over and he couldn't have played the final two games, as he was confined to barracks. In reality, Bill was not yet *in* the barracks. That first night in the hut had turned into a week and given the way things were going, Bill wondered whether they would ever move. They would probably shift two hundred miles to Aldershot before moving two hundred yards to The Dale.

As it was, they moved on 12th June. The barracks were crowded, with twelve in a room as opposed to the normal eight. The shift to No. 2 Company also brought a change in leader. Sergeant Cobb was an Irishman of quite some stature at over six feet tall, with a torso akin to an upside-down coat hanger. Bill got off to a good start with him and was made night marker which meant he was in charge of the room. He was also the gatekeeper for the bathroom. Entrusted with the key, he was told to ensure that nobody except No. 2 squad and No. 13 squad used the facilities.

In the classroom, tactical lectures from superiors gave Bill renewed hope about the war. He became more positive and regarded the Allies' prospects with quiet confidence, communicating the same to Lisbeth.

'Hitler may make advances but at a terrible loss and I think we shall retreat (within the bounds of safety and sanity) until he is sufficiently weak to bash through.'

Subsequently, hopes faded as word spread that the lads in mainland Europe were retreating fast. He began to doubt whether the Germans *could* be pushed back. Matters were not helped with news of the French surrendering and Bill feared the consequences if the Germans got their hands on the French Navy and Air Force.

Bill, Ken (Kenneth Morgan) and Dunc (Duncan McInness) were out for supper one evening at the YMCA and met a British Expeditionary Force sergeant from the Cheshires, not long back from France. Based on a long discussion with the chap who had been at the sharp end, Bill offered the following hypothesis to Lisbeth.

> All our troops will come back from France to this country and all troops will go on home defence, apart from the East, where replacements will come from Australia and New Zealand so that no troops will leave this country. As all our aircraft, bombers and fighters will be operating from this country, Germany's planes will have too much opposition to force us to give in to air attacks alone.

> We shall apply the blockades twice as fiercely as Italy's leak is now stopped and Germany can't do anything about it. [Hitler] has so many people to feed, including the French, that a second winter will finish him economically. Russia will also come in — there's no doubt about that — she will be in at the kill and America will give us enough planes to squash the Jerries by next spring. It's a cinch and I'm glad I'll not have to fight in France. I'll feel better on my own patch.

Bill was trying to strike a balance between caution and reassurance. Just twenty-four hours later he wrote:

> You must look after yourself these days. We are certainly seeing history being made. However, I can assure you we are quite ready to meet any Germans who try to land here. Remember they can't drop seventy-five ton tanks by parachute and only a limited number of troops.

By 18th June, there was still no word about Aldershot, the mobile column changed from a machine gun company to a rifle company and Bill was made a section commander. In anticipation of a German invasion, Bill found himself digging trenches for the first time. It was a laborious, dirty, sweaty activity he became very familiar with, but at this time, he and his friends were also enjoying evenings off, playing snooker and bridge, or venturing to the Regal for the latest showing.

Ken was a soft-spoken chap from some unpronounceable place in South Wales. Dunc, 'the fighting parson' was from Glasgow. He'd belonged to the Ministry for a while but gave it up as it interfered with his drinking. He was a decent lad with a hilarious turn of phrase. The company was an eclectic mix of personalities brought together by war. However, playing bridge could only assuage their fears and anxieties for brief periods. Bill didn't know whether he was standing on his head or his heels most of the time and in an instant would shift from pensive to carefree mood and back again. By now, Bill believed that the war was likely to last two or three years, unless they could get a sufficiently large air force to drive the Germans out of the skies.

'Improbable unless the Yanks do their utmost,' he concluded.

With the first bombings from the air, Bill felt apprehensive. One of his good friends since school days, Bill Brydon, had been captured and another friend, John Craig, had been killed in France. He warned Lisbeth to remember the air raid precautions and advised her not to wander too far from the shelters. Bill's first air raid warning in Chester came on 23rd June 1940.

The increased threat from the skies coincided with a reduction in food provisions for the lads. No jam and less bread, which did not please a man like Bill who liked his grub. Sports afternoons were also abolished. Bill thought about home a lot, especially of Lisbeth, Mother, golf and football. He later joked with Lisbeth that these priorities changed depending on how he was feeling at the time.

Back in training, Bill continued to contemplate the possibility of a commission. The Argyll & Sutherland Highlanders, Cheshires, Northumberland Fusiliers, Middlesex Regiment and 8th Battalion Gordons were the only machine gun regiments, so if he got a commission, it would be with one of those five. A posting back to Edinburgh would do him just fine, but there was as much chance of that as finding a snowball in hell!

As it was, Bill travelled to Malplaquet Barracks, Aldershot, with seven other men on 28ᵗʰ June 1940. The trainee officers were in huts with spring beds — twenty-six chaps to a hut. Of the seven men from Chester, five were with Bill, including Dave Robertson from Peebles. The other two were next door. The huts were collectively known as the spider, on account of the interconnecting corridors. Above each bed was a shelf. Hooks and lockers were outside in the passageway. The only unpleasant surprise was that the officer cadet training course was to last five months, and the sergeant confirmed it had never been shortened. This meant Bill and Lisbeth might have to postpone their wedding.

The first month in Aldershot was spent in the recruit company, meaning foot-drill and arms-drill all over again. On the plus side, the army taught all recruits to drive lorries and ride motorbikes and the news that orderlies would be sweeping out the huts and washrooms was equally well received. Being told to dig tank traps, however, was not.

Every other week, the recruits were confined to barracks; this was known as duty company. When permitted, lads made their way to town, a distance of just over a mile. It was walkable, but if the weather was bad, they could pay 2½ pence for a single bus ticket or 4 pence for a return. Aldershot was expanding with the influx of troops, Canadians and Anzacs among them. There was a post office nearby and a club on camp, run by the Navy, Army and Air Force Institutes (NAAFI). Whilst the prices were higher than at Chester, they still represented good value. Bill thought the food was decent, and they ate from porcelain bowls instead of the tin they'd had in Chester. Progress!

After some days in Malplaquet Barracks, the routine took shape and Bill wrote to Lisbeth confirming the hours he was keeping. The bugle call (reveille) was at 6am, and days were filled with parades; lectures in map reading, principles of war,[16] weapon training and gas training; and periods outdoors including PT and drill. The busy nature of a soldier's day at least meant that life was economical; Bill was surviving on the 5 pence a week his mother sent. He could ask her to send 10 pence if the need arose, but in the meantime, digging tank traps and trenches was cheap.

Air raids were now commonplace up and down the country. One afternoon, Bill was being interviewed by the commanding officer when the siren wound up and there was a series of almighty explosions. Bill grabbed his helmet and respirator before flinging himself into a trench. Perhaps the physical effort spent in creating it had been worthwhile after all. He looked skyward and saw the Jerries heading towards the coast, pursued by a British fighter. The all-clear came a full hour later and Bill made his way back to the commanding officer, throwing glances to the sky as he went.

The following morning, news filtered through that the German bombs had landed about three-quarters of a mile from camp creating some four or five decent holes in the road. One civilian was killed and another two were injured. British retaliation came the following day with three German planes shot down in the district.

On the same day, Bill's mother wrote to him confirming that a letter had come from the Scottish Football Association; Polkemmet had signed him on again despite the circumstances. However, sport was becoming a distant memory. Bill got down to the golf course in Aldershot, but only to undertake concealment, camouflage and disguise exercises. The sight of heather reminded Bill of the Pentland Hills and made him homesick. He promised himself he would never grumble once the war was over with. If he ever felt low, then he would remember jumping out of bed at 3am, patrolling lonely lanes, watching the dawn break whilst feeling the wet and cold cut through

---

[16] Bill referred to the principles of war as 'surprise, mobility, offensive action, security, economy of force, concentration and cooperation'

his clothing.

With increasing uncertainty about the future, many couples were tying the knot. Lisbeth had seen a number of weddings take place in Edinburgh, and asked Bill about the correct attire for a soldier's wedding. Bill replied that one would require two sets of dress. In a Scottish regiment, battle dress would comprise tunic, kilt, tartan trousers, glengarry and balmoral. In an English regiment, it would be tunic and two sets of trousers. Bill would have to purchase battle dress, but there were ways and means of acquiring it cheaply through the quartermaster's stores. The couple were still to arrange their wedding date.

Bill was twenty-four on 16th July 1940. The day was busy enough with the usual routine, but he also took his turn as acting sergeant and there was voluntary (meaning compulsory) drill practice after tea. This ate into the time Bill set aside for writing and his letter to Lisbeth on this date reflected his temper — short! The good news was that Mother, Auntie Meg and Auntie Ruth had all sent birthday money meaning Bill's financial situation was further eased. The only gift from the army was a little white band to be worn on the shoulder. If the lad's hats were off, the white band confirmed they were from the OCTU. 'Marvellous!' scoffed Bill. But wear it he would — the Regimental Sergeant Major (RSM) was in no mood for messing. Like all RSMs, he was a thunderbolt of a man, but had a vocabulary of words and phrases that tickled Bill, appealing to his sense of humour. During drill one day he'd barked at a lad:

'You're like a pickpocket at a nudist camp son. You don't know where the f--- to go!'

Bill and others strained at the gills to contain their laughter.

The irony of all this training and preparation was that air raids were commonplace in Edinburgh where the civilians were living and less frequent down in Aldershot where the number of troops was growing. Lisbeth reported that bombs were being dropped, mainly to the north of the city. This was a cause of considerable angst for Bill.

Month-end at Aldershot brought with it the first reports on cadet performance. The company commander wrote of Bill:

'an average cadet, not outstanding so far but will improve.'

Buchanan, the platoon commander told Bill that he was considering giving him a 'B', but had opted for a 'C' to encourage self-improvement. Overall, the platoon registered three Bs, eighteen Cs and three Ds. It was much the same in other companies. A platoon photograph was taken and Bill sent a copy to Lisbeth. In doing so, he pointed out Dave Robertson and suggested she may be looking at his best man. Lisbeth studied the photo and requested an explanation of the cadet NCO ranks, perhaps casting a hopeful eye on her fiancé's future, and Bill replied.

> The cadet company commander gets the company on parades, gives them the right dress [and] calls the roll. He then marches the squad onto the parade ground. He takes over certain duties from the company commander in organisation, if we are going into the field etc., and marches at the head of the column.

> The cadet orderly sergeant has to ensure that the company is present at reveille and last post, and report accordingly to the guard room. He sees that blackouts etc., are attended to — and no more noise after lights out, charging those who disobey. He also accompanies the orderly officer on his rounds.

> The platoon sergeant hasn't much to do. He does the donkey work for the platoon commander and gets the platoon out for parades, gets them dressed and in open order ready for inspection. He marches in the rear of the platoon.

Just twenty-four hours later, Bill moved to No. 6 Platoon 'A' Company. His new abode was a single floored brick building, similar in shape and size to the huts and plumb opposite the post office. There were twelve men to a room and Bill felt he could not have improved on fate's choice of his fellow roommates. He also managed to scrounge a lovely soft pillow.

That first evening, Leslie Henson, the comedian, actor and producer, brought down the cast of a London show and gave a free performance to all members of the 170th OCTU.

The 29th July 1940 was a significant day for Bill. Up to that point, his motorised transport training had been theoretical only and whilst the lectures were interesting, he was keen to try out the real thing. His first opportunity was in a truck. A driver took him out and showed him how the gears, clutch, brakes and accelerator worked. Swapping seats, Bill was both excited and anxious as the instructor told him to move off, navigating his way around two carts with horses, several tanks and some lorries. His confidence was building as the instructor told him to turn into a cart track, but he approached too sharply and caught the edge of a ditch running alongside. The resulting lurch forward resulted in Bill putting his foot down and accelerating straight across the road and into a field. Just as the instructor went to pull the handbrake on, Bill applied the footbrake with a force that brought the truck to an abrupt halt. The jolt took his passenger by surprise and he lost his false teeth!

Bill was not alone in his calamitous first outing. One lad scraped his side badly after smashing his motorbike into a pillar and another was nursing injuries after ploughing headlong into a hut, again on two wheels. Officer cadet training was evidently not yet complete.

'Malplaquet Barracks, Aldershot, 1940'
Bill Sinclair (front row, fourth from left)
Dave Robertson (front row, fourth from right)

WEDDING BELLS

Early August saw German aerial attacks against strategic targets, both during daylight hours and after dark. The Germans coined the phrase 'Eagle Day' which signified the start of a more intense campaign for dominance over British skies. The concentrated aerial bombardment thus began on 13th August 1940 with waves of Luftwaffe attacks over the south coast of England. With more planes than the British, the Germans were confident of success, but a staunch British defence limited the damage inflicted.

Just two days later saw the largest deployment yet of Luftwaffe planes and a broadening geographical scope of attack, including a significant fight in the skies over the Firth of Forth. The British raised a formidable defensive force against the mass daylight raids in what was the heaviest aerial fighting of the Battle of Britain.

The following day once more brought a concerted effort by the German aggressors, only for them to suffer significant losses as British fighters defended the country. After the Dunkirk evacuations, Hitler assumed Britain would capitulate, yet by the middle of August she was still standing strong. The nation's fate was dependent on the RAF's continuing defence. Churchill made clear reference to this reliance in his address to Parliament on 20th August.

> The gratitude of every home in our Island, in our Empire, and indeed throughout the world, except in the abodes of the guilty, goes out to the British airmen who, undaunted by odds, unwearied in their constant challenge and mortal danger, are turning the tide of the World War by their prowess and by their devotion. Never in

the field of human conflict was so much owed by so many to so few.

On 7th September, the Germans switched tactics, moving from the aerial bombardment of RAF installations to an all-out attack on London. Hitler ordered the Blitz to bomb Britain into submission and facilitate plans for a land invasion. But once again, the Luftwaffe overestimated the damage. RAF installations had recovered and British production lines were now churning out aircraft in volumes that outstripped the German factories.

The 15th September was a turning point in the Battle of Britain. Despite a day of sustained bombing in London, Britain's superior aircraft and pilots were overcoming Germany's Luftwaffe. The attempt to blitz the British into submission would ultimately fail. The message was clear; the British would stop at nothing to defeat Nazi Germany. Despite a monumental effort, the Germans never achieved superiority in the Channel and on 17th September, Hitler postponed plans for an invasion on British soil.

Ten days later, Hitler met his Axis counterparts and the tripartite (Axis) pact was signed in a show of force, attempting to dissuade the Americans from entering the war.

With Hitler's postponement of Operation Sea Lion, the threat of invasion was diminishing. Whilst the German U-boats were proving effective in attacks on Atlantic shipping[17] they would be of far less use in a cross-channel invasion. Britain had overall naval superiority and the weather was also a factor. Hitler's attention would turn away from British shores as he focused on plans to invade Russia.

Elsewhere, the Italians had invaded Egypt in mid-September and were heading east to take control of the Suez Canal in an attempt to expand the

---

[17] Throughout the period, German forces continued with targeted attacks on Atlantic shipping. The second half of October saw record losses for Allied ships due to sustained enemy action

Italian Empire. A little over a month later, the Italian Army invaded Greece in what was the start of the Balkans war.

*****

It had been eleven weeks since Bill kissed Lisbeth at Chester Station on Sunday 19th May 1940. If he could not manage a weekend away from Aldershot soon, it would be another fifteen weeks before training finished and he could take a week's leave. Could their wedding coincide? Bill hoped so. As he could not get away, Lisbeth would have to manage the lion's share of arrangements. The only thing Bill could confirm was his choice of best man; Dave Robertson was a real gent. Bill referred to him as 'economical yet generous — a true Scot!'

They would like to have spent their honeymoon on the east coast of Scotland, but Dunbar had become too military and the frequency of air raids ruled out Elie, North Berwick and St. Andrews. The west coast was further to travel but at least it was peaceful. Turnberry, Troon, West Kilbride, Millport and Oban were all possibilities.

It was a busy week at Aldershot. 'A' company had been on guard and Bill had worked hard digging defence trenches. In the evenings, he lay on his bed resting, and cast his eyes around. Behind him hung his respirator, great coat and battle dress, and just above was some shelving on which he stored books, magazines, cleaning equipment, shaving tackle, washing gear, boots and gym shoes. To the left of his bed was a small sideboard and just in front, there was a wooden chest in which he kept the rest of his belongings and secreted treasures, including letters from Lisbeth. Atop the wooden chest sat a mess tin, water bottle and tin hat. The space was tight, but manageable. The fire was close by, which would be just fine if Bill was still there when the temperature dropped.

He pulled the small Boots diary out of his pocket and read back through his entries for the previous four days:

5th Aug: Week Out. Demo thirty yards range, lecturing all afternoon.

6th Aug: Stayed in and played billiards.

7th Aug: Digging all day at Risely Mill. La Scala with George.

8th Aug: MT [Motorised Transport], out with new instructor.

Bill turned the small blunted pencil between his thumb and forefinger, sat up with knees bent, looked at the blank space for Friday 9th August and simply wrote, 'main guard.' In the memo section at the foot of the page he recorded, 'fourteen weeks to go.'

Instead of putting the diary back in his pocket, he casually thumbed back through the pages, and his mind returned to those few days in Chester spent with Lisbeth. The weather had been unkind, but the rain hadn't dampened their spirits and they'd dived into the cinema to escape the downpour. How he wished he could be back there with her, rain and all. Bill made a mental note to write more clearly as some of his diary entries were difficult to decipher. Could someone else read it? Should they be able to? Would this small diary still exist in say seventy-five years' time? Would the nation still exist?

The Germans were making progress and Bill had to acknowledge the possibility of war crossing the Channel. A wry smile came over Bill's face as he imagined some poor soul trying to read his diary in years to come; trying to untangle the scrawl made with that blunt pencil, words joined that shouldn't be, military acronyms only known to the informed and involved. He closed the diary, slotted it back into his pocket, turned to one side and shut his eyes.

The following week brought exams. Bill was still hopeful of a commission, and so he swotted as much as time allowed and felt quietly confident. Machine Gun practical: 2 hours, Machine Gun written: 1½ hours, General Knowledge: 40 mins, Map Reading practical: 2 hours. He had prepared as well as he could. The day of the machine gun written exam wasn't helped by the Aussies and New Zealanders driving down the avenue in tanks, kicking up a right old racket. He would just have to wait and see if this disturbance had affected his performance.

Bill was in his seventh week at Aldershot and the countdown clock was ticking ever faster. He was concerned about German air raids on the south coast, but made light of it to Lisbeth, writing that Hitler's strategy was to send all his planes up to get 'bumped down into the Channel.' Maybe there would soon be enough German wreckage for Hitler to 'build a bridge, over which his tanks and infantry can invade Britain!'

Being on emergency squad, Bill was confined to barracks and the restriction was frustrating — especially as there had been more air raids in Edinburgh. The desperate trainee would willingly do time in the glasshouse[18] if it meant he could get back to Scotland for a day or two, but it was impossible. Instead, he took his turn in the guardhouse. It was small and had no natural light on account of the blacked-out windows. Everyone hated the guardhouse.

On 17th August 1940, the air alarm sounded at 12.30pm, just before dinner. The men remained in the trenches on the sports field for an hour, but saw and heard nothing. At 5.30pm, the sirens went off again. The lads donned gas capes, respirators, eye-shields and tin bowlers — quickly making their way back to the trenches. Alert, they waited, hearts pounding, adrenaline flowing. After a time, there was a terrific noise above them, but the sky was overcast and they could see nothing but cloud. Some of the group were familiar with the droning sounds, referring to them as the current buns, or the hums. The enemy passed over and the lads assumed that was that. Relax. Moments later, however, the 'dirty dogs came down

---

[18] Military prison. The name, glasshouse, originates from Aldershot military prison which had a glazed roof

through the clouds about a mile away' and headed straight towards the waiting troops, presumably sighting the aerodrome. Bill remained in the trench, gazing up at about a dozen enemy aircraft. He described their payload as 'rather like baby aeroplanes floating away.' The men crouched down, faces pressed into the dirt, while those on the Bren and Lewis gun posts fired away. The planes disappeared back into the cloud, one of them smoking like a furnace, just as the bombs hit. The sound was like nothing Bill had heard before. Each strike seemed louder than the one before. The ferocious racket finally ceased, but not before some debris came crashing down close by.

'Damn it!' exclaimed Bill, as he lifted his head and glanced around.

'You okay?' said the next lad.

'I'm fine, but unfortunately, so is that blessed guardhouse!' replied Bill, and a ripple of nervous laughter made its way down the trench.

The runway at Aldershot had suffered some slight damage, but properties on the Farnborough Road had also been hit. One house was blown to pieces and another three wrecked, but there were no casualties. They received the all-clear around 7pm. Bill later referred to it as an 'entertaining day.'

Despite the dark humour, moments such as these brought home the importance of family. It was now thirteen weeks since Lisbeth's visit to Chester, but only another thirteen weeks (less two days) until Bill would see her again. He brightened up and considered the programme for the week ahead. Monday: machine gun, Tuesday: motorised transport and field engineering, Wednesday: unit exercises, Thursday: examinations, Friday: machine gun. On Friday night he would be on guard, again, in the — still standing — guardhouse.

Sunday, 1st September 1940 signalled the first full year of engagement for Bill and Lisbeth. Bill spent the first part of the day in a trench; in the afternoon, Dave Robertson called him into action of a different kind. Fighting was a regular part of a trainee's life and was encouraged to toughen up the chaps, as long as there was no real ill-will — there rarely was. On this day, Dave had taken on two lads from a rival platoon, Ken McEwan and another six-footer, Mahony. Mahony was otherwise known as *Mahogany* and for good reason. As Bill heard the battle cry go up, he raced towards the noise. Dave was struggling to fight off the two lads he'd just surprised. A scrap ensued with another six of Mahogany's mates piling in. It took a good while for them to drag Bill and Dave out which Bill was proud of, though it took four days for his cuts to heal over. He needed to lay off scrapping if he was going to look civilised for his wedding.

A few days later, Major Dolley published the exam results. The company commander informed Bill that he was first in 'A' Company with a score of 215 out of a possible 270, a performance which reinforced his hope of a commission. Fingers crossed.

Military routines continued throughout September: section drill, machine gun, motorised transport, tactical exercise without troops (TEWT), ensuring kit was blancoed,[19] digging trenches, guard duty, night ops and standing to. Sirens interrupted these activities almost daily, requiring the lads to grab their respirators, helmets and gas capes, and then head for the trenches. In reality, there had been no more bombings, and the lads now found the whole process exasperating. Funny how such events quickly become the norm, Bill thought. There were, however, reports of serious bombings in London and Bill reminded himself of the horrors other people were facing. Indeed, Auntie Meg couldn't stick it any longer and was clearing out of the capital.

In Edinburgh, Lisbeth continued with the wedding preparations. Ideally,

---

[19] Blanco compound was used to clean and colour equipment

she would have dressed in white and Bill in a kilt, but the expense was too great and they would have to compromise. She looked at possible venues for the reception, arranged for the banns to be read, purchased a ring and detailed the order of service. The major variable in all this planning was the wedding date itself. At least the cake was simple to sort as Uncle Andrew was taking care of that. Lisbeth herself had agreed to play Liszt's *Liebestraum* at the service, as requested by her mother, and Auntie Lily had agreed to sing a solo.

Thoughts of the west coast as a honeymoon destination were dropped in favour of somewhere closer to home, such as St. Andrews, or inland, such as Pitlochry. Despite the air raids, given its proximity, beach, and choice of houses in which to stay, Bill favoured St. Andrews, but Lisbeth would make the decision.

Bill finally asked Dave to be his best man, and he accepted, gladly. He had put his name forward for a commissioned officer position in India, but it wouldn't affect his ability to attend the wedding and perform his duties, as both men would complete their training at Aldershot at the same time in November. Dave would then have two months' leave. Bill decided almost immediately that his gift to the best man would be a Sam Browne and Brace.[20] There was no doubt in Bill's mind that Dave would make the grade as an officer.

On the same day that Bill gained a best man, he gained the accolade of corporal under the section commander. Dave would be one of the gun numbers in Bill's two sub-sections. In the event of an invasion, they would be together. Another pal, Jimmie, was also assigned to the section as a range-taker. Good news. Being a section corporal would put Bill alone in handling the gun. He felt proud of the faith his superiors were putting in him and

---

[20] Name given to the wide leather belt with cross-strap worn by British officers

would endeavour to meet their expectations.

The first flying column practice was the following day and Bill took his position as No. 1 with the section commander on the machine gun truck. In the afternoon, all the lads received their latest report covering the previous month in 'A' company. Bill's grade was C+, and his report read:

'Will make a more than average officer, shows a definite ability, keen and shows good powers of leadership.'

Dave also received a C+ while Jimmie's star was glowing with a well-deserved B. Bill expected the next report within days and hoped for further improvement in pursuit of his commission.

The word in camp towards the end of September suggested the likelihood of a German invasion was receding. 167th had stopped their flying column and were to have weekend leave reinstated. Bill hoped the 170th would follow suit.

At this point the wedding date had still not been set. Bill reckoned they would finish training on 15th November, making the 16th a possibility. Perhaps they would even get away on Thursday 14th. If not, they would catch the Flying Scotsman on the Friday and get into Edinburgh at around 7pm that night. What could go wrong?

In his next report, Bill got 772 marks out of a possible 1000. The second highest score in the platoon and fourth equal in the company.

57 / 100	General Knowledge
69 / 100	Tactics
74 / 100	Map Reading
250 / 350	Machine Gun Written
80 / 100	Machine Gun Practical
242 / 250	Machine Gun Fire Orders

Being fourth in a company of seventy-five men was no mean feat, but this moment of pride didn't last as the air raid siren went up again. Bill wrote to Lisbeth about it.

'Lone raiders passed over and back again, dropping what they had at various places.'

The lads in Aldershot were spared once more and as the all-clear sounded, Major Dolley called Bill in to see him.

'I have some good news for you, Sinclair.' His tone was pleasing.

'I have written down, this cadet is showing ability very much higher than average and will make a first-class officer. I have every confidence in his ability to do very well.'

Bill was chuffed. 'B+ rating,' he muttered, as though he needed some convincing himself. Now, the commission had to be in the bag. As he made his way back to the hut, Bill was completely unaware that the area around his first school — Dalry Primary — had been bombed, along with other well-known landmarks in Edinburgh. As such, Bill only wrote to Lisbeth asking about the progress of their wedding arrangements and confirmed his four preferred hymns.

Oh perfect love

How welcome was the call

Oh happy home

The voice that breathed o'er Eden

Lisbeth wrote that Minister Blackburn would like to see the groom before the banns were read, but Bill replied that there was 'more chance of Hitler winning the war' than there was of him being able to get away. However, second-in-command, Captain Griffiths, had been with No. 4 Platoon on night ops, twenty-four hours earlier, and had a different opinion. Given the reduced threat of invasion he was confident of the lads getting two weeks leave at the end of training. Bill made a mental note to ask Platoon Commander Hughes the following day, but before he had a chance, the men were told that all four OCTU's at Aldershot (167th to 170th) would shift to

Droitwich on 15th October. Bill mulled it over. If he was to go to Droitwich, then at least he would be nearer to Scotland. He didn't want to get his hopes up and focused instead on his wedding plans. In all the malaise, however, he forgot to wish Lisbeth a happy twenty-fifth birthday on 6th October, apologising profusely in a letter written a couple of days later.

On 10th October, Dave heard that he was not going to India, though where he would end up instead was a mystery. Unlike his mate, Bill had not been interested in India and was thinking of the Argylls (Argyll & Sutherland Highlanders) instead. 'D' Company had received notice of their postings ten days before leaving Aldershot and ninety percent were successful in their first choice. If Bill's training finished on 15th November, he hoped he would find out his next move early that month.

Before that, he had to submit a request for leave on urgent compassionate grounds, so he could get to Edinburgh and conclude wedding arrangements. Hughes had already checked with Major Dolley and confirmed to Bill that he would get a free rail warrant, though he would have to be flexible on routes. London may have to be avoided. Bill wasn't fussed as long as he could make it to Scotland. He would need to see the minister, but that would take second place to his visit to Jardines the outfitters, where he was having a fitting on the Saturday.

There were a million and one things to do, and the army could easily throw a spanner in the works at the last moment. Bill warned Lisbeth to prepare for disappointment, just in case something went wrong.

The pass that Bill so desperately wanted was signed on 16th October and he also received his free rail warrant. He wrote to Lisbeth in what was to be his last letter before seeing her for the first time in almost six months. He asked her not to meet the train, as it was liable to be late, and anyway, there was no guarantee he'd be able to catch the 7.15am from Kings Cross, as news suggested the Aldershot to Waterloo line had been damaged.

The very next day, Bill sent a wire to Lisbeth to say he would not be coming home at the weekend after all. As feared, the army had put a spanner in the works and cancelled all leave. Bill would still finish training on 15th November, so the wedding was provisionally planned for the day after.

In the meantime, Bill received his next report. Major Dolley awarded him an A grade and wrote:

'This cadet has a better all-round grasp of the work than any other cadet in the platoon.'

Bill was thrilled, and in addition, Dolley had selected him to play football in a team covering *all* OCTUs. They would play against an Aldershot Command team. Bill's side included Swift of Manchester City and four former English league players. Great news, but Bill was convinced they would be thrashed. The opposing side included six English and one Scottish international. Bill knew of Henry Wright (Derby), Walter Crooke (Blackburn), Joe Mercer (Everton), Tommy Lawton (Everton), Ralph Birkett (Newcastle), and Don Welsh (Charlton). He was less familiar with McKenzie (Dundee), Martin (Arbroath), Barret (Chester), Cann (Charlton), and Cornwall (Stoke). The game took place on Sunday 20th October. It was the best match Bill had played in since leaving home — and he scored! Sadly, this was his side's only goal and they went down 4–1.

The following evening, all hell broke loose regarding leave arrangements — again! For some reason that was never explained, the lads were given three weeks of leave from 23rd October, extending the duration of the course and scuppering plans for a 16th November wedding. It would have to be sooner.

Everything was hastily re-arranged. Minister Erskine read the banns at Saint Andrew's Church, George Street, Edinburgh, on 20th October and arranged to take the wedding service on the 28th. Jardines, Hill Street Halls (the reception venue) and all those required to deliver, provide or perform on the day, rallied round to bring it all together at short notice. Dave Robertson as best man and Ann Bathgate as bridesmaid were unflappable and helped Lisbeth pull everything together. The only casualty of the revised arrangements was the honeymoon, so Bill and Lisbeth resigned themselves instead, to ten days at Cowan Road.

On the evening of their marriage, Bill took out his diary and wrote: 'Married Lisbeth — definitely the happiest day of my life!'

'Wedding day, 28th October 1940'
William George McKenzie Sinclair & Elizabeth McGillivary Verth (centre)
Dave Robertson (left), Ann Bathgate (right)

DEFENDING FORT ELSON

O n 5th November 1940, Franklin D Roosevelt was elected to serve a third term as President of The United States (US). The US was already supporting British efforts in the Atlantic but wanted to remain neutral and avoid involvement in another bloody European conflict. Roosevelt had to tread carefully, but convinced Congress to step up efforts to support its British Allies.

On the European mainland, the Italian invasion of Greece from their Albanian base surprised many, including Hitler. Mussolini had kept the plans secret, even from some in the upper reaches of the Italian Army. The Greeks resisted, strongly. Despite being poorly equipped, they amassed many men with a good knowledge of the terrain. Within a matter of days, and in glacial temperatures, the Greeks forced Mussolini back over the Albanian border.

Elsewhere, the Luftwaffe continued to bomb British cities. The industrial centre of Coventry was attacked on 14th November, causing extensive damage, followed by Birmingham on the 19th and Liverpool on the 28th. Air defences offered little resistance this time and German bombers followed the fires laid down by advanced Pathfinder aircraft. Further fire raids followed in December with attacks on London, designed to destroy morale.

In the Western Desert, Operation Compass was the first large Allied military operation of the campaign. On 9th December, General Wavell's men advanced and overwhelmed the Italian defence before them. The Italians retreated and Wavell's Western Desert Force took Sidi Barrani and Sollum in little over a week.

The second phase moved into the New Year and into Cyrenaica, the eastern coastal region of Libya. After two days of aerial bombardment the

Australians took the seaport of Bardia on 5th January and the crucial port city of Tobruk on the 22nd. The Italians abandoned the region and the first major campaign in the desert was a success for the Western Desert Force. This success, however, was not exploited. Due to the Greek-Italian conflict, Churchill diverted troops to the Balkans — a move that radically changed the situation in North Africa.

Meanwhile, on 18th December 1940, Hitler authorised the invasion of the Soviet Union.

*****

Bill had been married for less than three weeks when he said goodbye to his wife on 14th November 1940 and caught the train with Dave Robertson from Edinburgh to Birmingham. After changing at Carstairs he fell asleep, only waking when the train ran into an air raid about thirty miles north of Preston. They crawled into Crewe two hours late and by the time they reached Droitwich, were three hours behind schedule. Bill pondered how long he would be at Droitwich for. He wouldn't have to wait long.

On 25th November, the lads were informed of their regimental postings. Bill and Dave were destined for the Argyll & Sutherland Highlanders, while Jimmie went back to his own regiment, the Middlesex.

The 170th OCTU had their final parade as cadets on 27th November. Bill was ecstatic. The platoon dinner that evening was a raucous affair reflecting the feelings of all those who had completed their officer training. Bill had just about recovered ten days later when he wrote to Lisbeth from the south coast. Second Lieutenant Sinclair (158883) had transferred to the Argyll & Sutherland Highlanders, 342nd Machine Gun Training Corps, New Barracks, Gosport.

The accommodation was more civilised than anything that had gone before. There was no toasting the King before dinner, and the food was good.

Pea soup, rabbit, potatoes, carrots, stewed fruit and sauce. There were all kinds of fruit and nuts on the table as well as biscuits and cheese. The Auxiliary Territorial Service (ATS) did all the cooking and provided waitresses, who served coffee after dinner in the anteroom. This good-sized room was rectangular, with two large windows at either end. The floor was carpeted and there were two fires. A large table sat in the centre of the room, with several leather arm-chairs and settees placed around it. It was all very comfortable. The refinement and service of the dining hall continued in the sleeping quarters with a fire and comfortable beds in each room. Bill would share with an assistant adjutant. On the first morning, he was woken at 8am by the batman assigned to the two of them. He provided a cup of tea before cleaning their kit, and Bill remarked, 'he made a very good job.'

The War Office would determine the duration of Bill's stay. They defined the requirements for army personnel and their regimental assignments. It worked on a first in, first out, basis. Bill bumped into an old colleague, Dave Thomson, from the Caledonian Insurance Company who had been waiting twelve months for an assignment, so Bill did not anticipate an imminent move for himself.

In the meantime, the boot was now on the other foot for Bill. He was in charge and was leading recruits in machine gun training, as well as taking on new responsibilities. He shadowed the orderly officer inspecting the guardroom, police room and cookhouse as well as examining rations.

Eating dinner at the barracks five nights a week limited Bill's outings to the pictures, but it did mean he had more time for reading and writing. He wrote to Lisbeth almost daily, and continued to correspond with Bingham and Old Murray at Invergowrie, along with relatives and friends in Edinburgh.

Bill quickly grew in confidence as an officer. He became accustomed to giving guard commanders a good dressing down for any inefficiency and his brief teaching experience helped when giving lectures to the platoon. On one occasion, when giving a machine gun lecture on identifying different targets and how to engage them, the colonel walked in. Bill stopped in his tracks but was given the signal to continue. The colonel sat quietly observing for thirty minutes before leaving as stealthily as he'd arrived. Bill later heard from the company commander that he'd been pleased with what he'd seen.

Despite a positive start at Gosport, Bill just wanted the rotten war to be over. He wrote to Lisbeth:

> [I want to] get back where I belong — with you, and trying to instil such ideas of friendships and give and take into as many school children as I can, to do a little to avoid the next generation having to live like this — constant partings and goodbyes from all the people you love, living miles away, learning how to be better killers.

Lisbeth had heard that bombing had damaged a picture house in Gosport and was concerned for her husband. Bill replied that it was not entirely true and that he was unaffected. In fact, Lisbeth was right. Three high explosive bombs had dropped outside the mess shaking the whole building and three men had died.

On 17th December, Bill wrote to Lisbeth warning of a new German incendiary device which had an explosive charge in it. They can 'take anything up to two minutes to go off,' he explained. The advice was to leave them for a few minutes and then follow the instructions he had previously provided. Bill added, 'if it is in a very dangerous place and you *must* handle it, then have your face screened, so that if it does go off, then you will at least save your face!'

Wednesday 18th December brought news of Dave Robertson's sudden departure — what was more — he was going to Edinburgh! Five men had been selected to go to the Royal Scots but one fell sick while on leave and Dave was picked to replace him for a six month stint in Auld Reekie (Edinburgh). So much for the first in, first out principle. Bill envied Dave, but was sorry that his best mate was leaving. It was likely they'd ship him off to a field battalion afterwards, by which time Bill would be goodness knows where, so that was that. The two friends promised to keep in touch and Dave would visit Lisbeth in Edinburgh during Christmas week.

The motorised transport course was going some way to brightening Bill's spirits. He became more expert in driving a truck, although he did have one accident. He thought the truck was in neutral but it was actually in second gear when he hit the accelerator pedal. This time he took out six yards of fencing and destroyed most of the cabbages planted behind it. The offside lamp and front bumper were damaged, but not as badly as Bill's ego. There were also trips out in an Austin utility van and a Morris 14 civilian car. The van was a more manageable beast than the truck with its synchromesh gears, but the car — despite being big — was the easiest of the lot to drive. Bill took the Morris down to Stokes Bay, Alverstoke and Lee-on-Solent. Unlike the trucks, the car was not limited, and he reached his fastest ever speed of 55mph along the Lee-on-Solent promenade.

In contrast, Christmas day 1940 was a muted affair. The ATS had decorated the dining hall with streamers and papers, but this didn't induce much Christmas spirit in Bill. He sat by the fire in the anteroom for a while, eyeing the tree adorned with ornaments and crackers. He'd received four Christmas cards and some cigarettes from Lisbeth. Dinner was a grand affair with asparagus soup, steamed salmon with parsley sauce, roast turkey with spuds and sprouts, and then Christmas pudding (plum duff) with various charms hidden inside. Bill was lucky enough to find a wedding bell just before he swallowed it. There was the usual fruit, nuts, cheese and sugared figs in boxes. All in all, there was plenty. An 'eloquent sufficiency,' as Lisbeth would have said. After dinner there wasn't much to do. The cinema was closed so Bill and Dunc corralled Drake and Major Shearer into a game of bridge to pass the time. Later that evening Bill wrote to Lisbeth and her brother Jack, before reading himself to sleep.

On 31st December, Bill wrote to Lisbeth for the last time in 1940. It had been his first year in the British Army and he wondered how many more he would face before life could return to normal and he could get back to his wife. He cheered himself up with thoughts of the wedding day, and their honeymoon period together at Cowan Road. Would 1941 see the end of the war and their reunion? What about children? Bill and Lisbeth had discussed the subject of children (wee red wrinklies) at length and had agreed to let nature take its course. Perhaps the Sinclair family might increase by one before next year was out.

1941 started as 1940 had finished with the normal routines of army life. Bill was becoming a capable driver, and the instructor remarked that he couldn't teach him anything more. Bill got 50mph out of a Bedford truck and his passenger didn't complain. He was a chap from Whitburn that had seen Bill playing for Harthill so the two had a good old blether whilst touring the countryside near Portsmouth. Not all the lads were enjoying such success. Drake had ploughed his truck into the back of a bomb disposal wagon. Thankfully, the wagon had been on its way to pick up a bomb — and not on the way back!

In the first week of January, Bill met George Emslie who ran the football team. George had been at Glasgow Varsity and had trained at Hampden. The impromptu meeting resulted in three games for Bill the following week. First up, was a match for the centre team, then an Officers vs Company game and a first round Cup game against HMS Collingwood a couple of days later.

On 8th January, Bill received an important letter from Lisbeth and responded by return as follows:

> If you are right in your supposition about a 'wee us' and I quite
> agree with you dearest, from the symptoms you describe, then I'll
> be the happiest man on earth.

Thoughts of a baby Sinclair were immediately put to one side. There were several air raids in January, as though the Germans wanted to begin the year with a blast of activity. On the evening of Friday 10th, Bill was duty officer. The sirens went off at about 6pm and within minutes, incendiaries were dropping by the hundred, followed by high explosive bombs and then more incendiaries. It went on until 10.20pm. No sooner had Bill rested his head than the thunderous noise kicked up again. This time the all-clear was not given until 3.45am, by which time Jerry had wreaked havoc. Numerous fires burned so brightly that you could have read a newspaper outside in the middle of the night. Firefighters from as far away as London were trying their level best to get on top of the flames, but bombs had hit the power station so Bill was forced to work by lamp-light. When daylight came up, he ventured into Gosport and discovered a tragic scene. The Ritz cinema was gutted and several pubs and shops were destroyed — many still burning fiercely. There were people standing in the streets outside the ruins of their former homes, clutching odd pieces of rescued furniture. There were more explosions as buildings that were no longer safe were demolished. Bill spent that day dealing with the aftermath.

Following the bombing, Bill was asked to take thirty-seven men to Fort Elson with orders to guard British shores. On taking over the fort, he felt like a feudal lord. Entrance to the defensive structure was through a wrought-iron fence some fifteen feet high, followed by a main street, with derelict buildings on one side and more habitable places on the other. On each side was a tunnel: one led to a compound surrounded by an iron fence, the other to a smaller square and a habitable building where the men would sleep. The smaller square was also home to several huts and Bill took one of them for himself. He posted a main guard and compound guard so that access to Fort Elson 'would be more difficult than an entrance into heaven.' He put up his first orders and felt bucked with himself: WGM Sinclair, Second Lieutenant, Officer Commanding, Fort Elson.

On the first full day at the fort, Thursday 23rd January, a German raid began at 6pm and continued for five hours. Enemy planes droned overhead and anti-aircraft fire banged away in response. It was Bill's first taste of live action whilst assuming sole responsibility for a group of men outside of the barracks. It was also the day Lisbeth confirmed she was pregnant.

Bill and his men spent three weeks at Fort Elson, and in the main, it was quiet. The most hunting the lads did was out in Elson woods, capturing wild goats for whom the forest was home. The goats provided milk and kept what little grass there was down to an acceptable level. Eventually, they were released back into the wild.

Bill was enjoying his new authority and created a good rapport with the men under his command, although he had to deal with the odd misdemeanour. Having confined one lad to barracks for seven days for stealing army cigarettes — he was caught red-handed with 200 Players — Bill sat back in his chair and concluded that it was just fine to sit on this side of the desk. He drew up an inventory of goods and chattels at the fort so that any further thieving could be detected.

While at the fort, Bill also managed to play football. The first round Cup game against HMS Collingwood was a match like no other. At half-time the score was 1–1. In the second half Collingwood went ahead with two goals in quick succession, only for the officer's side to hit back with two of their own. With fifteen minutes to go and the sides level-pegging at 3–3, Bill thought they had the momentum, but when the final whistle blew it was 11–3 to Collingwood.

'What the hell happened there?' he called out.

Nobody answered. Bill had not been part of a team demolished like that before. As he lay on his bed listening to the wireless that evening, an organist was playing *Smiling Through*. Bill shook his head at the irony.

One afternoon in his third week at Elson, Bill was on top of the fort when a German aircraft took advantage of the low cloud and glided down towards him. It dropped two bombs about a quarter of a mile out to sea, aimed at the vessel out in the Channel. Four more bombs hit the ground, close to the compound. Thankfully, no-one was hurt.

Bill took his mind off the war briefly and wrote to family members and friends, informing them of the wonderful news about Lisbeth's pregnancy. Letters of congratulations came back from all corners, including one from Auntie Kate and another from his new brother-in-law, Jack, who remained in Ireland doing goodness knows what with the Pioneer Corps.

At the end of January, Jack returned to Auld Reekie for seven days' leave. Bill was envious. There was no leave in the offing for him. He could only hope that his time in Gosport would soon be over and facilitate a shift back up to Droitwich where he might be able to see Lisbeth for the first time since confirming her pregnancy. In the meantime, he could only go about his duties and relax by playing darts or going to the local pictures. *Foreign Correspondent* was one of the best action films he'd seen — a fine slice of propaganda.

At the end of that week, Bill's duties at Fort Elson came to an end and the men made their way back to Gosport barracks as instructed. The routine of drill and machine gun practice was a stark contrast to the freedom enjoyed at Fort Elson. The little 'jungle station' had been a break from the norm and Bill had enjoyed the responsibility, though the food had been sparse — even ghastly at times.

On Wednesday 5th February, Bill received the fantastic news that he would leave Gosport for Ayr, not Droitwich, along with nineteen other lads. 'Take me back to bonnie Scotland,' he wrote to Lisbeth. Bill was assigned to one of the young soldiers' battalions to command lads aged between sixteen and twenty. Would Lisbeth be allowed to join him? Whatever the move brought, they should take the chance to get together as soon as possible, for as long as possible. Bill was to report to Ayr on the following Monday, before which, he would spend the weekend with Lisbeth. He sent a wire asking her to wait for him at home and he travelled to Edinburgh via Kings Cross on Friday 7th February.

ON THE MOVE FOR DRAFTING

I n North Africa, British and Australian soldiers continued their push west entering Benghazi on 6th February 1941. On 12th February, General Rommel arrived in Tripoli with his Afrika Korps to address the situation.

Later that month, Churchill diverted troops from the region to support the Greek effort against the Italians, but also to prepare for a likely German invasion of Greece in Hitler's bid to protect the Balkans and important oil-fields. Diverting British troops left their counterparts in North Africa vulnerable and the Germans would show themselves to be a formidable force in the desert wastes.

By the Spring of 1941, Germany was on the move on two fronts. Rommel launched an offensive across the Libyan province of Cyrenaica and made excellent progress, taking the vulnerable Western Desert Force by surprise. El Agheila fell, followed by Mersa Brega, Benghazi and Sollum as the Western Desert Force retreated east. Rommel also had the Allied garrison of Tobruk surrounded.

Elsewhere, Germany invaded Greece and Yugoslavia on 6th April, overwhelming Greek and Allied troops from the air and on the ground. By the end of the month, the Greek Army had surrendered, Athens had fallen and the British were evacuating.

On 6th March, Churchill issued his Battle of the Atlantic directive to address the U-boat and surface warship menace upsetting supplies coming into Britain. The directive introduced a range of measures to combat the threat, including protecting merchant ships and improving port defences.

In the same period, Roosevelt signed the lend-lease bill that permitted the US to support its war interests without being involved in battle, address-ing the desire of the American population to stay out of the conflict. At the end of March, the US Navy began patrolling the Western Atlantic to protect its interests.

British interests were very much under threat at the time as the Luftwaffe continued to attack from the air in the early part of May with a renewed focus on city bombing, including major raids on Liverpool and London. However, with attention eventually turning to an offensive against the So-viet Union, the Blitz diminished.

Back in North Africa, Wavell launched Operation Brevity to strike a blow against Rommel's advance and achieve a long-term aim of relieving the besieged city of Tobruk. In doing so, Wavell's force cleared the Halfaya Pass and retook Sollum. The success was short-lived. By the end of May, Rommel had once more forced the British back. Wavell tried again in June with Operation Battleaxe, but the Afrika Korps destroyed British tanks en-tering the Halfaya Pass and the order to retreat was given. Frustrated with the lack of progress, on 8th July, Churchill swapped out the Commander in Chief Middle East (Wavell) for the Commander in Chief India, General Sir Claude Auchinleck.

By the time of Auchinleck's arrival, Hitler's Operation Barbarossa — the invasion of the Soviet Union — was underway. Stalin called for a 'scorched earth' policy, laying waste to any land before giving it over to the advancing Germans. As the Nazi's moved deeper into Soviet territory they began to annihilate entire Jewish communities. On 31st July 1941, the order for the Final Solution was approved, authorising:

'all necessary preparations with regard to organisational, practical and financial aspects for an overall solution to the Jewish question.'

*****

It was Bill's first weekend with Lisbeth since he'd left her for Droitwich on 14th November and their first meeting since confirming Lisbeth's pregnancy. The train from Kings Cross arrived just twenty minutes late and Bill made his way to Cowan Road as planned. Lisbeth jumped into his arms; an embrace which lasted until Bill's mother rushed out to greet her returning son.

During his stopover in Edinburgh, Bill received a wire from the army informing him of a change of plan. He was to be posted to the north east of Scotland rather than Ayr, where his bags were waiting for him.

'You couldn't make this stuff up,' exclaimed Bill, as he read the wire for a second time. It wasn't the new location that bothered him, but the last-minute change and associated inconvenience.

That weekend, the young couple alternated between Cowan Road and Northumberland Place for meals, paying due care and attention to both sides of the family. The weather was kind and they revisited old haunts and special places. There was a long walk out from Liberton to Roseburn, and a trek along the foreshore of the Pentland hills and reservoir, to their private nook overlooking the city. The little fir wood and the valley below was where they'd first declared their love for each other, and revisiting that spot, Bill couldn't believe how 'in the pink' Lisbeth looked. Neither knew what the future held; the war meant taking each day as it came.

The following morning, Bill travelled north by train. It was a long walk from Stonehaven Station to the bay, but Bill found it with ease and reported to the orderly room where the commanding officer and adjutant sat chatting. The commanding officer, Lord Rowallan, seemed like a decent sort, but wasted no time in giving Bill his instructions. Stonehaven housed Headquarters (HQ) and 'A' Company; Bill was to travel to 'C' Company at Peterhead as soon as his luggage arrived from Ayr, the next day. Bill enquired as to the frequency of air raids in the area.

'Once in a blue moon,' came the response. 'There's a slim chance of spotting dirty dogs in the sky and the odd mine blowing itself up on shore. Apart from that, it should be quiet.'

With that, Bill retired to the Bay Hotel. Having settled in and enjoyed a great dinner, he made his way to the cinema, watching Mickey Rooney in *Young Tom Edison*.

The following morning, Lord Rowallan drove Bill to Peterhead, some fifty miles away. The journey took an hour and a half, including the crossing through Aberdeen. Rowallan's skill behind the wheel impressed Bill, referring to him as 'some driver.' Their journey ended at a new vulnerable point[21] just outside Peterhead at Blackhills. From the following week, it was to be manned by an officer, sergeant, corporal and eighteen men. Newly built huts joined a large farmhouse and several smaller properties in readiness. Lord Rowallan told Bill to explore the site and take a property for himself. Perhaps Lisbeth would be able to join him. In the meantime, Bill would stay at the Royal Hotel some three miles away in Peterhead. It would cost £2 per week, to be paid from his own pocket, but at least he had a motorbike at his disposal for the duration of his stay.

The first day proper, Bill took charge of the gas drill and weapons training. He quickly observed two extremes of young soldier. On the one hand, there was the son of Sir Robert Brooke. He was from London, working for a commission, and looking to stay in the army after the war. On the other hand, there was a rat from Blackridge, West Lothian, who had already been given the birch and had a civilian crime sheet a mile long. There were many absentees and prisoners on detention among the young soldiers and the local police were frequent visitors, enquiring after various robberies and house breakings. On his first day, Bill received a letter from the police

---

[21] Place of importance to be protected

asking if the army would keep all the sons from a particular family away from their district for as long as possible — and that they were eternally obliged to the Germans for taking one of them prisoner!

The work was challenging, but after only a day, Bill was quite enjoying it. There was more discipline than at Gosport and Bill had every intention of upholding it. Rowallan appointed him to the role of sports officer and he wasted no time arranging boxing for the lads. Football followed soon after. The young soldiers played their first match at Peterhead's ground against a navy team. Bill's ragtag side lost 5–2 with the heavy pitch taking its toll on the boys, but Bill was starting to win over some of the hard cases, and for a first outing, was not unhappy at the result.

On his first Sunday, Bill stood up in church and gave a lesson in front of a hundred young soldiers. Argylls, Royal Scots and Royal Artillery were all represented, though Bill noted they didn't pass a plate round after the service.

'They'd have lost the plate *and* its contents with these Argylls,' said Captain McDonald. 'You've got your work cut out.'

Bill smirked and nodded in agreement. He would need to put a bit of distance between him and the boys at the end of a day and decided to take lodgings as far away as he could. There was a school house just over the hill on the camp boundary. It was a very nice stone building with two sitting rooms downstairs and two bedrooms upstairs, plus a kitchen. There was no electric light and no gas, but it looked comfortable and Mr Reid, the headmaster, and his wife, seemed very nice people. All three were hesitant about broaching the question of money, but Mrs Reid eventually asked.

'Would 15 shillings per week be too much?' Bill had been expecting at least 20 shillings, so was quick to agree.

'That would be just fine.'

Bill moved into the school house on 20th February 1941 and wished for

Lisbeth to join him just as soon as she could. There was a slight delay, as her mother was unwell and Lisbeth had to attend an appointment to check everything was going well with the pregnancy. She finished work at the Caledonian Insurance Company at the end of February, and contrary to Bill's advice, she did not tell Mr Watson to 'go hang himself.'

Lisbeth travelled north on 3rd March. She took a train to Aberdeen and then on to Peterhead, arriving at 5.50pm. Dr Robertson, whom Bill had got to know playing solo and bridge, kindly offered to take them up to the school house in his car. For the first time, Bill and Lisbeth would share life as a married couple expecting their first child. Bill would go about his duties as and when required, and Lisbeth enjoyed the company of Mrs Reid in his absence. She would also stride out to Peterhead and the surrounding area whenever the weather permitted. But by the end of March, Bill was on the move again — destination unknown. Mr and Mrs Reid gave assurance they would take good care of Lisbeth until Bill called for her to join him, and so Bill travelled north and east along the Moray Coast to Cullen.

The 26th March saw a freak spell of terrible weather. Road, rail, telephone and every conceivable means of transport and communication were cut off by eighteen inches of snow and biting winds. Bill laid up in the Grant Arms Hotel at Cullen, while Lisbeth did the same, fifty miles south east in the school house near Peterhead. Bill and the men at Cullen could do little other than clear the billets and the streets of snow as best they could, but they were no match for the drifts brought in by a raging gale that chilled them to the bone. The snow *had* been forecast and was preceded by a spell of weather that left the roads like sheets of glass. Bill had found this out the hard way, taking two tumbles on his motorbike the previous day. Halfway between the school house and Peterhead he came a cropper, sliding twenty yards with the bike on top of him. He'd escaped with nothing more than a good soaking and a staved finger, but then had to endure a train journey in dripping wet gear with no prospect of a change.

Following a break in the weather, Lisbeth joined her husband in Cullen on 1st April, but Bill wasn't there for long. He understood his new destination to be either Stirling Castle (HQ and No. 1 Recruit Company), or nearby in Tillicoultry (No. 1 & 2 Training Company). The adjutant and commanding officer met Bill on arrival at Stirling and directed him to No. 2 Company, where it was thought he would be for around six weeks. Bill enquired about he and Lisbeth living outside of the barracks, and whilst the noises were positive, nothing was agreed. This situation continued until May when Bill enquired again. Eventually, the commander said:

'Of course, lad, get yourself out there and look for a house for you and your good wife.'

Bill didn't wait for a change of heart. After running around and looking at various places, he found a most acceptable property about a mile and a half from Stirling town centre with a nice bedroom, a lovely view and a shared lounge. He wrote to Lisbeth asking her to come, and they settled together for eight weeks at 15 Randolph Road, Stirling.

Throughout April, rumours of draft abounded, but Bill ignored them. A year's experience with the British Army had taught him that nothing was certain until it happened. Even when formal documentation passed his way on 23rd April, he only gave it a cursory glance. His superior told him he'd be in Stirling for at least another three weeks and that was as far as the horizon stretched.

Bill was enjoying his time with Lisbeth so much he didn't want to contemplate separation, though knew it would come. Even if the army weren't to force it, the baby would. By June 1941 Lisbeth was almost eight months pregnant and needed the support and comfort of the family home in Edinburgh.

Bill was now alternating between six and forty-eight hours' notice to leave. In a last-ditch attempt to preserve his position in Scotland he'd put in for an intelligence testing job, but the adjutant had informed him soon after that his name was not being put forward on account of the draft.

Lisbeth's absence hit Bill immediately. His mother recognised it in his letters and went through to Stirling with Auntie Ruth to cheer him up. It was a welcome distraction and fine weather enabled the three of them to venture out. They sat on a seat in Kings Park until hunger pangs got the better of them, then they took the back way up to McCulloch and Youngs department store. After lunch, they rode the bus to St. Ninians and sat in the park enjoying the sun, before boarding another bus, this time for Callander. There, they sat on the banks of the river staring up at Ben Ledi. With the warmth of the sun — and the company — Bill's anxieties flowed away from him like the trout in the Teith. They made a final stop at Cambuskenneth Abbey near Stirling, before Bill waved the two ladies off on their return train to Edinburgh.

The following day he was back to normal duties. The fine weather continued and Bill took his platoon for a route march in tin hats, tropical shirts and kilts. They went off up the Dunbar Road and back via Cambuskenneth where Bill had sat not twenty-four hours earlier with Mother and Auntie Ruth. That evening, Bill sat talking and playing cards with two blokes he'd met for the first time at Stirling; Bill McIvor and Bill Taylor became good friends in a very short space of time. With the prospect of draft and what lay beyond, they quickly formed close and common bonds.

Bill had had no privilege leave since November 1940 but didn't hold out much hope of getting any more. He joked with his compatriots that he would hop and skip all the way to Bannock Burn via Polmaise Way if the army sanctioned any.

'Looking forward to seeing that already,' quipped McIvor in response.

Needless to say, Bill didn't hop and skip to Bannock Burn, but he jumped into the air and clicked his heels when finally, a week of leave *was* granted. Fantastic!

Bill spent the week in Edinburgh with Lisbeth. Given her condition, walks were kept to a sensible distance, so the couple sat and talked, wondering what the coming days and months would bring. Nobody knew. The return to Stirling came all too soon, and when Bill kissed Lisbeth goodbye on the Sunday, he had no idea that they would not see each other again for some considerable time.

Back at Stirling Castle on 10th July, the men were now on a fortnight's notice. Skelton had changed over with McIvor who was now on Bill's draft but that was the sum-total of news. The following day, Bill started on a three-inch mortar course which was a welcome relief and set to last a fortnight.

'Fiddling about with mortars on the grass, instead of dealing with the platoon is fine by me,' he said to McIvor.

Bill celebrated his twenty-fifth birthday on 16th July 1941 and responded to the crack about senility that Lisbeth had made in her letter by reminding her that she had already celebrated her twenty-fifth and was therefore in no position to be taking the high ground. He also reminded her that baldness was not necessarily a sign of antiquity. Bill celebrated his birthday with some lads down at a local hotel with a few games of pontoon. He remained sober and emerged 6 shillings and 3 pence richer — a most satisfactory result.

The following day brought news that drafts, beginning with R.F.Z. were heading for Egypt while others, beginning with R.A.G. were Singapore bound. In theory, Bill was in the latter (R.A.G. XK), but either way, he was in for a long journey.

That journey began on Sunday 20th July 1941. As always, Bill had no real idea where he was heading. All he knew on that Sunday was that he was to pack his bags in readiness to head south. Two days later, he wrote to Lisbeth from the Royal Artillery Mess, Ashfield House, Burton-on-Trent, Staffordshire.

The Midlands was an unfamiliar area for Bill. He studied a local map to get his bearings and traced his finger across village names; Bramshall, Marchington, Doveridge and Kingston.[22] His finger moved south from Uttoxeter and stopped at Abbots Bromley, pausing for a moment while trying to recall where he had heard that name. It meant something but it took a minute to register. 'Of course,' he finally said out loud. The connection was with Cock O' the North. In the decade before, Cock O' the North had become the official regimental march tune of the Gordon Highlanders. An annual Horn Dance took place in the village of Abbots Bromley where the tune was reputed to have its origins.[23] When he'd heard about it, Bill hadn't bothered to find out anything more about the English village, and now there it was staring up at him. That day, Bill made himself a promise. If he got out of the war alive, he would journey back to the Midlands and call in to Abbots Bromley to see the village for himself.

That was a distant prospect. By now the reality of going to war had well and truly dawned on Bill which he acknowledged in a letter to Lisbeth.

> I'm afraid that there is very little chance of us seeing each other again until the war ends. Bill Taylor, McIvor and I are sailing on Thursday morning. The others sail tomorrow night. It is quite a blow dearest as you can imagine as we were certain that we would be here for a while. We are taking 297 men and 2 sergeants each with us — quite a responsibility…….. We are sleeping here tonight and tomorrow we are going to Uttoxeter to collect our men.
>
> There is a rumour that we are sailing from Leith but some say

---

[22] Later known as Kingstone
[23] Bullen, 1987, *Country dance and song*, p. 11

Newcastle, so I am afraid that it will be neither. However, if it is Leith, I will definitely be in to see you on my way. It is, as I say, quite a blow isn't it darling, but I know that you will keep your chin up and we'll come through smiling after it is all over and have that long-awaited good time.

    I'm afraid that my thoughts are a little scattered, my darling, as you will well understand, and as it is getting very late, I'll close for tonight. I do hope you are keeping fine and please try not to worry too much for little [baby] ----'s sake. I truly love you Lisbeth, you and only you forever. Your <u>very own</u> husband…Bill

The following day, Bill wrote his correspondence address on the reverse of the letter and included the latest information on arrangements, including a change to his expected draft:

    We are leaving from Liverpool tomorrow (Thursday) darling

    158883 Second Lieutenant Sinclair W.G.M.

    RFZ XA

    C/O A.P.O. 1000

When Bill recorded a diary entry on 23rd July 1941, it was the first since he'd graced the small Boots diary with the words: 'Married Lisbeth, definitely the happiest day of my life!' His wedding day felt like a distant memory. The two occasions that caused him to put pencil to paper could not be further from each other, but the strength and depth of feeling of each event was ironically similar. On 23rd July his diary entry read as follows:

    Left Burton by truck for Uttoxeter 10.45am — collected our draft of 297 [men] — wandered round Uttoxeter all day with BT [Bill Taylor] — went to pictures at night. Late at night being very browned off, got very "happy", playing pokey-di.

Whilst Bill was not a big beer drinker, he had his fair share that evening. It helped settle his nerves about the following day's manoeuvres and morphed into a final opportunity to let his hair down. He and Bill Taylor explored the Staffordshire town of 'Utcheter' and its endless supply of pubs. They toured (and staggered) around the Market Place, Market Street, Bridge Street, up the High Street and along Carter Street having at least one in each pub: The Black Swan, The Old Swan, The Olde Talbot, The Vaults and The White Hart. Their adventure ended in The Old Star where they found some new mates. Soon enough the Scots' version of 'Ay up me duck' was being used to greet all and sundry. Feeling the effects of the local ale, they stepped outside for a gulp of fresh air and a fag. Bill tripped over a short wall, performing something of a pirouette, before steadying himself and trying to look sober.

'Mark my words, some poor soul will break their bloody ankle because of that wall!'

His drinking partner was bent double laughing at Bill's acrobatics. Finally, the lads settled themselves, called it a night and got back to their billets early enough to be fresh the following day.

By 9am the men were on a train travelling from Uttoxeter to Birkenhead. Bill wrote to Lisbeth reconfirming his latest postal address and reminded her (whilst still on British soil) of the secret code they could use to pass information back and forth. Lisbeth could decipher the code by taking the second letter of the first word, the second to last letter of the third word, the second letter of the fifth word, and the second to last letter of the seventh word before starting the cycle again on the eighth word. The sentence used would be unique, to signify it contained a code. This could take the form of a phrase or series of words that Lisbeth would recognise as not being of Bill's typical style, or an obvious omission or spelling mistake.

'Across the seas I will always remembers your smile,' Bill wrote in his letter of 24th July. 'Remember our code darling, here is an example.' Including an 's' on the end of the word 'remember' showed the sentence contained a code. 'Across the seas I will always remembers your smile. That spells "Cairo". We can try it anyhow,' he wrote.

That same evening, Bill's feet were still on dry land. 'Bloody war,' he cursed. They hadn't gone direct to Birkenhead to embark, but instead, marched across Liverpool on their way to a transit camp. There were three groups, the first led by Taylor, the second by Bill and the third by McIvor. All three boarded a subway train at Liverpool Central, alighted at Birkenhead Park Station, and marched a further mile and a half to the camp. Bill, Taylor and McIvor would stop at a grand mansion at 4 Devonshire Place, Oxton, Birkenhead. It was a strange situation; the men had prepared themselves mentally to leave British shores for what could be the last time, only to find themselves in a transit camp, sitting and waiting. The three officers attempted to keep the men amused and motivated with billiards and similar activities. It was difficult though, and Bill sent a snorter of a letter to the War Office to complain about the arrangements, or rather lack of, and the ample opportunities the men had to skip.

'If we had had a bunch of Argylls and had taken them in the ordinary civilian subway like that, we would never have got half of them here!' he wrote to Lisbeth.

Bill had not received a letter from Lisbeth for two days and wondered whether she had gone into labour. He nagged Bill Taylor to go with him into Liverpool and take his mind off things. The two officers took the subway under the Mersey Tunnel to the city centre. They wandered around for a while, taking in the extent of the devastation caused by the German bombing campaign in May. Empty shells stood where great stores had once plied their trade and sold goods to the Liverpool faithful. The two pals ended up in the Paramount pictures and saw *A night in the Tropics* and *Call of the Wild*.

Later that evening, the major informed the officers that their men were likely to be used as a pool, taken in small groups over the next few days to fill space on various boats. Bill had given up worrying. His greater concern was for his wife's welfare and the imminent arrival of their baby son or daughter. The following morning, he received two letters from his wife; as of 28th July, baby had not yet appeared. The men were now confined to barracks for a possible departure in the next two or three days. Bill busied himself around the billets, doing what he could to keep the men engaged, focused and happy. He scrounged some fags for the Gunners who were squawking like gulls and a YMCA van provided tea and buns to placate the tetchy troops. Two more days ticked by.

Bill and Lisbeth Sinclair
1941

Elizabeth Sinclair
(Mother of Bill Sinclair)
1941

Lisbeth Sinclair and brother, Jack Verth
1941

Jack Verth
1941

SAILING OVERSEAS

On 1st August 1941, the US announced a ban on oil exports to the aggressor states, including Japan. The situation in South East Asia had been deteriorating for some time and the embargo followed the freezing of Japanese assets in the US. Japan relied significantly on imports and felt the squeeze. Meanwhile, the US continued to supply China in their efforts to repel the Japanese.

With the German occupation of France, the Vichy Government agreed to Japan's occupation of its Indochina colonies. This potentially provided the Japanese with control over resources such as rubber and tin, which were so important to the West.

Elsewhere, Roosevelt and Churchill gave a joint declaration known as the Atlantic Charter. Although the US was still technically neutral at the time, the Charter set out its support of Great Britain in its war effort and defined eight principles that both countries would be committed to in a post-war world. It was supported by several other countries in what was the forerunner to the United Nations. Following the declaration, Churchill hoped to draw the US into the war; Roosevelt was hoping to dismantle Britain's colonial power. Neither got what they wanted, but the Charter symbolised an alliance that Germany and Japan interpreted as an act of aggression.

In Eastern Europe the German offensive continued throughout August. Amid fierce opposition from stoic Russian defenders, the Germans took Novgorod on 16th August and surrounded Leningrad on the 19th. The following day, the main railroad from Moscow was taken, isolating the city.

By this time, an Anglo-Russian offensive in Persia, codenamed Operation Countenance, saw Britain and Russia invade Iran to gain control of

Iranian oilfields and secure supplies. Iran also became a major transport route for channelling military aid to the Soviet Union.

In the Mediterranean region, German firepower and aerial threat forced British shipping bound for the Suez Canal to travel around the Cape of Good Hope. The Atlantic was also treacherous as demonstrated by President Roosevelt's broadcast of 11th September. The 'shoot on sight' campaign came in response to the German attack on US Destroyer, Greer, a week earlier. The American Atlantic Fleet would now even escort convoys containing no American vessels. The US edged closer to full involvement in the war.

At the same time, in an attempt to stem the loss of Axis ships and protect supplies to North Africa, Hitler ordered U-boats into the Mediterranean. To get them there, the German submarines had to navigate the British controlled Straits of Gibraltar and suffered significant losses.

September 1941 also saw the beginning of atrocities that the Nazis would become forever associated with. On 3rd September, six hundred Soviet prisoners were killed in the first tests using Zyklon B gas. This became the blueprint for future mass exterminations.

*****

30th July 1941

Probably the most exciting and sad day in my life. Heard at 4.30am that I was the father of a bouncing baby girl, and so Elizabeth Ann Sinclair makes her bow. Terribly happy about this because 'both are well.' Looks as though I'll get home according to the major. Good news confirmed by wire at 1.30pm. At 2.30pm sad news comes that I have to embark immediately.

Around 4.30am on 30th July, Bill Taylor woke to a loud knocking at 4 Devonshire Place. He opened the door to a policeman who greeted him with news that a baby had been born to Lisbeth Sinclair up in Edinburgh, and that Bill Sinclair should be informed. Taylor woke his friend with news of the birth of his baby daughter. Elizabeth Ann Sinclair (always known as Ann) was born in Elsie Inglis Maternity Hospital, Edinburgh, on 30th July 1941, at 3.10am, weighing 6lb 6oz. Lisbeth and Bill named their baby Elizabeth, after her two grandmothers, and Ann after her Godmother, Ann Bathgate.

It was the last day of official confinement and despite Bill's excitement, he could do nothing about getting to Edinburgh, so he sent a telegram to his wife and daughter. A few hours later, Bill caught the major at lunch. He seemed to be in a cheery mood, so Bill asked about getting away to see his wife and new baby. Initially, there seemed no hope, but shortly after lunch, the major discovered that their draft wasn't required at all on this convoy. Bill tried not to get his hopes up.

A congratulatory telegram from Lisbeth's mother and father arrived stating that Ann had popped out around 3am on 29th July. Bill was puzzled. He knew this couldn't be the case as he'd now received a letter from Lisbeth dated 29th July with no mention of a baby! He wrote to clarify the timing.

[Born on 29th July at 3 am] 'If that is so, Ann must have been born and then you left the wee thing to be off with your mother to the bank! I knew you were wonderful darling but…….'

A request from the major to see Bill interrupted his thoughts. Bill hoped upon hope it was good news — instead, he was shattered. They were embarking that day at Liverpool. Bill had heard, however, that they may sail to Glasgow before venturing further. Perhaps that would provide an opportunity for a quick visit. He feverishly scribbled a letter to Lisbeth and his very first handwritten words to his new daughter.

My darling little Ann,

This is all for you. Always do as your mummy tells you and remember to stick up for yourself and your rights. You and mummy will always be with me wherever and whatever happens.

Your one and only father xxx

The letter was posted and Bill readied himself and the lads for travel. It was a titanic mental struggle. Along with Sergeant Bradley, Bill McIvor, Bill Taylor and twelve others, he climbed aboard the waiting truck and departed, followed by more trucks transporting the men under their command. They journeyed through the Mersey Tunnel and arrived waterside a short time later. There was a mass of ships and men carrying kit bags as far as the eye could see. Confusion abounded. Bill and the men received their orders and worked their way through the heaving throng and cacophony of noise to reach the 23,500 ton troopship, Orcades, at 5.50pm. Departure was at 6pm. Bill got the lads settled in and then saw to his own arrangements. He was sharing a cabin with three others, all RAF personnel. On board there were a total of 3,500: 3,000 RAF, 300 British Army and 200 crew.

His Majesty's Transport (HMT) Orcades was a beautiful ship with marvellous accommodation and fittings reflecting its more leisurely past as Royal Mail Ship (RMS) Orcades. It had received some modifications as part of its conversion to a troopship, including an anti-submarine gun affixed to the stern, but in terms of sleeping accommodation and facilities it was a complete contrast to anything Bill had experienced for a long time. At supper, the lads all concluded the same.

'Oranges for dessert? You wouldn't think there was a war on,' shouted McIvor gleefully.

Having moved out into the estuary, the ship had come to a stop with Bill contemplating his destination and avoiding the other men and their jolly moods. He moped about after eating and retired — still somewhat forlorn — at 11pm.

31st July 1941

Ann now 1 day old — her first birthday — wish I could get her something but it's impossible. I keep thinking of Lisbeth and Ann all the time. I wonder how long it will be before I see Lisbeth again and Ann for the first time….. Boat does sail at 7pm out into the sea. Plenty of wrecks lying about. Wonder where I am going.

Bill rose on the morning of 1st August to find he was sailing up the Clyde — no surprise given the rumour of recent days. He desperately enquired as to a route off the ship and a means to travel to Edinburgh to see Lisbeth and Ann. They were already in Scotland, there was no word of departure — surely it was doable? Alas not. Bill was instructed to stay put with the others for a further day. He could only cast his gaze out to Greenock and recall a previous time there with Lisbeth. Bill considered his predicament. Like waking from a deep slumber and trying to recall the previous night's dream; the closer one is to doing so, the further away it seems to drift. That sense of wanting something so badly and having it cruelly snatched away was difficult for Bill to manage. Over the previous twenty-four hours he'd moved physically closer to Lisbeth and Ann, but there was to be no opportunity of seeing them.

2nd August 1941

Still anchored off Greenock. Try to get ashore but impossible. Write letters to Lisbeth, one to Mother. Still always thinking of Ann and Lisbeth. Wonder how they are. Sail at 7.15pm. Take my last look at Clyde for some time I suppose. Never thought I loved the home country so much. Swear I will never leave it again once I get back (if possible). Throw goodbye kisses to my darling wife and daughter — God bless them both. Pretty near to tears.

Lisbeth and Bill had made a pact that when they were apart, if possible, they would set aside a moment at 7pm every evening to imagine the other doing the same and try to let each know what the other was thinking. Anchored off Greenock, Bill closed his eyes and tried to imagine what Lisbeth and Ann would be doing, but he could picture nothing. The Mull of Kintyre was the last piece of Scotland Bill saw as the Orcades sailed away into the Atlantic, linking up with other vessels to form convoy WS10.[24] As it did so he whispered to himself:

'I will see you again and until I do, every spiritual, ethereal, and mobile part of me is with you and never forget it.'

Bill was still uncertain as to exactly where they were heading or how long they would be at sea. They were likely to make stops before reaching their final destination, but he didn't know where, when or for how long. He would attempt to cable Lisbeth whenever they reached a port and in the interim, he could send an air mail letter every week, an air graph every fortnight and a long letter via sea mail whenever possible. Bill would begin numbering his letters — a routine that continued for the duration of the war. This ensured Lisbeth knew in which order to place the letters regardless of when they arrived.

Life on board was lazy. A steward brought a cup of tea and a biscuit to Bill's cabin at about 7am. This was followed by a leisurely wash and shave and then breakfast at 8am. From then until 11am there was little to do,

---

[24] Holdoway, *Military Convoys WS.10*

except pace the deck, read and write. Deck drill took place just before lunch. It involved donning life jackets and moving to allocated spaces before being reviewed and released by the ship's captain. After lunch, Bill would read and sleep until 4.30pm. After dinner, the chaps would play bridge, talk and stroll about before retiring to bed around 10.30pm. The bunks were comfortable, if a little narrow and Bill had no problem sleeping.

Bill acknowledged to Lisbeth in writing that it may be a couple of years until the war was over and it was unlikely, he would get back beforehand. As he tried to accept this prolonged separation, he imagined his homecoming at Waverley Station — Lisbeth looking as lovely as ever, with wee bonnie lass Ann in tow. He would play this scenario over in his mind innumerable times.

'We are playing today for the grand time we must have tomorrow and so we should do it gladly,' he wrote in a letter to Lisbeth. 'It is better to pay and then enjoy than to enjoy and know that you still have the reckoning to come.'

The middle of August brought an intense heat making it difficult to sleep at night because of the stifling air. It was, however, warm enough to swim. There were two swimming pools on board which gave some respite from the heat. The men took a plunge early in the morning before dressing in tropical kit for the day: shorts and open necked shirt. In the evening it was kilt, collar, tie and jacket for dinner. Deck games of tennis and quoits had started and the ship's passengers began to form bonds. Bill started to enjoy the company of other people for the first time since leaving Greenock.

As the days rolled by, the temperature rose. Bill had never experienced heat or humidity like it. To stand and shave with the sweat running down his face was a new experience. The sea was so still that nothing seemed to move for days. And then, finally, came the sight of land. They reached the port of Freetown (which Bill referred to as 'X' in letters to Lisbeth) on 17th

August. It was a short stop, and quite a few passengers disembarked creating more room on board. For Bill and the rest, the journey continued, crossing the equator on 23rd August. With it came a dry and more acceptable heat. Bill saw his first palm trees (outside of the Edinburgh observatory), and long golden beaches; albatrosses tracked the convoy.

The daytime routine stayed much the same, but in the evening fantastic concerts were put on by the crew. The compere was excellent — as good as Bill had seen anywhere. Various turns performed, all of which were very entertaining. Three of the twelve lads that had boarded with Bill in Liverpool entered a novices' boxing competition. All of them got through the first round, but then passed out — one of them, literally. There was also a cinema, which Bill enjoyed, despite the re-running of old films.

Bill didn't know where they were going next, but an engineer who had boarded at Freetown suggested they were heading for the only place he would leave Scotland for. Bill was intrigued.

On 3rd September 1941, HMT Orcades approached the port of Durban (which Bill referred to as 'Y' in his letters home) for an extended stay of five days. Swarms of native bumboats came alongside the ship selling bananas, mangos, coconuts and sandals.

Bill stepped onto dry land for the first time in over a month at Durban which was as grand and beautiful as the engineer had described. All along the front was a marvellous beach stretching for miles with large skyscraper like hotels to the rear of a wide promenade. Rickshaw drivers dressed in all kinds of exotic fashions and feathered headdresses made their way along the road. Some carried bells to attract attention, others would whistle and some rattled beads. The size and style of the buildings and properties signified wealth — as did the number of American cars fighting for road space with trolley buses. Bill, two chaps from the Army Post Office (APO) and Bill McIvor sat in a café watching this new world. Two lads Bill had known at Chester Castle joined them. Three footballing mates from Stirling also appeared. 'Small world,' one shouted in surprise as Bill rose from his seat to greet them. A striking sunset came and went with darkness falling around 6pm. Dark skies triggered bright lights — a wonderful sight for men who'd endured blackouts in Blighty for so long. And the song of crickets accompanied the magnificent light show.

After a while the group headed for a hotel — the grandest in town. Standing outside in their kilts having a smoke, a man approached them with his wife, son and daughter. The man had a clear and familiar accent; they were from Larkhall. Mr and Mrs Welsh took it upon themselves to chaperone the friends throughout their stay, starting with a lavish dinner and champagne. No expense spared.

The next morning Mrs Welsh took Bill to a local market where he purchased two ornamental elephants and a wooden box for Lisbeth. Mrs Welsh offered to post them. Later the same day, five of the lads piled into Mrs Welsh's car and they climbed up and away from the city, visiting a sugar plantation some forty miles distant. The visitors each broke off a piece of cane and sucked up the sweet sugar, before returning that evening for another lavish dinner.

The following day required some time back on Orcades. Some passengers, including Bill and McIvor, packed up and transferred to a Dutch ship. Going back ashore later, they bumped into Roy and Judy, the Welsh's children. Bill accompanied the youngsters around the markets before being taken for coffee and cigars back in the family's hotel suite. He concluded that Mr and Mrs Welsh were the kindest people he had ever met. On Monday, they planned to join them again for shopping and sightseeing, but it was not to be. The ships set sail on 8th September and a blissful few days ended.

The new ship was much bigger than the Orcades and a good deal faster.

Fitted out equally as well, Bill thought the cinema was a thing of beauty, seating over four hundred and doubling-up as a church on Sunday. Boxing, tug-of-war and tunnel-ball tournaments continued to provide entertainment, and late in the evening Bill would play bridge or solo, with lights going out in the saloon around 11pm.

By now, Bill guessed he was heading for Suez on a journey that had taken him around the Cape of Good Hope, thus avoiding the Mediterranean with its inherent threats. Bill was buoyed with the news of Roosevelt's speech, first broadcast on 11th September 1941.[25]

> One peaceful nation after another has met disaster because each refused to look the Nazi danger squarely in the eye until it had actually had them by the throat. The United States will not make that fatal mistake.

> No act of violence, (or) no act of intimidation will keep us from maintaining intact two bulwarks of American defense: First, our line of supply of material to the enemies of Hitler; and second, the freedom of our shipping on the high seas.

> No matter what it takes, no matter what it costs, we will keep open the line of legitimate commerce in these defensive waters of ours.

> We have sought no shooting war with Hitler. We do not seek it now. But neither do we want peace so much, that we are willing to pay for it by permitting him to attack our naval and merchant ships while they are on legitimate business.

Bill crossed the equator again on 12th September. This brought a further increase in temperature. At 7.30am it was 81 degrees in the shade and Bill felt as though he was burning up. Small hand towels were placed around

---

[25] 'On maintaining freedom of the seas' radio address

the men's necks to prevent sweat from running down their backs. By noon it was unbearable and at times, unable to cope with the climate, Bill bordered on delirium. He took refuge in his cabin and imagined a damp morning on the Pentlands with cool mist descending.

The cabin was spacious, even with four berths (as opposed to the standard two). He was sharing with Bill McIvor and the two postal captains they'd gone ashore with at Durban. Overall, it was quite a comfortable space. It was an inside cabin with no porthole, but it had a revolving fan and two ventilators (forced air) which kept the place as cool or as warm as anywhere else on the ship. Carpet covered the whole floor and there was a chest of drawers and writing-table. The table was mostly the domain of Bill, and he used it to craft letters to Lisbeth, complaining of the incessant heat.

'It's supposed to be winter around here. If that is the case then I hope I'm home again before summer,' he scrawled, adjusting the towel around his neck. He also hoped his return trip would be via the Mediterranean and not the frying pan of the Red Sea. 'Little gusts of air when they come are regarded as manna from heaven,' he wrote.

The men arrived off Suez on 19th September, disembarked into small boats and made their way to Port Tewfik quarantine quay. There was a cup of tea and a two hour wait, before boarding a train similar to those back in Blighty. The painted carriages were silver-grey in colour and had a veranda at each end. The major difference was in the quality of fitment. 'First class carriages not as good as our third class,' Bill noted in his diary that day. It was his last entry. Bill was now on active service — no diaries.

The swimming pool on board HMT Orcades
© Australian War Memorial (Catalogue No. 030390/01)

Native fruit sellers alongside HMT Orcades
© Australian War Memorial (Catalogue No. 030115/06)

HELIOPOLIS AND A CAIRO PENSION

In a move that would have significant bearing on the Second World War, Eighth Army was created from the Western Desert Force in September 1941 under the command of Lieutenant General Sir Allan Cunningham. The first offensive undertaken by the newly formed Army of Commonwealth troops was Operation Crusader, which ran from 18th November to 30th December. At the time, it was the only British Army engagement with German forces on land. Auchinleck replaced Cunningham with acting Lieutenant General Neil Ritchie on 27th November.

Around that time, an ambitious and charismatic soldier, David Stirling, was trying to find support for a niche mobile commando unit. Stirling pitched his idea to Ritchie who took it to his superior. General Auchinleck subsequently sanctioned the formation of 'L' Detachment, Special Air Service (SAS) Brigade. The LRDG, with their specialist navigation and survival skills, provided transportation and support for the new unit in daring raids behind enemy lines.

In North Africa, raging battles ensued with successes for both sides until Eighth Army finally forced Rommel to retreat, initially to Gazala, west of Tobruk, on 7th December, and further to El Agheila by 30th December. The campaign, though partially successful, did not achieve its ultimate objective of completely pushing Axis forces out of Cyrenaica and North Africa. Rommel now had the advantage of shorter supply lines. What had been a major issue for the Axis forces striving east, now proved to be the same for Ritchie in the opposite direction, as he experienced the difficult environment and stretched lines of communication and supplies. Perhaps the best assessment of desert conditions was given by General von Ravenstein, the captured commander of the 21st German Armoured Division.

'The desert,' he said, 'is the tacticians paradise, but the quarter-master's hell!'[26]

By late January 1942, Rommel, who had re-equipped and bolstered resources, initiated a brutal offensive against the tired and stretched force of Auchinleck. Eighth Army was subsequently pushed back to the Gazala Line to take up defensive positions just as the Germans had done the previous month.

In Eastern Europe, Hitler launched a strategic offensive against the Russians with the intention of taking Moscow. Multi-layered defences of a resolute Soviet Army combined with terrible conditions and extreme cold were too much for the exhausted German force. Hitler issued a halt order on the general offensive and assumed direct command of armies in the field. The Germans abandoned their attack on Moscow and retreated.

On 7th December 1941, the Imperial Japanese Navy attacked the United States naval base at Pearl Harbour to damage the US Pacific Fleet. America had been supporting the Allies with weapons, equipment and supplies. The day after Pearl Harbour, the US declared war on Japan and formally joined the Allied effort.

The Arcadia Conference was held in Washington two weeks later to develop a war-winning strategy. Despite the American public's desire for retribution against Japan, it was agreed that the focus of Allied efforts should be on the defeat of Germany. Churchill and Roosevelt achieved their conference objectives and American forces were soon mobilised and established bases in Britain.

*****

---

[26] Ministry of Information (for the War Office), 1944, *The Eighth Army (September 1941 to January 1943)*

For almost all passengers on the train to Cairo, this was the first time they had seen the desert. In the first few hours of rail travel Bill only saw two trees. He'd spotted wandering Arabs with herds of goats and the odd camel strolling about, but nothing more. He also experienced a mirage for the first time. Having sworn the train was approaching a shimmering lake, no matter how far the train travelled, nothing more than silky smooth sand came into view. Eventually, the train reached a more fertile spot with date trees, palms, fig trees and vines before coming to a halt. The lads climbed out of the carriages into the baking hot sun before shifting to Geneifa, an infantry base depot just outside Cairo. There were some hutments but the camp was mostly an all-tent affair. Bill and McIvor were thrown together in a large bell tent dug into the ground. They would receive 3 shillings and 6 pence per day colonial allowance, plus 2 shillings per day field allowance, reserved for those living in tents. Bill's allowances were paid locally so he opened an account at Barclays Bank, Cairo.

For the next three days, their time was their own. There was a tramway-cum-train that ran from Heliopolis to Cairo, so the two friends set out to see the sights. The hustle and bustle of the city characterised by the febrile behaviour of the locals, mesmerised Bill. The traffic had them in a quandary and there were hawkers and touts everywhere, from shoe blacks to vendors of cigarettes, postcards and razor blades. The friends took refuge for a while in a French hotel to observe the chaos outside before plucking up the courage to venture out once more.

Over the next two days they became accustomed to the ways of the Egyptians and settled in. There was an excursion to see the sights of Mena, and shopping back in Cairo combined with a visit to an open-air cinema. At the Pyramids, a fortune-teller told Bill that he would have two children, the first of which would be a boy.

'Really? Well something's already gone wrong there then.'

At the end of the first three days Bill had seen as much as his wee brain could take. He hadn't spent much money up to that point and decided to purchase a camera to record his memories, plumping for an American Vokar. It cost £5, including an astigmatic lens and distance regulator.

The imposing domain (tent) at the infantry base depot, Heliopolis, was named *Dunedin* after Edinburgh in old Scots Gaelic. The lads rigged up a table from suitcases. They also had two chairs and a washstand. Boots, boxes and sundries were shoved under their respective camp beds. The central tent pole doubled as a hanger and whilst it could never be described as luxurious, the tent was homely.

On 1st October, McIvor's GHQ posting came through and he left the same day. Bill had been pals with McIvor since Stirling and they had rarely been out of each other's company, save when Bill was playing cards or writing and McIvor was reading. The two friends took several snaps outside Dunedin and McIvor went on his way.

Bill missed his wife dreadfully and longed to see his daughter. On 29th September, he wrote his first letter to Lisbeth on an air mail letter card in what was the start of a fastidious routine. In his second letter, he asked her to forward a full description of wee Ann: weight, height, hair colour, eyes, feet, hands, sounds. Bill had a photo of Lisbeth in a frame fashioned from cardboard on his makeshift table. He desperately wanted a picture of Ann to accompany it. Bill felt rather depressed and, with no letter from Lisbeth, his mood worsened. Trust between man and wife was of the utmost importance. Tales of indiscretions back home were commonplace and it would be all too easy to allow jealousy, that most destructive of emotions to take hold. Letters were crucial because anything left to the imagination could weigh heavily on the mind.

'If you let jealousy get to you, then you may as well dig a trench and throw your marriage into it,' Bill was told.

He reminded himself that he and Lisbeth had a beautiful baby girl to look after and raise together, although it troubled him that he wasn't at home to share in the early days and weeks of Ann's life and to help Lisbeth with everything she would have to contend with. He would just have to make up for it with the next wee red wrinkly. Bill told himself he was just marking time before being able to live a normal happy life with his wife and child. For now, he could do nothing but deal with whatever came along.

Bill made enquiries about two posts; one cipher and one statistical. The adjutant had put him forward for a role in Adjutant General 1 (AG1) branch at GHQ. At the interview, Major Bailey accepted him within five minutes. Bill wrote to Lisbeth to tell her the news, although he couldn't include any detail for obvious reasons. His job involved 'figure work,' in line with his expertise and he looked forward to giving his brain a mental shakeup. To be near to the job, Bill moved out of Dunedin to a pension in the suburbs run by an old French lady and her daughter. Bill was sitting in the lounge when one of the other lodgers came home from work that day — it was McIvor. Beaming from ear to ear Bill spurted out, 'Of all the pensions in all the places!'

McIvor shot back, 'I was only saying in the office earlier that I hope I've seen the very last of that chap I've been stuck with since Stirling.'

The men smiled broadly and shook hands. The two pals were together again. Bill made do in the lounge for a few days and thereafter shared a room with McIvor.

McIvor was now a three-pip (captain) working in public relations. Bill had found himself a staff lieutenant's job that paid 2 shillings per day on top of his wage. He would pay £11 per month for his lodgings compared to around £18 if he was living in the city. This meant forking out an additional £2 per month for travel, but it was still the more cost-effective option, at least in the short term. Bill's hours were 8.15am to 1pm and then 5pm to

8pm. Half a day off was allowed per week (any morning or afternoon) and one full day per month.

McIvor joined the Gezira Sporting Club for £1.10 per quarter, plus fees for the various games. Bill's role wouldn't afford him more than an hour and a half free time in the afternoon, so he couldn't justify the expense. Instead, he would spend recreational time and money at the pictures. There were four cinemas within a five-minute walk of his pension — all open-air. There were two showings nightly with the second one starting around 9.30pm. This was perfect for Bill. In what became his favourite cinema, the wicker seats were all on one level with the screen at the far end. With the moon out, the stars twinkling and trees gently rustling, it was an unfamiliar setting in which to watch a film, but he became used to it. Before long, he considered it a fine way of passing a few hours and relaxing.

The sun blazed during daylight hours but it grew chilly after dark requiring one to wear service dress. When Bill and McIvor had spare time, they ventured out together to see the sights. One Sunday they went to the zoo and Bill took snaps to send back to Lisbeth. Back at the pension, he asked McIvor to take one of him as he wrote to his wife, so that she could picture him thinking of her, with pen in hand.

The war was a curse but it was teaching Bill a lot. The change in environment and the difficult circumstances brought into sharp focus just how fortunate he was in his civilian life. Bill longed for a cloudy day, full of rain, and wrote to Lisbeth that he would 'never grumble about the Scottish climate again.' He would give pounds just to sit in his chair and read, or listen to the radio and warm his hands by the fire. How he longed for the warmth and comfort of home. The Sinclair family had never had much, but Bill didn't need much — just the simple things in life — home and family.

In November, Bill revisited his decision about living at the pension in the suburbs. The rate had been increased and he had become frustrated by the lack of time for himself owing to the amount of travelling he had to do. Sadly, Bill left McIvor and moved to new digs in the city. Whilst right in the city centre, his sixth-floor room was high above the noise and it was much closer to GHQ. Initially, he shared with an RAF flight lieutenant — a decent chap who worked for Metro-Goldwyn-Mayer in London before being called up. Bill's move coincided with a promotion to lieutenant, which brought with it a further 2 shillings per day pay and 2 shillings and 6 pence per day staff pay.

Now that he had more free time in the afternoon, Bill wanted to get back to his football and he heard there was a league of service teams in Cairo. He resolved to get a game as soon possible and he didn't have to wait long. Bill found a place on the 'A' branch team and soon after, on the GHQ first team (as outside-left). As time went by, he also played a few games for the Imperial Chemical Industries side as centre-half. 'You can never say I'm not getting around,' Bill wrote. By December, he had taken over the running of GHQ football.

With his promotion to a two-pip (lieutenant) Bill was getting a succession of *brass* and *red bands* knocking on his door. As a result, he was privy to a lot of *griffin,*[27] almost all of which he had to keep to himself. Soldiers were not supposed to keep diaries during the war, but many of them did. Bill did not. And while his letters to Lisbeth contained a volume of information, they generally said nothing of his work. In his letter of 19th November, however, Bill referred to the 'big show' that had started the day before. Operation Crusader involved a plan to take on Rommel's Afrika Korps, and relieve the besieged garrison of Tobruk. This reference to military operations was a rare exception and was explained by the publicity that accompanied the operation. This coupled with the time it would take for

---

[27] Inside news or secret information

Bill's letter to reach Lisbeth, meant there was zero risk of confidential in-formation being passed. Bill was optimistic about the British offensive and by the time Lisbeth received his letter, he hoped that old Jerry up in 'the blue'[28] would have had quite sufficient. By the end of January his view would change.

The 30th November was St. Andrew's Day; Bill had never celebrated it. However, being so far away from home, national days became more signif-icant. Bill and three mates took dinner and then visited the cinema to see *Lady Hamilton*. Bill Taylor was in 2nd Echelon (02E) and the one who had announced the birth of baby Ann. Alex Howie was also in 02E and had been with Bill from Stirling to Burton. The other man was none other than Bing-ham from Invergowrie. It turned out that Bill's RAF roommate, Flight Lieutenant Dick Johnson, knew Bingham and had figured out that his friend and Dick's roommate were one and the same. The two Bills met the next day with Bingham remarking, 'I felt compelled to trek three thousand miles and seek you out to ensure you'd gotten over that incident with the use of the church organ?'

'Have never given it a second thought,' Bill replied with a grin.

Bingham was a platoon officer in the RAF and had only been in Cairo for three weeks. His call-up should have been as a maths and science man, but he'd opted to join the RAF in the munitions business. In a quieter mo-ment he confided in Bill that he was missing his wife terribly. She was pregnant, with her baby due the following March. Bill tried to cheer him up.

'Something to celebrate then Bingham my man. Instead of blue bonnets over the border, we shall make it blue bonnets over the desert tonight!'

News that a fellow in Bingham's office was going back to Scotland

---

[28] 'the blue' was a general term used to describe the desert area stretching up to and including the fighting front line

bolstered Bill's mood still further. The soldier was returning on health grounds, but he could take small parcels back with him. Bill had already sent one by sea to Lisbeth, but that would not reach her until March. Sending something back with this chap would be much faster. Silk stockings were purchased. Small and light, they could easily be carried and they were not available back home. Bill wrote to Lisbeth with all the news and concluded, 'for the first time since landing I am now beginning to feel more like myself.' With Stalin and his boys doing their level best to keep the war short, Bill was hopeful of a return to Scotland before much longer.

On the morning of 25th December, Bill rose to wish Lisbeth's picture a Merry Christmas. Wondering if she'd hung Ann's wee sock up, he smiled at the thought of how little one could squeeze into it in the way of gifts. He had had an expensive week with one thing and another. Contributing to presents for the clerks and wassies (South African ATS), plus the typist in the office, had left his wallet light. Two girls from the Women's Auxiliary Air Force (WAAF) who had sailed out with Bill on the Orcades threw a party, so naturally, he'd taken them a gift. In contrast, the only thing Bill received on Christmas day were two cards from Lisbeth's mother. 'It's a good job I'm old enough to know better,' he mused. 'If not, then I would be taking a very dim view of Santa Claus!'

On 26th December, Bill saw his daughter's face for the very first time. Lisbeth had posted the snap weeks earlier and it finally arrived on Boxing Day. He was happy and sad in equal measure. He was so pleased to see Ann for the first time, but ached to rush home and hold her.

For Hogmanay, Bill opened his door to all the Scots who wished to celebrate in the time-honoured fashion. The four corners of Scotland (and beyond) were well represented and after a while they moved to the larger pension of two Scottish captains to sing traditional songs such as *Auld Lang Syne*, the *Wee Cooper O'Fife*, and the *Road to the Isles*. Singing was only interrupted by drunken debates about Scottish football.

In the first days of January, Fayoum Sporting Club played host to the GHQ XI. It was seventy miles away from Cairo. Bill was managing the team, not playing, and took about sixty supporters including his roommate, Dick. They were introduced to the only Englishman in the province, a bank agent who had organised a terrific lunch. He treated them to the closest thing to good home-cooked food they'd had in months. Bill was introduced to the governor of the province and his chief of police. The game was a close affair with the visitors running out 5–4 winners. The governor complimented the referee on his handling of the match though Bill's opinion was, 'the referee didn't know much about the game.' A nice tea gave way to speeches before the party journeyed back to Cairo.

There was no set day to play football. The committee decided which teams should play, but the clubs concerned arranged the day between themselves. With an hour per day allowed for sport this was difficult, but manageable. Bill Taylor was running the football in 02E, so he and Bill arranged friendly games between their first and second teams. The second teams met on 27th January with the GHQ XI running out 6–3 winners. Bill knocked in two goals.

Pitch surfaces were often of hard sand — brutal if one took a tumble. The GHQ pitch was slightly more forgiving as it was grass covered, though Bill still described it as being, 'hard as a bone.'

The end of January brought with it the first round of the Cairo Cup. The GHQ first team annihilated their opposition 14–0. The second team also won their match 5–0 with Bill scoring a hat trick. During the same week a new branch league started and Bill repeated his hat trick in a 5–0 win. He wrote to Lisbeth the same day and told her all about it.

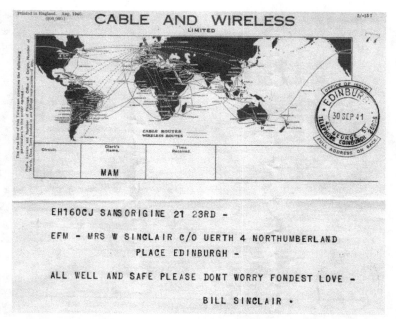

Wire sent on arrival in North Africa, 30th September 1941

'Outside Dunedin'
Bill Sinclair, 1st October 1941

Bill Sinclair, October 1941

'The veranda outside our bedrooms. One fond husband writing to his darling wife'
13th October 1941

Lisbeth and Ann Sinclair
Queen Street Gardens 1941

Sixth floor-lodgings, Cairo City Centre
Bill Sinclair, December 1941

HOSPITAL LEAVE

By the beginning of February 1942, Eighth Army was dug in at the Gazala Line, desperately holding on against Rommel. Churchill needed a public relations victory; he continued to badger Auchinleck for positive news in vain. Auchinleck needed time to regroup and build a force capable of countering the onslaught. His request for a major general led to the arrival of Dick McCreery.

The Russians were also struggling against the might of the Germans. After the relative success in the winter defence of Moscow, the Red Army was pushing forward in an attempt to relieve the beleaguered city of Leningrad but they were no match for the German fortifications in the dense forests. The Eastern Front pulsed as both sides attempted to gain ground.

In February 1942, the US agreed a billion-dollar loan to Russia in order to support the Red Army on the Eastern Front. At the time, a mutual aid agreement was signed between the US, Great Britain, Australia and New Zealand; and American troop numbers in Britain increased in advance of the planned invasion of German-occupied Europe.

The RAF intensified the bombing campaign against urban targets, attempting to disrupt German production lines and their ability to feed the Führer's army. Bomber command targeted civilian areas of industrial towns in the hope of destroying morale. The Rhine-Ruhr area, with its coke plants and steelworks was attacked extensively.

*****

Fighting to win

When the sun goes down on the desert waste
And the soldiers go to sleep
They shed a tear for the staff back here
And the ceaseless watch they keep

Battling along in Cairo
Taking it on the chin
Fighting the fight for Britain
Fighting the fight to win

Writing each other letters
Drowning each other's noise
Rallying round Gezira
Roughing it with the boys

Struggling along in Cairo
Straining our expert eyes
Fighting a serious battle
Foiling the subtlest spies

Knowing our proper worth
Ignoring ignoble jeers
Rallying around Gezira
Buying ourselves three beers

W.G.M. Sinclair 1942

In the second round of the Cairo Cup on 12th February 1942, Bill scored twice against a First Division side and the match resulted in a 2–2 draw. A branch league game the following day ended in a 10–0 win with Bill bagging five goals. He was feeling the magic returning to old lefty and looked forward to the Cup-tie replay to be held two days later. Unfortunately, the

GHQ second eleven went out in that game 2–1. Bill pinned his hopes on the first team.

Air graphs, air mail letters, and sea mail letters continued to drip through to Bill in batches from various sources. Auntie Meg, Auntie Lily, Ann Bathgate and Lisbeth's brother Jack were all writing to Bill and he replied whenever he could.

He had also been corresponding with his cousin Hamish for a time when he received a letter from him asking if they could meet. Hamish was also in Egypt. Bill's location was out of bounds for Hamish due to the nature of GHQ work, so Bill would travel to him. The fellow in charge of transport was a former Heriot's pupil and so Bill managed to secure a staff car and driver for the purpose.

Bill and driver, Mick, set out across the desert, guided only by empty tar barrels spaced every three hundred yards. The Ford handled itself well on the tougher terrain. The flared wheel arches allowed for the use of oversized wheels and desert tyres, which gave greater ground clearance than the standard Ford. British Army staff car M713026 was comfortable and provided a luggage rack on the roof and space for a spare wheel on the rear if required. Bill hoped there would be no need to change the wheel as the spare on this car was non-existent. The men saw nothing for miles and miles and hit a few soft patches, digging themselves out three times. Eventually, the surface became firmer and they made better progress. Finally, Hamish's camp came into view. He was let off for the day, but with no suitable place to go in camp, they headed back toward GHQ. Hamish drove with Bill sitting at his side and Mick laying at ease in the back. They had a good blether before arriving back at the Alexandria-to-Cairo road and taking refreshment at an eating establishment known as Halfway House. As a *pipper* (soldier with rank), Bill had to stand lunch for the others before ferrying Hamish back to camp. Bill then drove all the way back to GHQ for practice.

In March, the powers that be told Bill to take seven days leave before the hot weather started. His first choice was Palestine, otherwise he would journey to Alexandria (Alex). Whichever, there would be a change of scene and a well-deserved rest. Bill had been very busy both in and out of the office.

As it was, Bill didn't get to go anywhere, because on 13th March, he was admitted to hospital. A swelling on his finger had gradually become worse over the course of five days. He went to see the medical officer but continued to feel dreadful and so they admitted him. The swelling continued unabated and Bill began a routine of six pills per day and bathing — hand to elbow– in hot iodine. 'An Egyptian insect of some kind,' the medical officer surmised. Bill's mates suggested it was just the laziness coming out of him.

This kind of insect bite was commonplace in Cairo, along with gippy tummy, scabies, dysentery, boils, and infections related to the city's nightlife. In hospital, though, there were more serious injuries that made Bill realise just how lucky he was. One chap had bought a shell all to himself up in Tobruk during Operation Crusader and was in a terrible state. Bill was impressed by the skill of the surgeons.

'The things they had done and were doing to that lad were unbelievable. He still hopes to be able to play golf again, and I believe he may do it yet.'

It wasn't all doom and gloom in hospital. On the very first night a boxing tournament was put on for the patients. Bob Scally, the Scottish Heavyweight Champion from Leith gave a fantastic exhibition. And to make use of his time, Bill censored air graphs. This prospect did not excite him, but the very first one he looked at caught his attention. A bombardier, G.A. Latta, was writing to an address in Blackhall, Edinburgh. Bill used to play golf with Ian Hunter and a George Latta from Blackhall. It was the same man.

Another writer referred to Harthill in his air graph and Bill was reminded of his time at Polkemmet Juniors, and his old team mates.

If he hadn't been sent to hospital, he wouldn't have seen those air graphs, or struck up a friendship with the nursing sister. Situations where people's worlds collided based on seemingly random events or chance were intriguing. The seriously injured chap in the next bed had never met the medical staff attending to him before, yet they were now the single most important group of people in his life. They would determine what sort of existence he would have when he left hospital, yet, when they discharged him, he would likely never see them again.

Bill was discharged on 23rd March and although he had to report to the medical inspection room for the next few days, he went straight back to work as duty officer. Shortly afterwards, he moved into new lodgings. This time, he was living with a Scots couple at Atholl House. There were two beds in Bill's room but nobody had taken the other. His previous roommate Dick was sharing with an RAF pal elsewhere. If the second bed remained unoccupied the room would be £14 per month all in. This was very reasonable, but if Bill could find a partner, it would drop to £12. The room was well equipped with a dressing table, large wardrobe, writing desk-cum-bureau and a cabinet with drawers.

Mrs Milne, Bill's new landlady, took him down to the markets in Cairo and helped him barter. How he could have done with her when buying his camera. He referred to her as being typically Glaswegian, a proper blether with a no-nonsense approach; they got on well. She spoke Arabic like a native and got the best deal possible for Bill when he bought some fabric with the money he'd put by, for his now cancelled leave. He was originally thinking of purchasing silks but they were too expensive, so he bought cotton instead. There were three pieces, each two metres long; one plain white that Lisbeth could embroider as she liked and another floral. Bill wrote to

Lisbeth letting her know to expect a package and to ask her Auntie Kate to see if she could work the patterned material up into dresses for herself and Ann.

Towards the end of March 1942, the heat intensified and insects swarmed. In spite of this, Bill was still playing football and his branch team had won the league, meaning they were through to a Cup tournament. The first Cup game was played in Alex. The team travelled on the fast train and drew the match 3–3 with Bill getting a late equaliser for 'A' branch. In the semi-final of the Cairo Cup four days later the GHQ first team went down 3–2. They had chances galore but hadn't taken them, and succumbed to a last-minute goal. The season finished on 19th April with a final inter-GHQ match: Scotland vs England. The temperature was almost unplayable for a bunch of hairy knees from so far north, but they coped as best they could and the *Auld Thistle* ran out eventual 3–1 winners, with Bill scoring two goals.

Bill was thankful for the opportunity to organise and play football; it kept him sane. Everyone found cipher work tough and there was quite a steady sick list, but Bill reckoned his GHQ work was fifty percent worse than ciphers. That said, he was just grateful not to be a PBI (Poor B------ Infantryman). In his letters, Bill wanted to tell Lisbeth about his work, but he couldn't, and offered the following words.

> There are of course heaps of things I could tell you but can't if you know what I mean darling! Actually, some of them are not even to be revealed after the war is finished, so Lisbeth, if on my return you find you have a young clam for a husband you will realise why!

Letters were their only line of communication and the only means of keeping their relationship as a married couple alive. On the days that Bill didn't receive a letter, he consoled himself with the thought that Lisbeth was reading one of his, and that she was as excited and thrilled in doing so as he was when reading hers.

With the football season over, Bill sought entertainment elsewhere. There were the usual visits to the cinema — and cabarets — although Bill didn't think much of these. His pension was conveniently located for the pictures so he didn't venture far and avoided the main town areas in order to keep away from potential trouble. He sometimes visited the famous Gezira Club, but it was full of young bloods returning from the desert, looking to release their pent-up frustrations, and things could easily end up in a mess. The bringing together of men from all corners of the globe amidst a haze of alcohol, and women, was best avoided as far as Bill was concerned, particularly given the confidential nature of his work.

Besides his normal duties, Bill took his turn on picket which involved patrolling the streets of the city to stop any army fights. His opinion of Cairo under any circumstance remained; it was a filthy, dirty city with few redeeming features. It was a hotbed of spies and merchants, pedalling mistruths and rumour. Some referred to Cairo as the mysterious city. From Bill's perspective, the only mystery was why it existed! He reckoned the GHQ lads stationed there should be awarded medals for 'long service in Cairo, demonstrating great fortitude in the face of Egyptian insects' and 'strategic withdrawals to places of coolness in the midst of an Egyptian summer' and 'brilliantly conceived road-crossings in the face of Cairo taxi drivers and other sundry assassins.'

Bill also struggled with the food. Mrs Milne did the best she could with what she had and meals were, at least, substantial and varied. They had bananas, melons and oranges in great profusion, but the staples of a British diet were more difficult to come by at a reasonable price. There were three meatless days per week, but Bill thought it 'rotten meat in any case.' Bread was hit and miss. Sometimes it was 'queer darkish brown stuff' that he speculated was made with maize and rice. Sporadically, it returned to something more recognisable, made with wheat. The only regular vegetables on offer except potatoes, were carrots. 'Only occasionally an onion floats past,' wrote Bill. Mrs Milne said that vegetable prices had increased ten-fold since pre-war times. Eggs, butter and milk were in plentiful supply, but the eggs were often rotten and milk had to be boiled before consumption on account of tuberculosis, rendering it tasteless. The butter was made with olive oil — acceptable for a Mediterranean, but not for a Scotsman.

'AG Branch football team at the Arsenal Sporting Club, February 1942.
Winners of branch league, lost only one point, goals for 34, against 4'
Left to Right
'Newman, Hutchinson, Courtney, Fellowes,
Stride, Warren, McInnes, Kilroy, "Wee Mee," McBrien [Mac],
[front] Wilson, Telfer'

'Sent to daddy with all the love
in the world.
From mummy and Ann'
Ann Sinclair, age 7 months
March 1942

'Hamish and I and the wagon at Halfway House, March 1942'

'Fruit-seller, boats, Nile and Gezira Island, Cairo May 1942'

GHQ PROMOTION

The period from May to July 1942 in North Africa was truly terrible for the Eighth Army and Churchill's pressure on Auchinleck for a counter-offensive continued. However, on 26th May it was Rommel who attacked. There were valiant efforts to resist the German offensive such as the Free French defence of Bir Hakeim, but the Allies were on the back foot. By 14th June, Auchinleck had lost the Gazala Line and authorised Ritchie to withdraw. The British garrisoned Tobruk and began the retreat to Egypt. Tobruk lasted a further week but fell to the German advance on 21st June.

Four days after the fall of Tobruk, Auchinleck felt compelled to sack Ritchie and took the position himself. *The Auk* was now Commander In Chief Middle East *and* Commanding Officer Eighth Army. On the same day, General Eisenhower was made Commander In Chief Europe.

Rommel continued his drive east and consumed Mersa Matruh on 28th June. By 30th June, the Allies were driven back further, taking up defensive positions at Alamein. Rommel was coming on fast; Eighth Army had their backs to the wall and Cairo looked to be under threat. In a panic, on 1st July, GHQ staff burned vast quantities of classified files, engulfing the city with smoke and debris. The day became known as Ash Wednesday.

Luckily, Rommel's forces did not consume Cairo as feared. In fact, Auchinleck's Eighth Army drove the Germans back in the so-called First Battle of Alamein that continued through July. Despite preventing Rommel from entering Cairo, Auchinleck would pay the price for what Churchill saw as the unacceptable situation in North Africa.

Churchill arrived in Cairo with Alan Brooke, Chief of the Imperial

General Staff on 5th August 1942. Churchill instructed Harold Alexander to take over Middle East command. Dick McCreery would become his chief of staff. That left the role of Eighth Army commander vacant and Churchill selected William Gott for the job; however, Gott was tragically killed when his plane was brought down *en route* to the region. Bernard Montgomery was second choice. Churchill asked Alexander to take charge of Middle East Forces on 15th August with Montgomery becoming Commanding Officer Eighth Army on the same day. Montgomery, however, appeared two days early in what was a slight on Auchinleck, but typical of Montgomery's character.

At the end of August, Rommel launched an offensive at Alam Halfa, but Montgomery had been warned about the plans through Ultra intercepts.[29] He positioned his forces appropriately and made best use of the RAF, forcing Rommel to retreat. Montgomery did not pursue, electing instead to build up his Eighth Army for a later, major offensive.

Elsewhere, the German invasion of the Soviet Union continued. By September, the German Army had launched a massive offensive on Stalingrad. Capture of the industrial city would provide control over important transportation routes east and access to the Caucasus and associated oilfields. While the German offensive had made solid progress, and despite a continued determination, their drive east was stumbling amid stretched lines of supplies. Operation Barbarossa was fading into memory but the German push continued. Supported by Luftwaffe bombing raids, the Germans entered Stalingrad and engaged in hand-to-hand battles with Russian troops in bitter and bloody fighting.

To negate the need for such close quarters fighting, during the period, both the Germans and Americans were working on separate weapons

---

[29] The Ultra team based at Bletchley Park had earlier cracked the Enigma code used for German communications

projects. In Germany, the first V2 flight was a failure while in the US, the so-called Manhattan Project, to create an atomic bomb was progressing.

At the same time, in Poland, the first deportations from the Warsaw Ghetto to Nazi concentration camps took place. Treblinka was open.

*****

Working in the GHQ office next door to Bill was a Canadian captain from Ontario by the name of McBrien, who Bill knew from the 'A' branch football team. Despite their day jobs, the two men organised football, rugby, hockey, tennis, cricket and swimming for those who wanted to take part. In civilian life, McBrien was a lawyer, and by May 1942 he was touted for a more suitable job. Bill would be sorry to see him move on, but was lined up to take the Canadian's role once it became vacant. The staff captain promotion would mean a pay increase from 13 shillings (plus 2 shillings and 6 pence staff pay) to 16 shillings and 6 pence (plus 5 shillings staff pay). He looked forward to the tidy rise, but it was a step up in responsibility, and Bill would have to work especially hard at a time when the war was not going well.

Auchinleck was rumoured to be under immense pressure and changes to Eighth Army command structure were in the offing. Bill saw Auchinleck with Dick McCreery at the Sunday service in Cairo Cathedral at the end of May. Whilst Bill had his own work pressures, he couldn't imagine what the men at the top of the command tree were facing.

Earlier in May, 'Freddie the print' had dropped a gift on Bill's desk.

'What's this?' enquired Bill, as a piece of paper landed in front of him.

'I know how you like your souvenirs Bill. Here's one for your collection. What do you make of that?'

Bill turned over the paper. His eye was drawn to Auchinleck's signature at the foot of what looked like a memo. Reading it through, it became clear that Auchinleck was giving Ritchie a dressing-down over the quality and discipline of junior officers, something that had long been a problem. Sure, the memo was framed in polite language, but the message was clear.

'I don't want to know how you came by it Freddie, but I'll take it, thank you.'

'My pleasure. You know I like to keep in with the lads with the hairy knees.'

Re-reading the memo later that evening, Bill concluded that the rumours were true that Commanding Officer Eighth Army, Neil Ritchie, was in trouble. Bill was in no doubt that Auchinleck was applying pressure to his subordinate just as Churchill was doing to him.

At the end of May, the colonel (now brigadier) summoned Bill to his office and offered him the role as McBrien's successor. McBrien (known as Mac) was to take up the position of Deputy Assistant Adjutant General (DAAG) in Eighth Army. The brigadier thought Bill rather young to fill Mac's boots, but he was to be offered the opportunity on merit. Brigadier (Brig) McCandlish also believed the promotion would be a fine opportunity to extend Bill's staff training, and there was potential for a DAAG role six to nine months later. He considered Bill better suited to a staff job. This meant Bill was unlikely to get the chance to kill off any Germans, but it *would* mean that a) his chances of survival would greatly increase and b) his prospects after the war would be enhanced financially.

June 1942 saw many men shift out of Cairo and into the desert. Bill was not among them; he began his new staff role. A change in working hours meant toiling through the heat of the afternoon during which the temperature rose to 99 degrees in the office. In his new role, Bill was privy to more confidential information and he took his first flight in a Martin Baltimore reconnaissance bomber. Bill needed to have eyes on the supply lines, and with negligible risk of enemy attack, aerial reconnaissance and recording was the most effective method of obtaining intelligence.

Rommel had become well-known as a master tactician back in Blighty and Bill was as eager as any to dent this reputation. In letters to Lisbeth, he insisted the lads were still confident. With news of the continued Axis advance, he was in reality becoming extremely nervous. In his letter of 26th June, Bill wrote:

'My next holiday will have to wait at least until we have fixed up Von R [Rommel] who is causing a few sandstorms.'

By this time, Auchinleck had removed Ritchie and was now commanding Eighth Army himself. A day after Ash Wednesday in Cairo, Bill wrote to Lisbeth to confirm they were about to 'fix Rommel up good and proper.' As the Afrika Korps pushed further east, he was trying to convince himself as much as her.

Bill tried to remain positive but it was tough. Months of separation from his wife were turning into years and Bill dreamed of returning home after the war. He wanted a teaching post in a small or medium-sized town in the country, preferably among hills, or by the sea. If not, he would seek a position in Edinburgh and the family could live out at Currie, Juniper Green, Fairmilehead or Liberton. He wanted to smell wet grass after a rain shower and feel soft yielding turf beneath his feet. 'The far coolins are certainly calling me away,' he wrote. Bill dreamed of a detached house with garden front and back, and space on at least one side. It would have to be in a quiet area away from the main road to be safe for Ann and any more children they might have. He desperately wanted to be a real father, playing a part in the lives of his family. But for now, he was stuck in North Africa.

One hot afternoon, walking through the streets of ash-covered Cairo, Bill was hailed from across the way by none other than Jack McKenzie, a good friend from Varsity OTC. Jack had recently arrived in Cairo as a second lieutenant in the Signals and brought news of pals back home and their temporary displacement around the globe. They found they had a lot in common and spent the afternoon on the blether. Jack had also entered into the teaching profession only to leave it behind because of the war. They shook hands and agreed to keep in touch as best they could. With that, Jack went up into the blue. Bill prayed Jack would be spared. So many of his acquaintances — old and new — had died in the African desert or further north in mainland Europe.

Given the reports of Axis advances, Lisbeth was anxious for her husband. Bill wrote to reassure her on 29th July.

> You seem rather pessimistic in [Postcard] 15 my sweet. Personally, I can assure you that you should not be so. We here are only waiting until the other German Army (the one the Russians are playing with) comes down to our part of the globe and then we'll really get started and wipe the park with both that one and this other one we've got tied up in the blue — s'fact! …

> …When I go to bed tonight, I'll be thinking how exactly one year ago I went to bed in a certain transit camp, only to be rudely awakened at approximately 4.30am with the information that I was the father of a bouncing baby girl. I'll never forget that day as long as I live.

> I wish I could be there tomorrow to wish Ann many happy returns in person but miracles like that just don't happen nowadays. Perhaps next year!..

> …I know now just what is worthwhile in life and what isn't. I'll tell you someday Lisbeth.

The day after his daughter's first birthday, Bill began recording notes to include in a formal publication: *Maintenance of the Eighth Army*. He would document events and lessons learned, starting with Eighth Army's predicament at the end of July 1942. The theatre of war was like a project with various phases, including a start, middle and end Bill thought. What did we do badly and would seek to avoid in future? What did we do well but would endeavour to improve? What did we excel at and would aim to repeat? These were questions Bill had a responsibility to answer for his part in the management and control of reinforcements (Rfts) and prisoners of war (PWs). His handwritten notes summarised his thoughts.

31/7/1942

Situation resulting from Rommel's advance from El Agheila to El Alamein

As the Eighth Army withdraws to El Alamein, the shortened lines of communication simplified the movement of Rfts from Base Depots to the army area. Consequent to the withdrawal however, considerable congestion of Rfts in rear areas was caused. In main, contributing factors were:

- Rfts were not reaching units as locations of individual units changed rapidly from day to day and transit camps etc., lacked necessary information to enable them to forward Rfts. These Rfts consequently were withdrawn as Rommel advanced, each withdrawal contributing to the growing mass of Rfts in Amiriya area.

- Casualties in Eighth Army necessitated speedy replacement as the situation in respect of Rfts in army area was not fully realised at base. Rfts continued to be despatched ex Base Depots, likely adding to the congestion.

This problem was partly relieved by the reduction of availability of Rfts for Eighth Army, owing to commitments in the nature of Defence Units specially formed under BTE from the Rft personnel in Base Depots. These Rfts were of course available in an emergency for units in Eighth Army. When the line at El Alamein was stabilised the Control Post which had been formed in Eighth Army some time previously proved of great value in sorting out the Rfts congregated between Alamein and Amiriya and forwarding them to units.

At Appendix [appendix number not yet confirmed] is a statement of Rfts despatched ex Base Depots during the month of July; only a small number of these reached their ultimate destination prior to 31ˢᵗ July 1942

The main lesson to be learnt from this phase of operations is that in a withdrawal, strict control of Rfts must be exercised both in the area of operations and in the base. To this end, a Control Post such as was formed is essential. This post must be kept fully informed of the changing situation and locations of units and formations.

Up to this point, Bill's office space had been his own, but this changed in August with the arrival of John Robertson. John hailed from Colinton; he was a sports writer with *The News* and was a member of Lothianburn Golf Club. He was in charge of news bulletins and communiques from an RAF point of view. The two men had mutual acquaintances back home and immediately hit it off. John was looking for a pension room and so Bill arranged with Mrs Milne for the two of them to share. Coming from the same part of the world and with similar interests, meant Bill and John were a great source of support for each other and soon enough they conspired to bring their wives together back home.

Later that month, Bill received a letter from Lisbeth along with a photo of Ann in Abercromby Gardens on her birthday. Bill so wished he could have been there. Ann seemed to have received a 'large batch of presents,' he replied, though 'you might, however, ask your Auntie Kate what a one year old wants with a dressing gown? That one has me beat, I must confess.'

Towards the end of August, Bill turned his attention once again to football. For the new season, they'd formed an area league based on zones. A team from each zone would also play in a league. In Bill's zone there were seven professionals, so his chance of getting a game was pretty slim. However, running alongside was the usual GHQ inter-branch league where he would be sure to take part. Either way, it would be a busy winter of football and he was looking forward to it.

Back at Atholl House, Mrs Milne also lifted Bill's mood by securing a cabbage. Bill had not tasted cabbage for over a year and savoured every mouthful.

'Now, if she could only produce a turnip,' he wrote to Lisbeth.

As the football season had started back home, Bill asked Lisbeth to send him the *Saturday News* with reports of the Hearts and Harthill games.

By mid-September, Bill had fallen back into a routine. Rumours of an imminent move had diminished and Bill thought it most likely they would be staying put for now. He focused on the future in his letters, and this wishful thinking kept him going. For others, there would be no future to contemplate. Lisbeth informed Bill of friends that had died. Of the twelve men that had come out on the Orcades, three had been killed and two seriously wounded. Bill Taylor's batman had also died. It was a stark reminder of the sacrifice some were making in pursuit of victory.

The football season started at the end of September with all units naming their teams after those back home. Hearts had already been taken, so Bill chose Aberdeen for his first team as it contained one Aberdeen professional and two juniors. He named the second team Celtic under pressure from some of the players. GHQ was now split into two halves for sport, with Eric Russel running one half and Bill the other. This naturally brought a sense of competition between the two. In the first game of the season, Bill's

Aberdeen side played Bolton Wanderers. Aberdeen were 6–0 up at half-time with Bill grabbing one goal and Hugh Adam (the Aberdeen professional) scoring the other five. Aberdeen laid low in the second half until Bolton scored two in quick succession. The full-time score was 8–3. As they left the pitch, Bill was delighted with the early promise shown by his side; he had high hopes for the season ahead.

John told Bill he should try match reporting after the war, and that he might be able to help him. Being paid 10 to 15 shillings for watching a game of football sounded inviting. John was proving to be a good friend and useful contact. He woke like an alarm clock at 6.30am every day and ensured Bill was up and about by 7am so that he could polish six pips, two regimental titles, one Sam Browne and one cap badge before breakfast.

With the build-up of Eighth Army resources (including the 51st Highland Division), Bill had been extremely busy with Rft business and had his first full day off in months at the end of September. He spent the morning Christmas shopping in Cairo with John before venturing to the zoo and taking tea. In the afternoon, they made their way back up the Nile in a traditional Egyptian Felucca, and rounded off the day with a trip to the pictures to see *The Chocolate Soldier*.

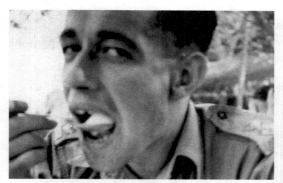

'Your long-lost husband indulging in the old-fashioned habit of attending to the inner man — pushing the old ice-cream back before it melts! June 1942'

'Abercromby Place Gardens'
Lisbeth and Ann Sinclair (age 9 months)

'Abercromby Place Gardens'
Ann Sinclair, age 9 months
May 1942

'This took ages to prepare. Old shirts, socks etc were picked up and stored away, the flowers were pinched from an adjoining room — what a job, all to show you how assiduously I write to you darling.
Cairo 1942'

Memo from General Sir Claude Auchinleck
to General Sir Neil Ritchie
6th May 1942
(see next page for transcription)

GHQ MEF.

BM/ 1GA / 37.

6th May, 42.

My dear Ritchie

1.   Criticism has reached me from various quarters regarding the way in which junior officers of certain units in the Middle East deal with the men under their Command.

2.   The importance of remedying any such state of affairs is obvious. In no campaign has individual leadership by junior officers been of greater importance, and in few have junior officers been in a position where less surveillance of their bearing towards their men has been possible. The value of an officer as a leader varies in direct proportion to the extent that he has the confidence, goodwill and respect of those under him.

3.   These qualities demand many things besides military competence, and it is in these respects that I think a number of our junior officers are lacking. This is not to be wondered at; in our search for officers we have cast our net wide, training has been in many cases insufficient, and has been carried out under conditions in which this most important subject of man mastership has been neglected. It is as important in administrative as in fighting units; in neither shall we get true and enduring efficiency without it.

4.   There are many outward signs of this, such as officers failing to return salutes, not addressing their NCOs and men properly, failing to consider the comfort of their men before their own, not identifying themselves with their men's interests and troubles, or trying to ingratiate themselves with undue familiarity.

5.   The root quality which is essential in the good Regimental Officer is unselfishness, a virtue which few of us possess by nature. The quality of thinking of others before we think of ourselves.

6.   But if we do not possess it naturally we can be taught or acquire it as a matter of duty, duty to the Army and those under us. It can be a very integral part of a Unit's pride in itself and its system.

7.   Its manifestation is the mark of a good Unit, and its encouragement the mark of a good Commanding Officer.

8.   Many of our Commanding Officers are excellent soldiers who are thoroughly competent to command their Units, but many of them have limited experience in Command of men, and still less of guiding and training their young officers. I wish this most important part of a Commanding Officers duty to be thoroughly impressed upon them, and I desire Formation Commanders to keep a watchful eye on the conduct of the junior officers towards their men. Nothing can be of greater importance than the inculcation of mutual trust, and nothing more disastrous than the lack of it.

Yours sincerely

C. Auchinleck

Lt.Gen. N.M.Ritchie,
G.O.C. Eighth Army.

My dear Ritchie

1.   Criticism has reached me from various quarters regarding the way in which junior officers of certain units in the Middle East deal with the men under their Command.

2.   The importance of remedying any such state of affairs is obvious. In no campaign has individual leadership by junior officers been of greater importance, and in few have junior officers been in a position where less surveillance of their bearing towards their men has been possible. The value of an officer as a leader varies in direct proportion to the extent that he has the confidence, goodwill and respect of those under him.

3.   These qualities demand many things besides military competence, and it is in these respects that I think a number of our junior officers are lacking. This is not to be wondered at; in our search for officers we have cast our net wide, training has been in many cases insufficient, and has been carried out under conditions in which this most important subject of man mastership has been neglected. It is as important in administrative as in fighting units; in neither shall we get true and enduring efficiency without it.

4.   There are many outward signs of this, such as officers failing to return salutes, not addressing their NCO's and men properly, failing to consider the comfort of their men before their own, not identifying themselves with their men's interests and troubles, or trying to ingratiate themselves with undue familiarity.

5.   The root quality which is essential in the good Regimental Officer is unselfishness, a virtue which few of us possess by nature. The quality of thinking of others before we think of ourselves.

6.   But if we do not possess it naturally we can be taught or acquire it

as a matter of duty, duty to the Army and those under us. It can be a very integral part of a Unit's pride in itself and its system.

7.   Its manifestation is the mark of a good Unit, and its encouragement the mark of a good Commanding Officer.

8.   Many of our Commanding Officers are excellent soldiers who are thoroughly competent to command their Units, but many of them have limited experience in command of men, and still less of guiding and training their young officers. I wish this most important part of a Commanding Officers duty to be impressed upon them, and I desire Formation Commanders to keep a watchful eye on the conduct of the junior officers towards their men. Nothing can be of greater importance than the inculcation of mutual trust, and nothing more disastrous than the lack of it.

Yours sincerely
C. Auchinleck

'Me in the front o' oor aeroplane.
Somewhere above the desert 1942'

Bill Sinclair, Cairo Zoo
September 1942

'Somewhere above the desert 1942'

'John on the roof of our abode
[Atholl House]. Not exactly the
background for tennis racquets but
since John fell heir to them, we
thought we'd better use them for
something!'
Cairo, September 1942

MOST SECRET MESSAGE OUT   OFFICER ONLY

TO :- TROOPERS
FROM :- MIDEAST
MOV.6A 48829   15/9   TOO 0915 GMT

Departing by Liberator AM 922 today Lt-Col Mc A STEWART

Major STRANGEWAYS(.) Live guinea pig for D of P in charge

former (.) Arrange reception

Degree of Priority :- IMMEDIATE

Officer i/c Ciphers

Please despatch IN CIPHER ONLY

Brigadier.
D.Q.M.G.(Mov & Tn).

Copy to :- AG M O2E File Mov.6A/101/7

Cipher message, date unknown

'Departing by Liberator AM 922 today Lt-Col Mc A STEWART
Major STRANGEWAYS(.) Live guinea pig for D of P in charge former (.)
Arrange reception'

SECRET   Cipher Message
                      IN

To:-   MIDEAST.
                                      Folio No. 38437.
From:-   EMBARKATION BOMBAY.   17.8.42.
                                      TOO 1145/17. THI 1146/17.
No.   4822.   TOR 0520/18.

Your MOV/5/36153.   Repeat after WINF ELD in para 2 to end of
para 2. Para 5 repeat number of foll wers IGSC
(I AM SO DRY DEAR MOTHER NOW)

MOV   7   ACTION
AG(2)   3   C.4. 0818/18.
G(SD)   3   T.T. 0820/18. MP.

Cipher message, 17th August 1942

'Your MOV/5/36153. Repeat after WINFIELD in para 2 to end of para 2.
Para 5 repeat number of followers IGSC
(I AM SO DRY DEAR MOTHER NOW)'

FOOTBALL SEASON AND THE SMALL MATTER OF ALAMEIN

T he 51st Highland Division (Heilendmen) were sent to the Middle East in August 1942. Their primary role was to support Montgomery's planned offensive. Whilst there were probing attacks at the end of September, the major offensive at Alamein only began on 23rd October. Churchill's demands for earlier action were successfully rebuffed by Alexander.

Eighth Army were well prepared for the battle, though initial gains were hard fought and progress through Axis lines was slow. Whilst the Allies had more men and equipment, Montgomery also understood the value of the RAF and, by the end of October, the Allies were seeing some success. Operation Supercharge finally broke through the Axis lines at Alamein and by 2nd November, Rommel signalled to Hitler that the battle was lost. Hitler ordered his men to stand and fight, just as he'd instructed the German Army in Stalingrad to do. It was too late. Rommel began to retreat on 4th November.

Churchill addressed the Lord Mayor's Banquet at Mansion House on 10th November 1942, and praised all those who played their part in the success at the Battle of El Alamein.[30]

GHQ Middle East could not rest on its laurels and assisted with preparations for Operation Torch — the mass landings on the North West African coast. Montgomery continued west with caution. The Axis powers were on

---

[30] During the address, Churchill uttered the famous words, 'This is not the end. It is not even the beginning of the end. But it is perhaps the end of the beginning.'

the run, but as they retreated, pursued by Eighth Army, so Allied supply lines became stretched once more. GHQ Middle East worked tirelessly to cope with this, until Tobruk, Benghazi and Tripoli were recaptured and provided additional routes in for supplies. Rommel continued to retreat west and eventually took up defensive positions at El Agheila. His last stand in Libya was effectively over by mid-December and the beleaguered Axis troops formed a rear guard near Sirte. By the end of December, Eighth Army had taken Sirte and reached the Buerat Line.

Away from the desert, on the Eastern Front in the Soviet Union, Hitler ordered troops into a second major offensive at Stalingrad with massive approaches from air and land. Savage fighting at close quarters ensued, as the Germans tried to progress towards the Volga. This continued throughout October and the first half of November, when the Russians launched a surprise counter-offensive in which they surrounded the German Sixth Army, closing in for the strangle in December.

*****

HMT Orcades sank on 10th October 1942, in a sustained torpedo attack. The converted troopship had set out from Africa and was heading for Liverpool. It was a sobering moment. The Orcades was the ship that had taken Bill from Liverpool to Greenock before sailing on to Freetown and Durban. It pained him to think of the former ocean liner lying on the sea bed, having steered a course through treacherous waters so many times in recent years. As usual, Bill had to digest the bad news and then move on. To dwell was not an option.

For Lisbeth's birthday, Bill had sent her a small card with his details on, displaying his change in rank. On the reverse he'd written a personal note and a few words to Ann. He also sent a cable with best wishes the day before Lisbeth's birthday. The couple had now been married for two years. Lisbeth was worried about where her brother might be sent, and so Bill asked her to send him Jack's Army Post Office (APO) number and draft letters because in his current role, he could establish where Jack was heading — if he was coming south east.

The new football season continued with Bill's first team (Aberdeen) coming out 8–4 winners in their second match. He scored three as did Hugh Adam, making the overall goal tally 16–7 for the two games. Bill also played a trial game as a representative of his zone — something he'd considered very unlikely given the quantity of professional players available. He spent five afternoons (in his free hour) per week watching, organising and playing football. He thoroughly enjoyed the distraction, even though it was hard work in the searing temperatures. The next game was played in unrelenting heat against 'A' Rifle Regiment; final score, 3–3.

The local newspaper published the results of games and occasionally a full match report. Bill liked to keep the clippings, so John Robertson promised Bill his paper after he'd finished with it. On the morning of publication, Bill was sitting at his desk working. Suddenly, his pencil was knocked out of his hand as a paper landed on his desk.

'There you go chap, as promised. You even get a mention Bill.'

Bill looked up. 'Great, thanks for that.'

He picked up the pencil from the floor. The paper was open at the correct page, with the heading: GHQ hit back and draw....three goal recovery.

Bill skimmed through the article.

> Adam, inside right, played a great game for Headquarters, and besides scoring two of his side's goals made the opening for the third. Sinclair, centre forward, was another <u>outstanding</u> figure, while Ford on the right wing sent in many useful centres.

John had underlined the word *outstanding* and, in the margin, he had written:

'He didn't mean this. What he meant to say was *standing*.'

The pencil Bill had picked up moments before was now winging its way through the air towards John.

'Hey, there's no need for that.' John was still laughing.

'Bloody news reporters,' scoffed Bill. 'Anyway, you're supposed to be busy. How have you got time to be fudgelling about?'

'Fudgelling about? I don't understand.'

'To fudgel, John. I believe the definition is something along the lines of pretending to work when you're not actually doing anything at all. And you're supposed to be the words man. I'm disappointed, given your most appropriate association with it.'

'Well you can just fu..........dgel off!' came the retort, as the pencil flew back through the air towards Bill. 'I believe that's your writing implement my friend. You should be more careful with it.'

Bill's mind remained on football with thoughts turning to the upcoming international match. It was an eclectic mix of the home-nations thrown together to form two sides. Scotland and Ireland took on England and Wales. The referee was Lieutenant Corporal Knight, who'd been the official at the GHQ vs Rifle Regiment game. The first half was goalless. In the second half, Scotland and Ireland scored, first through McIness with Bill grabbing their second. Henderson gave the opposing side a fighting chance with an own goal, but Bill scored his second, late on in the match to make the final score 3–1.

The day was made even better with news of leave for Bill. His previous leave allocation had been cancelled due to his spell in hospital. Now, in the middle of October, six days of leave were reinstated. He hadn't made any plans when John rushed in to announce he was going to Palestine on a job.

'You lucky so and so,' replied Bill. 'Even if it is work related.'

'Well, if you can be ready in fifteen minutes, there's space in the plane.'

'Are you serious?'

'Absolutely Bill. Come on.'

With nothing else to do, Bill raced round and gathered enough gear together for the two-day trip. An hour later they were in the air on their way to Transjordan. They travelled on the same type of bomber Bill had flown on during his first reconnaissance job. Looking down from the plane, he marvelled at the oases and spotted the odd camel and herd of goats like wee pinpoints down below. They flew along the shores of the blue Mediterranean for a while and had a bird's eye view of the breakers romping in. For the final leg of the journey (one hundred miles) the friends travelled by truck. Bill wasn't fussed. For him it was a jolly, and as they entered Jerusalem following a long day, he was happier and more relaxed than he'd been for a long time.

From Jerusalem they travelled across the Judean hills and through the plain of Jericho. They skirted the Dead Sea and then drove up through the mountains of Moab and on to Amman. The moonlight on this part of the trip was magical. As they climbed five thousand feet, the road turned and twisted like a coiled spring, with a three hundred-foot drop on one side and sheer cliffs on the other. Bill sat up front wrapped in an RAF great coat, while John lay in the back and covered himself with blankets. The driver adroitly made his way through every twist and turn.

The following morning John headed off to work. Bill took a car and a chauffeur for the day. He explored the local hills and visited a Roman amphitheatre, before travelling back to the mess for lunch. John joined him in the afternoon and the two men made their way down to Jericho. Thereafter, they crossed the River Jordan before going back into the Judean hills and on to Jerusalem. As darkness descended, they wandered the narrow streets of the old city, becoming disoriented more than once. Despite these historical surroundings, they ended up in the pictures! The following morning, they got cracking for the airport, climbed back on to the same bomber, and flew back to Cairo. Bill reflected on the trip for days afterwards and leafed through parts of the New Testament, now with first-hand experience of some of the places mentioned.

On returning from Jerusalem, Bill still had four days of leave left and travelled up to Alexandria to spend them at the coast. He found the most wonderful guesthouse, appropriately named, Villa Elizabeth, where he shared a room with a Major McCallum from the Royal Army Medical Corps — a Watsonian.[31] The food and attention he received was the best since being on the Orcades. The house was spacious; it had large balconies and was only a three-minute walk to the sea. Bill wrote to Lisbeth on 20th October, describing a lazy afternoon at the beach. He had swum about thirty yards out into the cool blue Mediterranean, turned on to his back, closed his eyes and allowed the breakers to carry him in to the shore.

One afternoon, McCallum and Bill borrowed their landlady's car and drove along the promenade, taking frequent stops to enjoy the sea-breezes and views. The journey was only twelve miles in total, but took the pair over two hours to complete.

The next day Bill played golf. He had been longing to play for what felt like an eternity. With the loan of clubs, balls and caddie, the whole thing cost 12 shillings and 6 pence — something equivalent to a fortnight's ticket at Millport Golf Club! In the end, he only managed sixteen holes. The heat, sweat, club grip and his lack of playing, resulted in four blisters that rendered him unable to play out the last two holes. Having put in a score of fifty-seven (against a par thirty-seven) on the outward nine, he started to find old form in the first seven holes of the back nine with a score of thirty. He enjoyed himself immensely, and for a short time he lost himself in the

[31] Former pupil of George Watson's College, Edinburgh

game and forgot about the war. The separation of thought didn't last long. Bill returned to Cairo just in time for Eighth Army's Alamein push.

'You will see by this time that we are having another crack at it, with a lot of Heilendmen to help us,' he wrote to Lisbeth.

Bill's role would become ever-more important as Rfts were a critical success factor for the drive west. Considering this, at the end of October, Bill penned the second tranche of notes for the *Maintenance of the Eighth Army* document.

1/8/1942 — 22/10/1942

Preparation for our advance from El Alamein

The problem to be faced in this phase was the building up of units and formations to enable Eighth Army to assume the offensive.

The availability of Rfts in Base Depots, the short lines of communication, and the facilities with which Rfts could be moved from base to army greatly simplified this problem. Careful control of these Rfts was exercised in the army area and ensured that they were put to the best possible use.

That the problem was successfully overcome proved by Appendix? which shows Eighth Army deficiencies as at 1st August 1942 and the numbers of Rfts received by Eighth Army for the months of Aug, Sept and Oct (total 41,925).

The lesson learnt from this phase was that the three requisites for reinforcing are:

- Availability of trained Rfts
- Adequate camp and station arrangements
- Strict control over disposal in army area

The end of October 1942 saw the brief return of Jack McKenzie from the front line. He was back in Cairo and doing fine, but only had until 24th November before his next stint up front. Despite sustaining shrapnel injuries to his shoulder in the recent Allied push, Hamish was also okay and glad of a role in the back-office area. Bill hadn't seen Bingham for months and assumed he'd been posted. John Robertson was extremely busy and working late virtually every night on account of the Allied offensive. As he was on the 'news bulletin racket' he was regularly up in the desert taking snaps and reporting stories. Bill received all the *dope*[32] about four days before it hit the newspapers.

On 3rd November, Bill wrote to Lisbeth about the push which had been going for eleven days.

> As you will doubtless know, we are now having another crack at sending all pests from the Western Desert and at the time of writing are doing very well. This is due in no small measure to the good old Highland Division. There are quite a number of my old varsity pals in this crowd....They are certainly doing great work and I try to keep them well supplied with men. Let's hope that this time we manage to obliterate the whole Afrika Korps. What would happen in that event we have yet to see, but here's hoping darling.

Guessing in letters about how things might go was as taboo as reporting facts, so Bill had to be careful in expressing personal opinions and details in writing to Lisbeth, but he was feeling more positive now it looked like the British Army could fight and beat the Axis. Amongst other things, Bill was responsible for processing enemy PWs and with ever-increasing numbers, he was now dealing with people going west *and* east. As always, when time allowed, football provided a welcome distraction.

---

[32] Inside news or secret information

Bill's first team was at last turning a corner. After three losses on the bounce, Aberdeen won their fifth game of the season on 7th November. Bill scored two as an outside-left. The second team, Celtic, were also doing just fine. Their next game was against the league leaders who had only given up three goals since the start of the season. The inside-left hadn't turned up, so Bill filled in despite playing only twenty-four hours earlier. He was chipper when Celtic ran out 5–1 winners against the table-topping side. The following week, Aberdeen achieved the same feat beating the league leaders, though it was a narrow 3–2 victory. Bill nodded one in with Hugh Adam bagging the other two.

From 7th to 10th November, John Robertson was right up at the battle-front and reported events back to Bill. Allowing for the requisite number of days to pass, Bill relayed the same to Lisbeth.

> Our local war effort is quite bright at present and looks like re-maining that way with the landings in West North Africa.[33] It seems as if we shall shortly control the whole of Africa, and consequently the Med [Mediterranean], as there is no use in Jerry staying in Trip-oli this time, if we are going to come at him.

Sadly, Lisbeth's response brought news that two more friends from the Caledonian Insurance Company had been killed, and that another was now a PW in Italy. Bill fixed his mind on the job at hand, determined to do what he could to positively influence proceedings.

During winter, the heat died down sufficiently for Bill to walk the twenty minutes into work. The alternatives were to take a tram (which was invari-ably crowded and filthy), a bus (just as crowded but not quite so filthy), or a taxi (cleaner and quicker, but expensive). By the time he got to work one mid-November morning, he'd formed in his mind, most of the notes on the

---

[33] Landing of troops in Operation Torch

pursuit to Tobruk.

23/10/1942 — 13/11/1942

The 'Break Through' and pursuit as far as Tobruk

Problems to be faced during this phase were:

-    The normal fortnightly Rft demand from Eighth Army had to be replaced by some method which would confirm that priority of movement was given to the Rfts most urgently required. Casualties sustained in the army altered their requirements daily.

-    Longer lines of communication necessitated the adoption of measures to assure speediest possible arrival of Rfts in army area.

To overcome these difficulties the following steps were taken:

-    A statement of requirements amended according to the changing requirements was despatched daily from Rear Eighth Army to GHQ. Based on this demand the available Rfts were despatched at the earliest possible moment.

-    The departure of Rfts ex Base Depots was timed to ensure their arrival at Amiriya in the morning. Close liaison was maintained between Rear Eighth Army and GHQ in respect of probable arrivals. This enabled preparation to be made for onward despatch by road transport without delay.

These measures were only partly successful. Rfts quickly arrived in rear army areas (according to Eighth Army requirements) but delays were caused in forward transit camps owing to a loss of control, consequent on the extended lines of communication.

It is considered that this difficulty would be overcome if there were established in the forward area a unit whose sole employment was the handling of Rfts *en route* from base to units in the army area; this unit must be in the nature of a transit camp capable of holding up to fifteen hundred Rfts, with the necessary instructors to continue training of these personnel detained through altering priorities.

By the end of the morning, the notes were typed up and set aside. Bill generally walked back to his pension at lunch time if he didn't have cause to stay around the office. If he did stay on, football was normally the reason. He would play for branch, the GHQ first team, take the second team somewhere to play, take the Cairo zone team somewhere, or play in a friendly game arranged for units ex the blue.[34] When he wasn't playing or arranging games, he would watch them. A rival team would be playing somewhere, so Bill would go along and observe their tactics. By the end of November, the results of Bill's teams were as follows:

Aberdeen: played 8, won 5, lost 3, scored 30 and lost 26

Celtic: played 8, won 5, lost 3, scored 39, lost 21

'A' branch: played 3, won 3, scored 16, lost 6

Aberdeen and Celtic were running fourth in their respective leagues while the branch side were the only team to have scored maximum points. Bill reckoned the standard in the Cairo league was roughly equivalent to English Third or Scottish Second Division. The scene was booming with virtually the whole Bolton Wanderers team being out in the Middle East. 'They must have joined up en-masse,' Bill wrote to Lisbeth.

In the six afternoons leading up to 20th December, Bill played four matches, watched one (his zone team), and refereed one. The four games included two for Aberdeen (4–1 and 7–2 victories) one for Celtic (0–0) and

---

[34] Units back from fighting up front

a game for the GHQ Officers against the 02E Officers. The latter was a team managed by non-other than Bill Taylor — his one-time shipmate and roommate.

Football continued to play a crucial role in providing some respite for the men stationed in Cairo and those returning from the front. Despite his machine gun training Bill was spared front-line action. He was never more grateful of this than when he heard of the deaths of friends and former work colleagues. In mid-December, Alex Howie informed him of another two. Bill Brechin and Freddie Sills were originally on Bill's draft but were delayed and had been routed out to the Middle East separately. Bill had seen Brechin very recently, as he'd dropped into GHQ before going back up into the blue. He died from wounds sustained in the fighting. They found Freddie Sills in a German-Italian cemetery. Bill could only assume he must have caught a packet in a raid. He relayed this latest information in a letter to Lisbeth and paid tribute to his two fallen colleagues.

> The war however is distinctly better, thanks to the efforts of fellows like Brechin and Sills in the Eighth Army, so let's hope that their efforts weren't in vain, and that soon we can all live at peace.

On completing his latest letter home, Bill got to work on tranche four of the maintenance notes:

14/11/1942 — 15/12/1942

The pursuit from Tobruk to El Agheila

The main problems in this phase were:

- Overcoming of the difficulties presented by an ever-increasing line of communications and shortage of transportation.
- The line taken in transit, making necessary a high degree of anticipation in respect of drafts to be despatched in order

that Eighth Army should receive these Rfts which were most urgently required at time of receipt.

The following steps were taken:

- Whenever possible additional trains were run to railhead which was for the greater part of this period at Matruh. Arrivals at Matruh were forecasted to Eighth Army in order that forwarding transport arrangements could be made. Road convoys could take a certain number of Rfts from base but the time taken rendered this method impracticable. Movement of Rfts by sea to Tobruk and Benghazi (when captured) was impossible owing to non-working of the ports and extensive risks involved until the closing days of the period.

- Forecasts of requirements (future) were made by Eighth Army wherever possible by units, failing which by formations. Drafts were accordingly prepared and could be despatched in receipt of a signal with minimum of delay.

That these measures had a certain amount of success is shown by the fact that approx. 11,500 Rfts were received by Eighth Army during this phase, an average of approx. four hundred per day, while casualties were [to be confirmed]. Differences in finding adequate transport for railhead caused delays in army area. The Rfts were forwarded as and when transport and mains stores convoys were going forward. That the correct drafts were received is shown by the fact that the same formations have been retained as spearhead for the common cause of the battle.

This phase re-echoed lessons learned before i.e. that strict control is essential:

- Over nature of drafts despatched.

- Over drafts en-route.

It also showed that in an advance, adequate transport arrangements for forwarding Rfts for railhead are essential to avoid unnecessary delays.

Bill's notes covered Eighth Army activity up to 15th December. Ten days later brought with it another Christmas away from home, but it was not all bad news. The food served up in the Kirk Hall on Christmas Day was a welcome change from the usual pension fare. There was a terrific crowd and the entertainment comprised dances: eightsome reel, parlais glide etc., a good many games organised by the Padre from Paisley, and two or three bouts of community singing. Bill joined in with *Mary's Argyll*, *The End of the Road* and *The Rose of Lalee*.

It was Bill's second Christmas in Cairo and his third without Lisbeth. Bill pictured Ann's stocking hanging up by the fire at Northumberland Place and blew an imaginary kiss into it. He prayed that next Christmas Eve he would be able to put a present inside instead. Bill saw 1942 out quietly in his room, writing his last letter of the year to Lisbeth.

G.H.Q. HIT BACK AND DRAW

THREE-GOAL RECOVERY

A Rifle Regiment 3 — G.H.Q. 3

A recovery in the latter part of the second half put General Headquarters football XI on equal terms with a Rifle Regiment after they had been three goals in arrears. Both sides played excellent football, the forwards combining well together.

ADAM, inside right, played a great game for Headquarters, and besides scoring two of his side's goals made the opening for the third. Sinclair, centre forward, was another outstanding figure, while Ford on the right wing sent in many useful centres.

The Rifle Regiment forward line was smart in combination, the forwards working well together, and often getting behind the H.Q. defence, Nastri, Barnford, Barton and Jones deserving special mention for the hard work they put in. Ingledew, centre half, supported his backs well, and cleared with long kicks.

He did't mean this what he meant to say was "standing".

Football match report 1942

"INTERNATIONAL" IN CAIRO

Scotland-Ireland Beat England-Wales

**Scotland and Ireland 3 —
England and Wales 1**

Scotland and Ireland won the return match with England and Wales 3-1 at the E.S.R.I. ground yesterday. The players were drawn from G.H.Q., M.E., and some excellent play was produced in spite of the blistering heat.

Scotland and Ireland were always the more dangerous in attack, although England and Wales did well enough until they approached their opponents' goal, when they could not place a shot right, their only goal being scored by an opponent, although the ball would have gone into goal even if it had not been diverted.

COMBINED WELL

The Scottish-Irish forwards combined well together, McInnes and Wright, the wingers sending some useful centres to Lt. Sinclair, who made good use of them, while Adam, the inside right, kept the rest of the forwards well fed with long passes upfield.

Play during the first half was fairly even, no goals being scored by either side. Soon after the resumption Scotland and Ireland went ahead.

F. Wright took the ball up, and after beating Tullitt shot at goal. Stubbs, England and Wales 'keeper, got his hand on the ball and diverted the shot but the ball went straight to McInnes, the latter unhesitatingly scoring with a hard return.

FURTHER AHEAD

Straight from the resumption England and Ireland went down in a determined raid and Barnard was called upon to save, performing his duties well. However, two minutes after their first goal Scotland and Ireland scored again, this time through Lt. Sinclair.

McInnes, Lt. Sinclair and F. Wright advanced on their own soon after, and it looked as if a goal was certain but McInnes was unlucky when his shot hit the bar after the 'keeper was beaten. Lt. Sinclair was also out of luck, his shot striking an opponent who was standing in the goalmouth.

Halfway through the second half England scored when Foster shot in, the ball going straight at Henderson, Scotland and Ireland centre-half, who was standing in the goalmouth. Henderson, in trying to clear, diverted it into his own goal.

SCORED AGAIN

A few minutes later Lt. Sinclair scored his second goal, manoeuvring himself into position before placing the ball well out of the goalkeeper's reach. Teams.

Scotland and Ireland. —Pte. Barnard; Pte. Aitken, Pte. Kilroy; Cpl. Herd, Sgt. Henderson, Cpl. Davidson; Pte. McInnes, L/Cpl. Adam, Lt. Sinclair, L/Cpl. I. Wright, Pte. F. Wright.

England and Wales: — Sgt. Stubbs; Spr. Tullitt, Cpl. Hutchinson; S/Sgt. Sharples, S/S/M. Stride, Pte. Day; L/Cpl. Foster, Lt. Birkett, Cpl. O'Shea, L/Cpl. Powell, L/Cpl. Brown.

Referee: —L/Cpl. Knight.

GHQ Middle East
1942
International football match report

'Jerusalem from the King David Hotel.'
October 1942

SECRET   TELEPRINTER MESSAGE   Folio No 80415
                              IN   7 Nov 42
                                                    TOO ----
To:- PAIC(L) GHQ IEF   HII 0945/7
From:- RSP ASLUJ   TOR 1609/7
No:- ----

Blood Orange three ASLUJ.   Completely happy, happily complete.
Possible non-starters 3 three ton 2 fifteen cwt. Will contact
SARAFAND.   Distance 180 miles very long for guns.   Suggest
farther first day. Request instruct 64 Fd REAR part obtain 3 air
bottles

Mov			7 ACTION
MO	2	E	3
AG(O)	3	X(1)	1
Q(A)	2	ST	2
Q(AE)	2	M	2
Mov	4	OS	3
AFV	1	EME	2
RA	1	Sigmstr	1
AA	1	PAIC(L)	2

                                    C4/1930/7
                                    T/12205/7/ JHRU.

Teleprinter message, 7th November 1942

'Blood Orange three ASLUJ. Completely happy, happily complete. Possible non-starters 3 three ton 2 fifteen cwt. Will contact SARAFAND. Distance 180 miles very long for guns. Suggest farther first day. Request instruct 64 Fd REAR part obtain 3 air bottles'

TRIPOLI TEARS

In the first half of January 1943, the Germans began withdrawing from the Caucasus. In Stalingrad, the German Sixth Army ignored demands for their surrender and the Soviets tightened the stranglehold. Eventually, starving and running out of ammunition, the Germans surrendered on 2nd February.

The Allied Casablanca Conference, to plan the European strategy for the next phase of the war, began on 14th January. In attendance were Franklin D. Roosevelt, Winston Churchill and Charles de Gaulle. Joseph Stalin did not attend due to the situation in Stalingrad. The conference resulted in the Casablanca Declaration: a demand for the unconditional surrender of Axis forces, and plans were made to achieve this ultimate goal. There would be a strategic bombing campaign against the Germans and an agreement to take the fight from North Africa, across to Sicily and thence to the Italian mainland. The military approach against Japan in the Pacific region was also decided.

At the Buerat Line in North Africa, Eighth Army regrouped and attacked on 15th January. Rommel retreated further and the Allies pushed on, entering Tripoli on 23rd January. New Zealanders, Highlanders and Desert Rats (British 7th Armoured Division) pounded the city's streets and Montgomery took the surrender. After a march of some fourteen hundred miles from Alamein, Tripoli was under Allied control. A fortnight later, Churchill arrived to address Montgomery and the men of the Joint Headquarters of the Eighth Army, and to witness the victory parade through Tripoli.

By this time, Axis forces had retreated across the border into Tunisia. Eighth Army entered Tunisia soon after, as Rommel headed for defensive positions at the Mareth Line. The Battle of the Kasserine Pass was the first major test against the Axis troops for the Americans who had landed in Operation Torch. They suffered many casualties and were quickly pushed back. However, as Axis attention returned to the east, the Americans fought back, and with the help of British reinforcements, they held the exits through mountain passes in Western Tunisia, defeating Axis forces.

On the Tunisian east coast, in March 1943, Montgomery faced attack from Axis forces in the battle of Medenine. The Allies had been forewarned of the Axis attack by the Ultra team at Bletchley Park and Eighth Army continued to benefit from the reconnaissance and spoiling activities of the LRDG, SAS[35] and Popski's Private Army (PPA). The attack was a costly failure and was abandoned by Rommel at dusk that day.

The battle of Medenine was the last in Tunisia for Rommel. Increasingly unwell, he left the Afrika Korps for good and returned to Germany, to be succeeded by General von Arnim, but the change in command made little difference and Axis forces retreated further to Wadi Akarit.

By the end of March 1943, Allied progress in North Africa, Russian advances on the Eastern Front, and US success at Guadalcanal in the Pacific turned the tide of the war.

*****

News coming back from the west via John Robertson, suggested good progress continued against the Axis forces. John had spent a few days up at the front, staying in a camp near *Marble Arch,*[36] Cyrenaica, and had reliable sources.

---

[35] SAS founder, David Stirling, was captured in Tunisia in January 1943, and despite repeated escape attempts, would spend the rest of the war in Germany at Colditz Castle

[36] Archway built by the Italians, marking the border between Cyrenaica and Tripolitania. It was nicknamed *Marble Arch* by Allied troops

Bill's work in Cairo, supplying the frontline thirteen hundred miles away, was all-consuming; it felt as though they were at the extreme limits of what was possible, operating from such a distance. He saw the potential for efficiency improvements, however, and suggestions were shoved under the nose of the colonel on a regular basis. Half were rejected; the remainder were published in General Orders, which meant Bill could get through his work faster. With supply lines extending ever further west, even small efficiency gains were key.

At the time, his boss, Major John Welch, was up for promotion and an associated move. Bill contemplated his own future. The brig had told the colonel he was thinking of sending Bill to the Middle East Staff School when the next vacancy arose. This would mean five months in Palestine. The alternative was a shift closer to the action with a slot in operational HQ. Whilst he wanted to stay in a staff job, if the next posting was in a Tripoli platoon then so be it. For now, all Bill could do was continue with the work in front of him. This included documenting the fifth instalment of maintenance notes.

16/12/1942 — 14/01/1943

The pursuit from El Agheila to Buerat

The problems were there of the previous phase being further aggravated as the army advanced.

The shortage of road transport for ferrying duties from Tobruk railhead had caused investigation to be made into possibilities of sea transport and efforts were made to despatch as many Rfts as possible to Benghazi by this method.

These measures were successful and approx. fourteen hundred Rfts were despatched during this phase by sea to Benghazi. In addition, the use of available space on road convoys from the Delta and the despatch of Rfts to railhead onwards by road made possible the fulfilling of Eighth Army's demand for this period, although the despatch of Rfts as a whole did not attain the proportions of previous counts. At the close of this phase small numbers of very urgently required Rfts were being sent by air as far forward as possible. The only new lesson learned from this phase was that in order to attain the best possible Rfts for army, every effort must be made to utilise all possible means of delaying — road, rail, sea, and air.

When not focusing on work, Bill's attention turned to football. In the two weeks since 7th January, there had been only one friendly game and a match against Fouad El Awal Secondary School at Abbassia. Bill played in the latter but didn't get on the score sheet in a 6–2 victory for his side. Lincoln had netted five of the Cairo team's six goals with McBeath grabbing the other. Post-match, the school principal gave an awful speech about politics, but praised the visitors as champions of liberty. Bill replied in style by telling just as many lies about his wonderful time in Egypt and the happy memories they would cherish.

At the end of January, John Robertson blew in for three days and gave Bill all the dope on the taking of Tripoli. He also gave Bill a copy of the *Tripoli Times* for his collection of souvenirs. Best of all, he offered Bill a trip west to assist with a forthcoming event. Major Welch approved Bill's leave.

Bill witnessed the victory parade through Tripoli at which Churchill was present. The event attracted thousands, all standing and cheering as troops and vehicles filed past. Bill's chest expanded with pride as the 51st Highland Division marched by. The drums and pipes evoked an emotional response and there were rumours that Churchill himself shed a tear as the lads came through. Bill wiped tears from his eyes as the lads played *Cock O' the North* — the regimental tune for the Gordon Highlanders.

'Bloody hell John,' he shouted over the noise as his pal approached. 'If Hitler and his cronies could witness this they'd roll over in a moment.'

Bill also saw Churchill's address to Montgomery and the men of the Joint Headquarters of Eighth Army. Churchill's closing words would be forever synonymous with the campaign.

'After the war when a man is asked what he did it will be quite sufficient for him to say, "I marched and fought with the Desert Army."'

It was a moment Bill would remember for the rest of his life.

When back in the Cairo Office, Bill completed tranche six of his maintenance notes.

15/01/1943 — 08/02/1943
The pursuit from Buerat as far as the border of Tunisia

Apart from the usual problems of means of transportation from base to forward unit, another problem to be faced was the recurring attempt to despatch to army, small parties of Rfts by private or unofficial means which invariably resulted in unnecessary delay to the personnel concerned. It was realised that the ability to despatch Rfts was not centralised sufficiently with the consequence that overlapping occurred, resulting sometimes in wastage of accommodation and personnel were despatched without regard to priorities of Eighth Army. This resulted from the reversion of method from a daily statement of requirements by Eighth Army to the original fortnightly overall demand. The following steps were taken to overcome these problems.

- More extensive use of shipping was made and by

coordinating rail and sea, considerable numbers of Rfts were despatched to Tobruk, thence by sea to Benghazi.

- The opening of Tripoli harbour in the later stages enabled the shipment of Rfts to that port. Close liaison between AG [Adjutant General] + SD [Staff Duties] ensured that units and drafts were received in the proper proportions and in the right priority, according to demands made by Eighth Army.

- In addition, all accommodation and stores convoys (and re-placement vehicles) ex Delta was utilised to the best advantage. To ensure that the Rfts despatched were as re-quired by Eighth Army, all Rft procedure was centralised under AG1 without whose authority no drafts could be des-patched. This necessitated close liaison between AG, 02E and Movements.

These measures were partially successful. The fact that the available accommodation had to be divided between units and Rat personnel [British 7th Armoured Division] as well as reinforce-ments restricted the latter to a total below the availability. The centralising of control ex base was also successful to a certain ex-tent but Base Depots, Schools etc., were still despatching individuals and small parties under their own arrangements, an ac-tion which invariably resulted in such parties arriving at their destination later than would have been the case under official ar-rangements.

Lessons to be learned were that still further endeavours should be made for additional transport accommodation and that control of Rfts ex base should be centralised. The centralising factor to ex-ercise the utmost control.

Bill wrote to Lisbeth on 11th February with two pieces of news. First, he'd played in the first round of the Cairo Area Cup which resulted in a 10–0 win. The second piece of news had a significant bearing on the remainder of Bill's war. Eighth Army had asked for his assignment to them as Staff Captain, Statistics, with a promotion to DAAG likely soon after.

> The brig is still wondering about it, but if he asks me, then by the time you get this darling I'll be on the way to somewhere near Tripoli. I'd love it. However, if it comes off, I'll send you a wire, so if you haven't got a wire by the time you get this [letter], then I'm not away!

There was no news on the Eighth Army posting the following week. In the meantime, Bill played in the second round of the Cairo Cup, beating a South African team 4–1. He headed in the first goal after only thirty seconds and that set the tempo for the rest of the match. The third-round tie would be played the following Saturday, 6th March.

As March arrived, things slackened off a little, and with a reduced work-load, Bill was able to watch some football during his afternoon breaks and venture to the pictures in the evenings. He also attended a three-day course culminating in hand grenade practice, and that evening, he made up a fourth at bridge. Only the army could have you watching football, going to the cinema, playing bridge and throwing grenades in the same week thought Bill.

His mind shifted to Lisbeth and Ann, and the green valleys and purple hills of Scotland. He pictured himself with his family gazing across Edinburgh City and the hills beyond to Fife, or wandering through the wooded dells of Colinton and Craiglockhart. He longed to be with fifty thousand others, shouting his head off at Hearts, or smacking a long drive off the fourteenth tee at Lothianburn, and watching it bounce and roll away down the hill. It all seemed so far away.

The colonel approached Bill on 7th March and told him that Eighth Army had asked once again for his services in Rear HQ. Bill reminded his superior that the brig had turned the first request down.

'The brigadier will let you go,' replied the colonel, 'but he only wants it to happen if you are to receive a promotion in the process.'

Bill would have to wait. He turned his attentions to the match that would see them into the last eight of the Cairo Cup. They were playing away to a team on the outskirts of the city on an awfully hard sand pitch. As it was, they won the game 6–2. Bill knocked the posts around but couldn't stick the ball in-between. His inside man had no such problem and scored five.

Eventually, the brig returned and confirmed Bill's new posting. This meant he would likely miss the semi-final of the Cairo Cup. He tried in vain to pull the game forward, but couldn't manage it, so he handed over the running of the Cairo City Zone to friends in the 15th Scottish General.

Before Bill left for Tunisia there was a day of leave. A close friend invited him to visit Memphis and Sakkara, around forty miles away. They arranged for a car and were accompanied by an Egyptologist. As they left the Delta and entered the desert, the sand whistled around the car, limiting their visibility and prolonging the journey, but it was worth it. Their Polish guide was a fountain of knowledge on ancient Egypt and helped Bill imagine the place as it would have been, thousands of years ago. They made their way to the step pyramid, reputed to be the most significant ancient monument in the world at over five thousand years old. Around the pyramid were arenas and tombs. The Egyptologist led the two men down into a tomb, forcing them to almost bend double. Bill marvelled at the inscriptions on the walls that were so lifelike, and the magnificent sarcophagus. After a hearty lunch, they travelled across the soft sand by donkey to visit the tombs of the sacred bulls, before heading back to the car and setting off for Cairo.

As his time in the city was nearing its end, Bill took his kilt and jacket

to the garrison tailor for cleaning and repair. His relief was due to arrive on
25th March and Bill wanted to be sure everything was in order. Morty Dykes
was a Walker Cup golfer from Bearsden and son of John Dykes, the rugby
international. Bill hoped to 'extract a few wrinkles on the old and ancient
game for post-war use.' Their shared interests led to an immediate rapport
and made the task of handing over simple. At the end of day one, Bill concluded that Morty was a decent lad and felt confident he was leaving GHQ
in capable hands.

In eighteen months of GHQ work, Bill had spent around eighty percent
of his time working on behalf of Eighth Army, and he felt it only fitting that
he join it out in the field. Bill reckoned the sixteen hundred-mile trip would
take around five days by road. As his departure day neared, however, there
was a change of plan. Bill would fly up as far as John's camp at Marble
Arch and a car would meet him there.

He made the most of his remaining days visiting friends and colleagues.
This included a dinner with Bill Taylor and Alex Howie. He wanted to see
Jack McKenzie and Cousin Hamish, but they had already moved west. One
of Bill's last tasks before doing so himself was to complete tranche seven
of his maintenance notes.

09/02/1943 — to date
The pursuit from the border of Tunisia onwards

No new problems have as yet arisen in this phase of operations
but the ever-increasing distance between base and forward func-
tions and the time taken for Rfts to reach their respective units
augmented the difficulties of i) transportation ii) necessity for accurate forecasts of requirements.

A further obstacle was the division of the formations in Eighth
Army between Tripolitania and Cyrenaica, necessitating accurate

despatching of Rfts to ensure that they arrived at proper destinations with the least delay.

Measures taken: To obtain speedy arrival of Rfts most urgently required, a fleet of aircraft were employed transporting personnel from railhead to a forward aerodrome. The personnel were despatched under arrangements made between SD, AG and Movements in accordance with Eighth Army priorities. Application for further sea convoys to Tripoli was successful and large numbers of personnel were forwarded in this manner. Road convoys going to forward areas were utilised as far as possible for transporting Rfts of lower priority. Rfts for rear formations were of a much lower priority and were despatched in road convoys destined for their area and by rail for onward by available transport. Forecasts of numbers of Rfts required were made by Eighth Army (by formations and arms) approx. every three weeks. This was facilitated by the presence of a liaison officer who could give Eighth Army a true picture of the situation at base and return with up to date requirements. The normal fortnightly demand was used as a guide to the ranks and trades of such Rfts.

The appendices show that considerable success was obtained in despatching Rfts. Reports by liaison officers have also indicated that Eighth Army is grateful at the numbers of Rfts received by them during the advance from Alamein. Abolition of practice of transit camps and the units illegally detaining drafts *en route* to two area for purposes of employment with these units.

In working for GHQ AG1 branch, Bill had supplied men to Eighth Army, the LRDG, SAS and PPA. He wondered how many of the 80,461 Eighth Army Rfts who had passed his desk between August 1942 and

February 1943 were still alive, and how many had made the ultimate sacrifice, enabling him to shift west in the hope of seeing out the war.

Bill's side won the semi-final of the Cairo Cup on 27th March 1943. The final was played on 9th April, but Bill was not there; he had taken up his new role in Tunisia as DAAG Organisation, Rear HQ, Eighth Army.

Sinclair's XI Beat Fouad El Awal

Capt. W. Sinclair's XI were the guests of Fouad el Awal Secondary School at Abbassia in a football match yesterday afternoon which the visitors won by six goals to two.

Early in the game Mc-Beath sent a neat pass to Sinclair and the latter came very near with a low shot. After ten minutes' play Lincoln scored from a pass by Sinclair.

A good move by the School halves and forwards resulted in Abdel Hamid equalising, but Lincoln added two more goals before the interval.

Shortly after the change of ends McBeath scored the fourth goal for Sinclair's XI, and five minutes later El Ginidy reduced the arrears.

Before the end Lincoln scored two more goals, making his bag five for the day and his side's total six.

Fouad El Awal Secondary School. — Ghayish; Abdel Aziz, Moustafa, El Khami, El Guindy: Abdel Hamid, El Ginidy, Hamid, Halim and Said.

Capt. W. Sinclair's XI. — Price: Wilcox, Stringer: Cook, Henderson, Kesteven; F/Lt. Collins, Norris, Lincoln, Capt. W. Sinclair and McBeath.

Football match report
January 1943

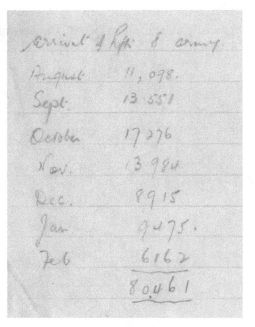

'Arrival of Rfts [reinforcements]
8 [Eighth] Army'
August 1942 to February 1943

Aug:	11,098
Sep:	13,551
Oct:	17,276
Nov:	13,984
Dec:	8,915
Jan:	9,475
Feb:	6,162
Tot:	80,461

Churchill with Montgomery behind.
51st Highland Division, Tripoli Victory Parade, February 1943

Churchill with (left to right), Alexander, Leese, Brooke, Montgomery
Eighth Army, Tripoli Victory Parade, February 1943

34904/'MS(SB)   SECURITY
URGENT MEMORANDUM   *dc/c)*   31 Mar 43

AG.1
To: MS Main Eighth Army

From: GHQ MEF   Copies: AG3(a)   C2E   Pay   Camp

1.   Lieut(T/Capt) W.G.M. SINCLAIR A & SH from S.C. AG.1 GHQ MEF
      has been selected for appt as DAAG Eighth Army with the Acting
      rank of Maj whilst so employed vice T/Maj J.R. McBRIEN RNF to
      ME Staff School.

2.   This offr will report for duty forthwith and be posted wef the
      date of assuming duty. Eighth Army will report to O2E on
      AF.W.3010 the effective date of this appt for Gazette action.

3.   A copy of this order will be handed to the offr concerned.

                                          S. Palmer
                                          S.V. Palmer
SVP/JC   for   Brig
                                          Dep Mil Sec.

Confirmation of role change and promotion, 31st March 1943

*' (T/Capt) W.G.M. SINCLAIR A&SH from S.C. AG.1 GHQ MEF has been selected
for appt as DAAG Eighth Army with the acting rank of Major whilst so employed
vice T/Maj J.R. McBRIEN RNF to ME Staff School'*

'A' Branch GHQ Team, March 1943
Bill Sinclair: back row, far left

*'Corporal Wright receiving a medal from Colonel Catherall
on my behalf after final of Cairo Cup, April 1943. If I'd been
there it would have been a winner's medal!'*

THE LAST OF NORTH AFRICA AND A PICTURE OF HOME

O
n 6th April 1943, Operation Scipio was launched against Axis forces along the Wadi Akarit. The Allies had reached the area a week earlier, but halted their march to allow British and American bombers to act first and facilitate the ground force attack.

The Battle of Wadi Akarit was won the following day and Axis forces retreated once more. Montgomery's Eighth linked up with the American led First Army and the Allies gave chase, taking Sfax and Sousse in the process. Axis forces eventually dug in again at Enfidaville. Its mountainous terrain represented a very different prospect for the Eighth Army with their desert fighting expertise.

On 19th April, Allied forces once more used a bombardment from the air coupled with artillery, to soften targets in preparation for a ground attack. Despite this, the combined German and Italian forces successfully countered on 21st April, and the strength of the Axis defensive positions became clear to Montgomery. The attack was suspended. This would be the last major battle for Eighth Army in Tunisia. It was subsequently split with some units moving to their American and British counterparts elsewhere.

Attempts to re-supply Axis forces defending the north east section of Tunisia had been successfully suppressed and on 7th May, the British 7th Armoured Division captured Tunis. The US II Corps took Bizerta.

On 13th May, Axis forces surrendered, and General Alexander informed Churchill of the same, stating, 'Sir, it is my duty to report that the Tunisian Campaign is over. All enemy resistance has ceased. We are masters of the North African shores.'

A quarter of a million German and Italian troops were captured and pro-cessed as PWs. The North Africa Campaign was finally at an end with the British having suffered some 220,000 casualties. Axis losses amounted to 620,000.[37]

Eighth Army's reputation and place in history was assured due to the units from Britain, New Zealand, Australia, South Africa, Rhodesia, Canada, India, Poland, Greece and the Free French. They had all played their part in the desert war of North Africa.

Victory on the ground was matched by domination of the skies and Mediterranean waters. This enabled the Allies to secure supply locations in North Africa and further facilitate the preparation and shift to Sicily. Churchill gained American commitment to this invasion at the second Washington Conference in May 1943.

By 11th June, the Italian fortress island of Pantelleria was taken after heavy bombardment. A day later, the Italian island of Lampedusa surrendered.

Axis powers were expecting an invasion of Sicily with the Allies using air cover from British bases on Malta. In preparation, they began to bolster defences on the island. To counter this defensive build up, an ingenious plan was initiated to fool Hitler into thinking the Allies intended to land elsewhere. The supply of false information in an operation, codenamed Mincemeat, worked and Hitler mistakenly shifted troops to Greece, thereby reducing the number left to defend Sicily.

With the SAS spearheading the assault, Allied forces landed on Sicilian shores on 10th July. Montgomery's Eighth Army headed up the east coast in the direction of Messina via the Catania Plain. The American Seventh Army, under Patton, landed in the south west. Within ten days they had

---

[37] Holocaust Encyclopedia, *Allied military operations in North Africa*

captured Palermo on the north of the island. Italian forces were now in dis-array and Mussolini was forced to resign on 25th July.

Amidst the German evacuation of Sicily, Churchill, Roosevelt and others attended the Quebec Conference in August 1943. As planning for the Normandy Landings (Operation Overlord) continued, it was agreed to pursue a diversionary front coming up from the south. With this, Eisenhower sanctioned an invasion of the Italian mainland.

An armistice was signed by Italy on 3rd September with the formal surrender following five days later. By this time, multiple amphibious landings were underway as Allied forces breached the Italian mainland, attempting to move up both east and west coasts. By the middle of September, the most fiercely contested of these landings was yielding results. The US Fifth Army led by Mark Clark was finally breaking out at Salerno.

Elsewhere, the period bore witness to the last major German offensive on the Eastern Front at Kursk in Russia. In some part this was due to the Allied progress in the Mediterranean, forcing Hitler to divert resources to meet the Italian offensives of Montgomery and Clark. The Russians took advantage with a strategic offensive at Kursk and a major tank battle ensued through most of July and August. Momentum was now with the Soviets and their push west. By the end of August, the Red Army was pursuing a multi-front offensive in Ukraine. Within days the Germans were evacuating.

*****

Belongings that couldn't be carried were sent on by road. As Bill boarded a plane on the evening of 5th April 1943, what he carried with him had to last until he and his kit were reunited. Goodbyes had been said, along with a final word with the colonel, who congratulated Bill on his promotion and wished him the best. A last minute change to the travel plans saw Bill's old Canadian colleague, Mac, meet him directly off the plane at Tripoli.

Mac took Bill by car up to Eighth Army Rear HQ which was rather different from the one he'd left in Cairo. This headquarters was more reminiscent of a Bedouin encampment, but with caravans, trucks and cars rather than camels and goats. At any rate, there was no mistaking that this was a mobile force. Home for Bill was a tent of about eighteen feet by fifteen feet. Mac bequeathed to Bill the Pointer puppy (Mick) he'd taken in as a stray. Bill also inherited Mac's batman and driver, Donnelly.

'What I've not worked out Bill is which one is the more difficult to control.' Donnelly was within earshot but he ignored the quip.

Donnelly was a first-rate chap; a tough character from Kirkintilloch near Glasgow, fiercely loyal and very useful to have around. Bill had a first-class staff sergeant by the name of Nicholls and a shorthand typist by the name of Lott. His staff captains, Johnstone and Chubb, were both intelligent men. They had their respective batmen, clerks, and the use of a fifteen-hundred-weight truck.

The Head of Organisation was Colonel Malcolm J Richards. Bill's first impression was that he was a square-shooting type who would not stand any *bull.* They would rub along just fine. There were one or two orderlies and clerks thrown into the mix and together the group formed the main components of Rear HQ 'A' Branch of the great Eighth Army.

The day after Bill's arrival, Mac took him up to the front to meet the opposite numbers in the corps. Bill was nervous at the prospect. He knew the main policies behind what he had to do, but everything else was new — not least the environment. Travelling up towards the front for the first time, with shells booming in the distance, had adrenaline rushing through Bill's veins.

Bill's new routine meant rising at 7am for breakfast, followed by a quick wash and shave, before settling down to work until bedtime with a short break for lunch and dinner. He began venturing up to the front, regularly, to liaise with the opposite numbers he'd already met, and find out how best to support them. On the journey he would eat by the roadside. Donnelly did all the driving as well as supplying the food.

'Where it comes from is a close secret between Donnelly and Mick!' Bill wrote. He'd wanted to send an earlier signal to Lisbeth to let her know he was okay but he was unable to, so Mac would send a wire on his behalf just as soon as he was back in Tripoli. Regardless, Bill would continue to trot out the usual air mail letter cards.

He had brought his camera but had forgotten to bring any films in the rush to pack and depart from Cairo. He would get some from Tripoli at the first opportunity. Somebody would have to go because soap, razor blades, fags and matches were difficult to acquire elsewhere.

Bill was writing a letter home on 15th April when several booms viciously shook the tent. He was getting used to the inherent danger of being closer to the front, and calmly continued writing.

> I am glad to know the stockings arrived and happy to know that you like them (Wow! — Charlie Hun just dropped a couple up the road — nasty bloke at times!!'). As regards the price [of the stockings] I honestly can't remember…'

He switched from pen to pencil part way through the letter as his pen ran dry. Replacement ink was with the rest of his luggage somewhere between Cairo and Tripoli.

On that day, Bill had moved two hundred and fifty miles with Eighth Army. They'd packed up the tent the night before, and slept out under the stars. Not wishing to travel in convoy, Donnelly, Mick and Bill had set off at first light. The countryside in Tunisia was far more colourful than the desert and Bill recalled a smashing lunch in a field of poppies, marigolds and marguerites. The two men swapped some fags for eggs with a local and had omelettes, eight rashers of bacon, half a loaf of white bread, a tin of potatoes and a tin of peas — each!

Covering long distances was something Bill had become used to in Cairo, but in Tunisia the distances were even greater. He would travel up to one hundred and thirty miles to liaise with forward formations, and the journeys were both tiring and dangerous. In addition, there was plenty of work to do back in camp. He soon came to realise the workload in Cairo had not been as intense as he'd thought.

On 18th April, Bill woke as usual with Donnelly standing directly in front of him. He was holding a cup of *shai* to start the morning, though Mick the pup was doing his best to get to it first. Being a Sunday, Bill attended the usual church service which was held out in the open. Monty addressed those in attendance, providing an update on 'the recent free fights and one or two other odds and ends.'

Bill had heard mixed opinions about Monty since his arrival in August 1942. Back then, he'd seen him occasionally, but working in Rear HQ he was now witnessing first-hand Monty's comings and goings. Nobody could dispute Monty's ability to hold a crowd and Bill would never miss an opportunity to hear him speak.

Three weeks into his new posting, there was little Bill missed of life in Cairo with one notable exception — football. Without the organisation of fixtures and games to play, Bill supposed he would have more time to himself in Tunisia, but this was not the case. The workload in Rear HQ allowed little spare time, even for letter-writing. Bill made sure he wrote to Lisbeth and Mother, but he didn't have much time for anyone else. Instead, Bill would ask Lisbeth how her brother Jack was doing and request she pass on his regards.

If supplying the front with Allied reinforcements wasn't enough, Bill was also responsible for administering German prisoners going the other way, from forward areas back to Tripoli. As a result, he was dealing with a plethora of incoming calls and was making just as many himself. Dealing with visitors and their requirements was heaped on top for good measure. From the day he arrived in Tunisia, Bill always retired to bed weary.

Back in Auld Reekie, Lisbeth was also feeling weary. Raising a *wain* (young child) was no mean feat at the best of times, but having no husband at home, the restrictions of rationing, and all the other implications of living through a war made her task even more difficult. Lisbeth did, however, have her parents, Bill's mother and plenty of friends, to help. This provided some much-needed respite.

In May 1943, there was a real sense of community in and around North-umberland Street, Edinburgh. There were a variety of shops within a short walking distance and everything needed for daily living could be found within a quarter-mile radius of home. Adams the grocer was on the corner of Northumberland Street and Dundas Street. Everything was bought by weight, from sugar — which was put into blue bags — to biscuits, which came from large tins behind the counter. Sometimes broken ones were available more cheaply. The shopkeeper sliced bacon on a machine and weighed tea out in quarter pounds from large canisters. Coffee was un-known.

Across the road from Adams the grocer was the dairy and further back towards home, the greengrocer. Both were below street level, accessed via steps from the pavement. Also, on Northumberland Street was Doctor Shaw. The dentist was around the corner in Dundas Street. Mr Hutton was a nice man, but patients dreaded visits as he rarely used anaesthetic. Lisbeth had been a regular in 1941 owing to a longstanding problem with a wisdom tooth. Mr Hutton's practice had cricket pictures on the wall, which Lisbeth would concentrate on whilst undergoing the torture and her fingers ached after gripping the arms of the dentist's chair. Later in life she could still recall those pictures. One didn't forget a trip to Mr Hutton!

In the other direction from Northumberland Place one could walk along a narrow lane and come out on Dublin Street to find Bootlands the bakery, the chemist, the butcher and the fish shop. Food was rationed: a few ounces of meat, butter, sugar and one egg per week for an adult although children had a higher ration. Auntie Kate saved her egg allowance for Ann so that the *wain* had extra. There was also dried egg which could be reconstituted and was a virulent bright yellow colour. All children under a certain age were entitled to orange juice which came in small glass bottles with a blue label.

If any unfortunate soul had an upset stomach, the remedy was Gregory's mixture. This was a dried powder which Lisbeth would mix with a little jam to make it more palatable. The alternative was castor oil which was vile. The solution for constipation was California Syrup of Figs. To boost vitamin intake there was Virol or Malt Extract, thick syrupy stuff, both of which Ann grew to love.

To help the diet, occasional food parcels arrived from South Africa where Bill's Uncle Dan and Aunt Hettie lived. Packets of fat juicy raisins and dried apricots were a treasure to behold and the parcels sometimes included colourful comics for Ann. The Verth family cleaned their teeth using Gibbs Dentifrice — a solid block of paste in a small round tin. Toilet soap was Pears or Knights Castile (Granny Sinclair's favourite). For kitchen use it would be red tablets of Lifebuoy.

At 4 Northumberland Place, wee Ann would lie in bed in the mornings with her maternal Granny while Grandad got up to make porridge. With the porridge ready, Ann had hands and face wiped with a warm cloth before being helped to drink a cup of hot water. Granny Verth would often sing the 21st and 23rd Psalms to her; Grandad Verth preferred *Mademoiselle from Armentières* and other songs from the First World War.

During daylight hours, Lisbeth strode out, pushing Ann in the new pram she'd purchased, to places like Queen Street Gardens, the Royal Botanic Gardens and Inverleith Pond. Queen Street Gardens were not open to the general public, but all the flats in close proximity had a key and Lisbeth went there often. It gave her an opportunity to clear her mind, though she often became anxious thinking and wondering about Bill.

The large glass palm houses of the Botanic Gardens were a favourite distraction for Ann. There were tanks of water at floor level around the inside walls in which goldfish swam. Ann would lean over, supported by her mummy and gaze at her rippled reflection staring back. Outside, the rock garden was a great attraction for a toddler, with its wee paths, nooks and crannies.

Granny Sinclair was still living at 48 Cowan Road, where she'd moved with her young son Bill in 1928. This was in the Shandon/Slateford area of Edinburgh, a good way out from the centre of town. Lisbeth took Ann over every Sunday, walking from Comiston Road by Ashley Terrace and over the canal bridge. The house was a good size, planned around a central hall area, where two portraits of Granny Sinclair's parents, Euphemia Scarth and George McKenzie, hung. There was a large bedroom, bathroom and a living room with a small scullery. These rooms faced north and looked over the railway shunting yards some distance away. All those who stayed at Cowan Road remembered the sounds from the shunting yards and the wind whistling down the chimney stack. On the mantelpiece of the living room stood a photo of Bill's father, with a poppy positioned in the frame. Granny Sinclair's bedroom was really a box room, but she had always preferred it. There were no exterior windows — the only natural light entering via a ceiling skylight. Finally, there was the good room, or parlour. This faced south towards the Pentland Hills and was very sunny but seldom used. The piano stood against the wall facing the window and an alcove beside the fire housed Chinese plates from Uncle Dod's naval exploits.

As Lisbeth made the best of it back in Edinburgh, Allied forces in Tunisia were making significant progress, and now that Bill was moving with the Eighth Army, he felt the tangible shift resulting from battles won. He travelled with Eighth Army Rear HQ from Mareth to Tunis via Sousse, El Djem and Souk-El-Khemis, along with Donnelly and Mick. Later in May they were joined by the roving reporter, John Robertson. As always, John was busy collecting stories from the front and linked up with Bill, Donnelly and Mick at Souk-El-Khemis for a night. By 12th July, Bill had shifted to Sicily, via Malta, still with Donnelly and Mick in tow.

On 15th July, Bill wrote to Lisbeth informing her he'd been in Sicily for three days during which he had been all over — at least those parts under Allied control. Using a motorbike and truck, he raced up and down between divisions and corps, planning for reinforcements and related matters. His mood was elevated as the Allies continued their progress north.

I have seen quite a bit of the battle (from a <u>nice</u> distance) and it has so far been very enjoyable. We are so far doing quite well. Long may it continue — knowing the Eighth Army I don't see why it shouldn't.

Details of the trip across are not easily told without revealing some 'unrevealable' items but the trip from Malta was quite good and fairly uneventful. We only had one visit from the Hun but he was much more interested in adjacent craft than in our 'wee boatie' so nothing dropped nearer than quarter of a mile.

Bill's mood at the end of July was still positive given the news of Mussolini being forced from power and his subsequent arrest. Writing to Lisbeth, Bill surmised if Italy as a whole surrendered, then it should facilitate a rapid conclusion to the European war. A little over six weeks later, on 8th September, Italian surrender was made public. Bill's letter of the same day conveyed his positive outlook.

Quite a bright and cheerful day this day my sweet. We have finally managed to get Italy out of the war....Seems funny to think that the Eighth Army with a bit of assistance from our own First and American Seventh has managed to make 'Musso's' [Mussolini's] eight million bayonets get a bit rusty....It is going be rather enjoyable to wander through Italy (if we do!) although I'd readily forego that for a one-way ticket to Blighty....Probably the brightest remark of the war came from an Italian officer who was speaking to one of our chaps in a PW camp just after he had heard the news. Says he, 'Well, we are in this thing together now.' There is a feeling around army tonight of, well, what now?

Bill also mentioned the visit of George Formby and his wife to HQ. It was the first show he had seen in quite a while and he thoroughly enjoyed it.

On 10th September, Bill stepped onto the toe of Italy, bringing up the rear with his HQ colleagues. Receiving a belated birthday package at the same time was most welcome. Quantities of boot polish, laces and toothpaste had been running low until the timely arrival of Lisbeth's parcel. Stepping back on to the European mainland for the first time in over two years, Bill wanted to purchase a memento. There was no time. After a slow start, Eighth Army was now travelling at speed, precluding stops in local towns for shopping, even for the bare essentials.

The scenery in the toe of Italy was magnificent. Bill almost resented the quality of the Italian roads hugging the coast, as the rate of progress meant the beautiful wooded areas flashed by before he could take in the views. There were small towns nestling in coves and terrific valleys to behold. The Italian mainland was greener than Sicily, but the fruit had all but vanished. Apples were appearing, but oranges and lemons were no more. The local population were welcoming and seemed to be on the side of the new arrivals. Bill's experience of Italy in those early days was positive. He mentioned to Lisbeth in a letter that he would love to bring her down to the *toe*.

By this time, only the breadth of Europe and the English Channel separated Bill from Blighty, but there would be tough days ahead before reaching the sacred shores of home. Thoughts of the Apennines and the Alps reinforced this. They represented a different challenge to those faced in the previous two years. The climate too was a significant departure and what faced the Allies in the last quarter of 1943 would at times be brutal.

On 19th September, Bill wrote to Lisbeth and apologised for missing the fourth anniversary of their engagement.

'Very sorry dearest, but we were due to start an invasion a couple of days after that and I'm afraid I just forgot all about it.'[38]

In the last week of September, Bill was heading north and, as usual, was splitting his time between front and rear. He went up to forward formations to meet with opposite numbers before heading back to create, adjust and implement plans. The Allies were averaging around one hundred and fifty miles per day. Retreating Germans did their best to constrain the Eighth's progress. They blew up viaducts and bridges causing Allied workarounds, which were costly in terms of time and effort. One such instance resulted in Bill, Donnelly, an Italian farmer and several villagers having to strap two Oxen to the front of the truck to haul themselves up the steep bank of a field they'd found themselves in. This involved much headshaking and swearing in English and Italian, and the incident cost Bill's party about four hours. Then, having run out of fuel, they lost a further two hours. A Signals chap kindly donated a couple of cans — enough to see Bill, Donnelly and Mick back to Rear HQ.

---

[38] The anniversary of Bill and Lisbeth's engagement was 1st September. On 3rd September, Allied forces made the first amphibious landings on the Italian mainland

As the journey north continued, there were short stops and hold ups in every village and town as the locals cheered and children dashed into the road to greet the Allied arrivals. Bill found the whole thing quite confusing, but then politics had never interested him.

Bill wrote to Lisbeth on 25th September with best wishes for her upcoming birthday on 6th October. Given Eighth Army's rapid movement, there had not been a moment to pick up a gift. Perhaps next year it would be different.

CABLE AND WIRELESS
LIMITED
"Via Imperial"   60

The first line of this Telegram contains the following particulars in the order named:—
Prefix Letters and Number of Message, Office of Origin, Number of Words, Date, Time handed in and
Official instructions—if any.

Printed in England. Sept 1942
(200,000)

Circuit.	Clerk's Name.	Time Received.	
	JPN	10·37 AM	

EH34 OVERSEA 26 10

NLT MRS W G M SINCLAIR C/O VERTH 4 NORTHUMBERL-

AND PL EDINBURGH -

ARRIVED SAFELY ALL MY LOVE DEAREST MY ADDRESS

IS DAAG/MAIN HQ 8TH ARMY MEF -

Wire sent home informing Lisbeth of Bill's new address
12th April 1943

'*John Robertson and I in car at Souk-El-Khemis, May 1943*'

'Peebles 1943'
Ann Sinclair (front) with grandparents
Granny Verth (left), Grandad Verth
(centre), Granny Sinclair (right)

Ann Sinclair, age 2 years   4 Northumberland Place, Edinburgh

WARRING THE WEATHER

By the end of the first week in October 1943, Allied action in Italy saw Clark's Fifth Army capture Naples and Benevento. The French island of Corsica was also liberated. Further east on the Adriatic coast, British Commandos landed at Termoli and linked up with Montgomery's Eighth Army. The Italians were turning. On 13th October, Italy declared war on Germany.

Despite progress, particularly on the Adriatic coast, the campaign was proving costly and troublesome. The extreme cold and wet of the Italian winter and terrain of the Apennine mountains favoured the elite German troops in their defensive positions. To compound the issue, Allied men and equipment were being diverted in aid of the pending Normandy Landings. Delay and disruption tactics were successfully employed by the retreating Germans. The laying of mines and booby-traps coupled with the demolition of crossings slowed Allied progress. For Eighth Army, pursuit of the enemy towards the Sangro River and the Gustav Line was immensely difficult.

During the same period, the United Nations announced the establishment of a War Crimes Commission (UNWCC). Members, were to submit information to UNWCC on war crimes allegedly committed against their respective nationals. UNWCC, in turn, would determine whether enough evidence for a case existed and periodically report its findings to the member governments. UNWCC would also prepare and circulate lists of war criminals among the member governments.[39] The first trial took place in December 1943, and the later Nuremberg trials of Nazi Party officials and

---

[39] National Archives, *Collection of World War II War Crimes Records*

high-ranking military officers became synonymous with Second World War crimes.

At the same time the Russians were advancing on a wide front. They took Kiev in early November and whilst the Germans had some success in repelling the Red Army further north, their position was looking ever more untenable. Eisenhower's reluctant decision to sanction an invasion of the Italian mainland was assisting the Russian advance in so much that German forces were now being stretched to breaking point.

The Tehran Conference at the end of November was the first joint meeting of the three Allied leaders: Roosevelt, Churchill and Stalin. Turkish involvement in the war was discussed as were proposals for post-war Poland, Yugoslavia and the division of Germany. Stalin gave assurances of support for the Allied fight against Japan, after Nazi Germany had been defeated. Roosevelt now had an ally in trying to persuade Churchill to invade Europe via Northern France.

Eisenhower was given the role of Supreme Commander of the Allied Expeditionary Force. Field Marshal Montgomery would provide tactical expertise. Montgomery gave a farewell address to his men in Vasto, Italy. His departure was a significant moment for all those associated with the Eighth Army. Montgomery was the individual most associated with it, from the break-out at Alamein and subsequent chase and expulsion of Axis forces from North Africa. The offensive was later enshrined in history with Churchill's statement on its success: 'Before Alamein we never had a victory. After Alamein, we never had a defeat.'

*****

Bill stood outside the tent and tipped his head to the sky with eyes closed. He enjoyed the simple pleasure of the water splashing onto his face and running down his ears and neck. He opened his mouth to collect the

moisture, drinking in its freshness — rain! Tunisia, Malta, Sicily and southern Italy had brought changing landscapes, but a continued lack of
precipitation. October 1943 brought showers and Bill's thoughts turned
again to home: the sights, sounds and smells of Edinburgh; the mist hanging
around the upper reaches of the Pentland Hills. Southern Italy was beautiful, but Bill would have walked over hot coals to get back to Scotland.

On 5th October, Bill played his first game of football in Italy. '*Per ardua
ad astra* and all that,' he wrote in his letter to Lisbeth of the same day. Bill
took an 'A' branch team down to quite a nice ground and they won 3–1.
Bill had knocked in a couple, but was stiff due to a lack of training since
leaving Cairo.

On the same day, Colonel Richards asked Bill if he was interested in
going to Junior Staff School (Middle East) as an instructor. Bill politely
refused. He was at last heading in the direction of home and was not about
to do a U-turn.

Lisbeth turned twenty-eight years old on 6th October. The last time Bill
had seen his wife she was twenty-five. In her snaps she didn't look a day
over twenty-two, and Bill wrote, 'they say that hard work and worry make
you look old, so perhaps that's why you look so young!' The sarcasm
masked a burning desire to jump over the Apennines and run the rest of the
way home to see the birthday girl.

The rain returned on 10th October and turned the camp into a sea of mud.
Colonel Richards told Bill it reminded him of Flanders, although it wasn't
quite as bad. In the Great War, the mud had come up to the men's waists.
At least now it was only up to the knees. With the help of a lot of pushing
and pulling using the four-wheel drive vehicles available, Rear HQ slid forward. Bill's joy at the cool refreshing rain just a few days earlier had turned
to frustration and annoyance at the 'ruddy weather.'

The convoy found the next site in the same condition as the one it had just left. There were two buildings by the roadside, the doors of which were persuaded to open by Pete Methven's broad shoulders and Bill's left foot. They were glad to be out of the torrent. Remaining positive, Bill considered the weather to be good physical preparation for returning to Scotland and over the following days it grew colder, just to reinforce this training. Time to revert to full-time battledress. Apparently, even Mount Etna was covered in snow.

Lisbeth's letters were now arriving a respectable fortnight behind. She had written to Bill about the Fifth Army who, according to news back home, were having a torrid time. Bill replied on 13th October with pride.

> I suppose they had until Monty came to the rescue... The Eighth always seem to be there at the right time — with the First Army in Tunisia, the Seventh Army in Sicily, now with the Fifth. The trouble is they cannot find another army to keep up with us!

John Robertson was just about keeping up. Bill had last seen him in Sicily and caught up with him again on 15th October. The two pals reminisced about old times, but both pined for home. John was fortunate because he was getting into local towns for rest, shopping and meals. Bill listened with envy as John described his latest digs and the food on offer. Whilst a Rear HQ cook could present *bully* (tinned, corned beef) in thirty-five different ways, there was no disguising it, and the accompanying biscuits were also dreary fare.

On 18th October, Bill had his second game of football in Italy: Main HQ vs Tactical (Tac) HQ. It was a 4–1 win with Bill scoring two, meaning his average was two goals per game.

Exactly a year on from the battle at El Alamein, 23rd October 1943 meant *Alamein Day*. It started just like every other day; however, 11am signalled kick-off for an Officers vs Warrant Officers and Sergeants match. A spirited 6–1 victory saw Bill score another two. Later the same day, Main HQ took on a Desert Air Force eleven and this time Bill was on the losing side. He couldn't even claim the one goal scored. Bill was tired having played two matches on the same day, but Rear Army were having a spread that evening and he didn't want to miss it. Local turkeys, chickens and vino had been acquired for the great Alamein celebrations, during which Bill was inveigled on to a football committee. At least this time he would not be responsible for all the work, as he had been in GHQ Cairo. Instead, Bill would adjudicate in team selection and use his influence to obtain kit and arrange matches.

On the morning of Sunday 24th October, an Alamein service was held. 'The old Padre [Montgomery] gave a real fighting service!' In the afternoon, Bill played the first game of a new branch league, losing 4–3 to Camp.

Around this time, he secured a new wireless set. Bill hadn't heard music since his old set had been declared defunct back in the Catania Plain. Having been starved of music, it was great to hear a tune again. Even better, would be sitting in the same room as Lisbeth and listening to her playing *Ave Maria*. Bill hadn't heard it since Auntie Lily sang it at their wedding and it put him in mind of his upcoming anniversary. On 28th October 1943, it would be three years since his marriage to Lisbeth.

Bill was momentarily distracted from his writing by the noise of some thirty horses and twenty cows chewing the cud, right outside his tent. 'Don't say I'm not practising for life in the country,' he added to the letter. Each cow had a bell around its neck and Bill likened the resulting noise to a low-grade orchestra tuning up. He was relieved when the metallic clanking of bells petered off as the herd ambled away.

Noisy cows were one thing, but contending with the cold and wet of an Italian winter was becoming more of an issue and the open nature of the tent only made matters worse. Any part of it that wasn't tied down flapped uncontrollably like a ship's sail. November arrived bringing more of the same weather with it and Bill struggled to write to Lisbeth in the evenings on account of his shivering, but something happened to help him put things in perspective.

On the ship over to Africa, Bill had met an RAF Padre who had sat at his table several times. Bill heard he'd been killed at Benghazi not long after landing in 1941. He was, therefore, surprised to see the same man wander into camp at the beginning of November 1943. At first, he didn't recognise the hollow-eyed, bedraggled man shuffling in, but on closer inspection, Bill realised it was the Padre. He had been taken prisoner in 1941, ended up in Italy and spent two years in a PW cage before being released on the armistice. After walking for seven weeks he made it to Bill's camp, resembling death warmed up. His wife thought he was dead. Bill attempted to lighten the mood.

'At least you've still got your teeth Padre.'

'What do you mean?'

'Remember that chap who came out on the ship with us? The one who went for a booze up on one of the escorting destroyers in Freetown. On the way back, he was as sick as a pig and his false teeth now repose gracefully at the bottom of Freetown harbour — quelle vie! Do you remember? We laughed like hyenas.'

His attempt produced a nod of acknowledgement from the exhausted and forlorn Padre. Bill reminded himself how he'd felt sailing away from Greenock without seeing his daughter, and someone had said that things could always be worse. As he looked into the Padre's eyes, he saw the man's angst and despair. Bill said no more, but stepped away to find the long-lost traveller a bite to eat instead.

During the first week of November — despite the weather — Bill played two games of football. The first was a match against a Rft camp. They won

8–0. The second was a branch league game and a little more even, but Bill's side still ran out 4–1 winners. He scored two and three respectively.

In the second week of November, Bill received word from Lisbeth that she had sent his Christmas parcel and included something for Donnelly. Bill's glengarry bonnet was also on its way, which was a relief. Lisbeth's brother Jack was home on leave and spending time with Ann, but as a result, Lisbeth reckoned on him returning to his unit wearier than he'd left it. Where do they get all that leave from? Bill replied in his letter of 9th November.

There was no chance of leave in Italy, but every now and again, the ghastly war afforded an opportunity for Bill to see wonderful sights. He had been down to Naples and the glow of Vesuvius, ripe for eruption, was an image he wouldn't forget. That evening he had also visited John Robertson's flat which was a thirty-minute drive away and was pleasantly surprised to see Eric Russel there. Eric and Bill had managed the Cairo branch league between them so there was only one topic of conversation for most of the evening, much to John's annoyance.

The latter half of November grew colder still with strong winds to boot. Despite his wee coke fire, Bill felt the raw of the cold whistling through the tent, which regularly did its best to take off. Donnelly and Bill worked hard at pitching to ensure this didn't happen, but it was a struggle. On these occasions, Bill's thoughts turned to the poor sods up front. He may be miserable, but at least he had a tent. Those lads ahead had no such comfort, out in the middle of the night on patrol or building bridges and the like. Bill admired them and their capacity to survive such harsh conditions.

The weather exacerbated Bill's low mood. He longed to tell Lisbeth everything, but couldn't. It was a cause of frustration — a constant feeling of constraint — unable to share with his wife the mental state into which he was frequently driven. All he could do was write in general terms about his days and describe his surroundings to give Lisbeth a picture of his exist-ence.

At the back of Bill's tent was his bed. As a coverlet, he used the travel rug purchased in Cairo. At the head was a small, shelved box that he used as a general holdall, and on top of this he stored his washing and shaving kit along with his towel. On the back wall of the tent hung Bill's great coat and raincoat. At the foot of the bed his suitcase sat on his trunk, and hanging in the same area were battle-dress trousers, clean washing and football boots. A large table stood at the front of the tent covered in tin trays, maps, an ashtray, ink bottle, packets of fags, newspapers and various odds and ends. Smack in the centre stood snaps of his wife and daughter. He had a camp chair with large sponge cushion, given to him by Mac and there was a standard wooden chair for visitors. An electric light hung down from the central tent pole and the wee coke fire generated a little heat.

After a first cup of tea in the morning, Donnelly provided hot water for cleaning and shaving. Breakfast was always porridge accompanied by tea, toast, butter and marmalade. There was also bacon or sausage and an egg made an appearance if Donnelly had managed to lift any.

There were three primary sources of work for Bill:

a) Files and stacks of paper, replies, and general moans and complaints.

b) Dealing with visitors who came from all angles and on all subjects.

c) The constant ringing of the telephone.

Bill concluded that the telephone was the most abnormal and disturbing influence that could ever enter one's life. He reckoned on an average morn-ing there would be fifty calls out and the same number in.

Lunch came in the form of potatoes, onions, cabbage, or another vege-table and some kind of meat. Work continued in the afternoon until 8pm with a half-hour break for tea and toast. Dinner was soup, a meat-course with veg and a sweet. Donnelly served up turkey every five or six days at a cost of around 10 shillings a bird. There were seven or eight hams on the go at any one time and sometimes there was fish. Bill never asked about the source.

Another win at the end of November, emboldened the reputation of the Main Army HQ football team. This time it was 3–1. They were beating teams of some repute by rather large margins. It had started in the lay-off period between Tunis and Sicily and continued on the Italian mainland. After this latest game, a future contest against the Scottish Command at Tynecastle was being whispered about. How likely this was, was anybody's guess. Bill figured the army publicised such events just to keep the lads positive.

Maintaining a positive outlook was often a struggle. Another of Bill's friends was killed on 28th November, a major in his regiment — a Divisional DAAG. He'd been travelling in a truck when he'd taken a direct hit. 'Another very nice chap gone west,' Bill wrote to Lisbeth.

In early December, Bill played in a match against one of the fighting units. His side were two down inside the first quarter, but recovered and got home by one goal (3–2) with only minutes to spare. Bill didn't get on the scoresheet but was happy to have played in what he considered to be the best match since Cairo. After the game, he made haste back to camp to pack up; they were on the move again. Bill longed for more substantial accommodation — even a bit of corrugated iron over his head — but the frequency of moves, precluded this. The longest stay to date had been six weeks, which warranted nothing more than the tent and the most basic and transferable of chattels. At least if he was moving north, he was edging closer to home.

As Bill stared through the celluloid window of his new office on 9th December, he took comfort from the four walls around him. His prayers had been answered — for now. Army HQ had taken over some buildings, so

Bill was for a while, living and working in a more stable structure. It was the first time in over six months. His bedroom was in a flat which constituted the mess. There was a wardrobe, a dressing table and a spring bed, on which he had his valise. His office was a short walk and quite comfortable, doubling into a bedroom for Donnelly and Mick.

Bill's Christmas parcel arrived on 13th December and contained socks for Donnelly and a Scotsman calendar for himself. Lisbeth also included the new glengarry bonnet to replace the other that had been worn to a shadow. Two snaps of Ann completed the gifts that gladdened the heart of a distant father. Bill noted to Lisbeth that 'this ruddy war has now lasted six days longer than the last one — a fact of which I take an extremely dim view!'

As Bill sat attending to papers, Donnelly wandered into the office with a cup of tea, accompanied by Mick. The sight of his batman at the door made him chuckle. He thought of Donnelly's gift to Ann and later wrote the following, by way of an explanation to Lisbeth:

> Donnelly has sent Ann a doll — and what a doll! It is about two foot long (or high) and all togged up. It was really rather funny as he was told the APO wouldn't accept it as it would be too big a parcel. So, Donnelly wanted to cut off the legs — says he, 'Ah'll send them oan in another parcel and then yer wife can sue them oan again!' I persuaded him to try the parcel on the APO first and they accepted it![40] He is truly an awful character is Donnelly, but his heart is in the right place and he is the best driver in the whole army, and is moreover a fairly 'handy' bloke.

'I'm happy wi at,' was Donnelly's response when Bill presented his pen portrait to him.

---

[40] The doll arrived intact at 4 Northumberland Place in the first week of January

Bill wrote to Lisbeth on Christmas day 1943 proclaiming, 'by the orders of Monty, we are only doing what is absolutely essential today.' In his capacity that day as chief provider for the mess, Bill organised quite a feed. For lunch he'd arranged cold pork, ham, pickles and sauces. For the evening's main event there was broth, turkey (four among sixteen), roast potatoes, cauliflower and green peas. There was Christmas pudding and date pudding, jelly and custard, pears and pineapple chunks. The NAAFI had been most generous in providing two bottles of beer and one bottle of whisky per head. Donnelly had made crackers and very creditable efforts they were too. Somebody had deposited mistletoe in the mess though even in Bill's wildest imagination he couldn't conceive of a use for it. Nevertheless, it was festive, as was the South African concert party that performed in the mess that evening.

The period between Christmas and New Year saw a return to business and Bill had his head down for three days. This coincided with the news that Monty was leaving Eighth Army. In his letter of 30th December 1943, Bill wrote:

> The Eighth Army won't quite be the same without him although Oliver Leese is a first-class General. Monty gave us a farewell speech this morning and wasn't far from tears himself. I think nobody except himself could possibly know exactly how he felt about leaving his army as he used to call it, but it was obvious that he was very, very sad about it. Having built this outfit up largely by merit of his own efforts and having accomplished so much with it, such sorrow is understandable, and if we felt like we all did at losing him, then how much more must he have felt it. Still, there it is and on he goes to bigger and better conquests. The general attitude now, of course, is to get to Berlin first so that we can turn around and say, you should have stayed with us!

BOGGED DOWN AT CASSINO

Montgomery's successor was Oliver Leese who had been with Eighth Army throughout the North African Campaign. Both Eighth Army in the east and Fifth Army in the west now faced the German Gustav Line, spanning the breadth of Italy. The road to Rome was Highway 6 via the Liri Valley at Cassino. In the first of four attempts to break through at Cassino, the Allies crossed the River Garigliano on 17th January 1944. Their American counterparts reached the River Rapido three days later. Combined Allied troops continued to push but the offensive was repelled. Attempting to support their colleagues at Cassino, amphibious landings were made at Anzio, north of the Gustav Line. The landings on 22nd January were initially met with little resistance but the Americans missed the opportunity to advance. By early February, a German counter-attack at Anzio and the halting of Allied forces at Cassino meant the offensive on both fronts had stalled.

A second offensive at Cassino started within days and the hill-top monastery, thought to be used by the Germans as an observation post, was flattened in a massive bombing raid as a prequel to ground attack. Despite the monastery's destruction, the subsequent Allied offensive including Indian, British, New Zealand and Ghurka troops, petered out. Further north on the coast at Anzio, a second German counter-attack forged a break in Allied lines. German and American forces slogged it out. Kesselring's German Army contained the American bridgehead, but no more. The result was stalemate.

Atrocious weather prevented a third attempt at Cassino until mid-March when the Allies tried again. By this time, Leese had shifted Eighth Army

HQ east from Vasto to Venafro in support of Clark's Fifth Army. On 15th March the third battle for Cassino began with Allied forces attempting to take the town and Monastery Hill. Again, this was preceded by a heavy bombing campaign. Some of the American bombing was wildly off-target and struck Eighth Army Tactical (TAC) HQ, damaging caravans and injuring four men.[41] The now twisted frames and rubble where Cassino buildings once stood proved immensely difficult to navigate. The Italian Campaign resembled that of the First World War in terms of approach, significant loss of life for little gain, and an obliterated landscape. Highway 6 was still blocked.

Over the following two months, the Allies re-grouped and brought in reinforcements for a fourth attempt at prising open the Gustav line and over-powering its German defenders. Combined forces of the Eighth and Fifth Armies launched a huge offensive (Operation Diadem) on 11th May, taking Kesselring's men by surprise. Bitter fighting at close-quarters ensued but the German Army was, at last, slowly being pushed back. They retreated to the Hitler Line on 15th May as the Allies moved into the Liri Valley. At Anzio, the American breakout began on 23rd May. Two days later, the Germans were in retreat.

During the same period, the Russian advance on the Eastern Front had seen them march further into Poland and Ukraine. They subsequently broke through on a broad front and continued their slog west through March, April and May.

*****

Almost a month had passed since 6th December 1943, when Bill's boss, the AAG, Colonel M J Richards, moved on and up to a brigadier role of another *Area*. Bill would miss the old boy. Being Regular Army, he'd

[41] Ryder, 1987, *Oliver Leese*, p.160

brought a wealth of experience and when the situation warranted, he also provided 'very strong backing.'

Colonel Richards' replacement was Edward Tilley. In civilian life he was a Lawyer from Oxford. Bill confirmed his early impression of Tilley to Lisbeth in his New Year's Day letter.

'It is hard to imagine a nicer chap [and] it is a very pleasant business working with him.'

Bill's thoughts turned to the recent change in Eighth Army command. Monty's departure coupled with the flattening of German cities would surely have the aggressors backing down and conceding defeat, Bill thought.

> May this year see all us together to have fun, to share our troubles and woes, and to live together as we should. I have been thinking every New Year since the start of this war that perhaps next year....but never have I been so sanguine of success as I am this time and I know that by far the great majority of people on our side, and I daresay a great many on the other side also think so.
>
> Nobody knows for certain when exactly Germany will be down and out for good, but my guess still remains autumn of this year. I'm afraid that this treatment that is being handed out to their civilians this winter, plus the treatment which will be given to their armies in the field this coming spring and summer will make the German nation as a whole think five or six times about undergoing a similar winter at the end of this year! At any rate I sincerely hope so for everybody's sake.

Tilley, like those before him, referred to Bill as Scotty. This had started on Bill's arrival in the Middle-East when Major Bailey used the nickname and there it had stuck, although some men called him Jock. He'd been known as Bill, Scotty and Jock depending on the context, although back home, Mother, Aunt's and Uncle's had always called him Willie.

As Bill woke on 6th January, he did so to light snowfall and solid puddles. He hadn't seen ice like it for three years. He got dressed and after breakfast spent a few minutes outside pressing his foot down on frozen pools watching the cracks expand out from under his boot with a satisfying sound. It was a moment of quiet until Mick came dashing out, darting from puddle to puddle. His delight at being away from the heat and dry of North Africa knew no bounds.

The previous night Bill had been down at Rear Army playing bridge. One player was an opposite number, a DAAG who took care of the non-operation side of 'A' – legal, discipline and welfare. He had been overseas for a month longer than Bill and was going home on compassionate grounds. The news put Bill in mind of former colleagues and their whereabouts.

Bill's best man, Dave Roberston was now a lieutenant in a machine gun battalion with the Manchesters. Bill wouldn't have swapped places for that. Mac the Canadian whose job (and dog) Bill was heir to, had gone to Staff College, but about three months later was back in GHQ Middle East in a DAAG role. Bill maintained Mac was too intelligent and forthright for them up at the Staff College and would have been unteachable. Whatever the reason for his release, Bill had a huge fondness for Mac and an admiration for his intellect. Bill Taylor was still ticking along in 02E, based in Algiers.

Thinking about old mates brought back memories for Bill. Whilst he missed little of Cairo itself, in Italy he was no longer able to get to the pictures or to see a show regularly. There was a mobile cinema that came around and he took in a film when time permitted, but standing out in the cold to watch it was less than appealing. There were visits from concert parties occasionally, and Bill would get out to see the ENSA (Entertainments National Service Association) shows when possible. His favourite was a group known as *Double Scotch*. Five men and seven girls made up the show which was easily the best Bill had seen. The Gibson Sisters brought the house down and the two Glasgow comedians 'with their wee peaked keps' had the audience, wiping away tears of laughter. The songs and tunes were mainly of Scots origin and raised Bill's spirit enormously. So much so, that he secured tickets to see them a second time. On that occasion they were joined by Tommy Trinder.

At the end of January, Leslie Henson was in camp with a party of six men and eight women. Bill last saw a Henson concert in July 1940 during his initial training. The concert party needed to move to Fifth Army HQ, some two hundred and fifty miles away and Tilley entrusted their safe passage to Bill. The day before they left, Bill spent the afternoon in the makeshift theatre wings going through details for the trip with Leslie Henson. After the show that night, Henson took Bill and a few members of the concert party to dinner. It was a fantastic evening which finished up back in the camp with a game of pontoon.

Bill managed to get some staff cars together and escorted the group to their next venue. He sat with Henson while Donnelly drove. Donelly spoke with the broadest East Dunbartonshire accent. For hours, Leslie Henson had said 'yes' and 'no' in response to Donnelly's chatter, only to confirm later that he hadn't understood a word. On the whole, the journey had gone well. They had encountered a bit of the heavy stuff coming over from Jerry but the arty (artillery) was banging the same back. No harm was done and Bill wrote, '[Henson] is just as funny off the stage as he is on.'

Bill started the month of February feeling nice and refreshed from his two day jaunt and was bucked to receive a couple of letter cards from Lisbeth. She wrote of her brother's promotion to corporal and the new lady in his life. Bill asked Lisbeth to congratulate him on both counts and to supply all the griffin on Vickie, Jack's new love interest. Lisbeth enquired as to the progress of the Eighth Army as she had heard it was slowing. Bill rebuffed the rumour.

'If anybody remarks to you that the Eighth Army is going on very slowly, just invite them to come out here and try it at my expense! At least it's flat in Russia!'

For the previous two days the rain had poured down and to make matters worse, it was cold. Further inland there was deep snow, accompanied by bitter temperatures. This, however, did not seem to stop John Robertson from getting about and in the second week of February he turned up once again. John's visit, on his way to the front line, was a fleeting one. He would later say that despite the poor weather and lack of progress, the lads up top maintained as optimstic an outlook as possible.

In early February, Bill was busy covering duties for the AAG who was away, and so was always at the beck and call of various brigadiers and major-generals. He craved the day when he would only be summonable by two people – his darling wife and daughter. He wondered how different his existence would be when he finally returned to Edinburgh. For a start, how would he conduct himself in the home? He was used to putting his feet up on chairs, flicking cigarette ash on the floor and leaving papers lying around, so he would need to be retrained in the habits of *homo domesticus*. For now he would just continue to leave his papers lying around.

In the middle of the worst Italian winter in living memory, Eighth Army men were bogged down by the weather; they were trapped and going nowhere. A lack of progress meant that Bill became a little quieter for a short period. That was just the nature of his work in handling Rfts and PWs. Being static presented fewer difficulties in shifting men around. Not so for those up front who were parked in their trenches when they weren't trying to break through the Gustav Line. Rain, sleet and snow all vied with each other in a struggle to make the lads' task more difficult. *Old man mud* reigned supreme. Trying to remain positive, Bill at least considered that the Fifth and Eighth Armies were holding down a considerable number of German divisions. He was also glad to hear that further east, the Russians were walloping along in style.

By now, Bill was certain that Monty and co. were preparing to start the much talked about second front. He could only hope that these combined operations would affect his early return to civilian life. Most important for those in Italy would be a turn in the weather. If only the sun could break through and provide a period of relative meteorological calm, then both Fifth and Eighth Armies would dart north like a scalded cat.

The weather finally turned in early March and Bill became busier with visits to Rft camps. He combined such trips with a hot bath and a good feed; boiled eggs on toast were the order of the day. In a letter to Lisbeth he apologised for his ravings on the subject, given the rationing back home. Bill also met up with John Robertson again. John had secured some film for Bill's camera and he assured Lisbeth of some photos in due course. He also met up with his old boss, John Welch, who he hadn't seen since Christmas.

On 10th March, Bill wrote to Lisbeth telling her he'd been up in the field for three days and hadn't time to read or write. The letter was special. Bill couldn't say why, but he referred to it as a regal letter 'to remind one in days to come of its importance.'

When the letter was finished, Bill changed into his New Zealand battledress, which he favoured (he also had American uniform), joined Donnelly and Mick (the dog) in the staff car and hit the road again. On this occasion, Eighth Army moved from Vasto to Venafro, linking up with the American Fifth Army. Mick enjoyed sitting up front between Donnelly and Bill but occasionally he was a menace. Bill often had papers and maps laid out on the seat, so Mick would get dumped into the rear of the car.

'Sit back there Mick, otherwise there's going to be a row.' Invariably,

Mick jumped back over on to the maps, at which point Bill would deposit him back again. Mick would then put his front paws on the back of Bill's seat and lick his neck with great energy.

At approximately fourteen months old, Mick was at the stage of having 'girlfriends' which Bill didn't mind, apart from when he started to bring them round on his *reveille* duty. One morning Mick came into the tent at 7am (which he always did) leaving his girlfriend waiting patiently at the tent entrance until Mick had enjoyed the normal fuss from his master. On trotting out of the tent, Mick's girlfriend trotted after him.

'Big shot is our Mick,' Bill wrote to Lisbeth. 'I'm watching his conduct with great interest these days to see if I can pick up any wrinkles on how to handle females!'

In the last week of March, Bill, Donnelly and Mick took receipt of a new vehicle. The staff car had for some time been causing problems. It had served them well but was no longer reliable and a new American Jeep (M5633126) took its place. It was a lighter, more nimble mode of transport, though exposure to the elements was a problem. Mick didn't appear to mind. The ability of Audrey (the Jeep) to go anywhere, obviated the need to bypass certain terrain that the old car couldn't manage. Donnelly soon got the hang of the Jeep's wee foibles and in Bill's mind he would certainly win the title of best driver, should Eighth Army ever hold a competition. Donnelly's skill behind the wheel had gotten Bill out of some serious scrapes during those treacherous first months of 1944 when the pair were running the gauntlet to and from the front in tough terrain and terrible weather conditions. It was perilous, and Bill depended on Donnelly, his batman cum driver. Running the death race between rear and front, the precarious and brutal Cassino was a far cry from the relative safety of Cairo where, to a large extent, Bill had been spared the physical and mental burden of the frontline.

As March drew to a close Bill was asked to arrange the odd football match and undertake the associated hunt for kit and players. Bill was acutely aware of how a simple game of *fitba* could raise men's hearts in much the same way as Montgomery's rousing addresses. Understanding how important a little respite was for the lads, Bill poured his energy into putting on games for the lucky few who were able to take part.

Whilst Lisbeth would often send photos of Ann, sprouting into a cheeky wee toddler, Bill was itching for a recent image of Lisbeth herself and had been badgering his wife for an updated snap. When it finally arrived, it took pride of place on his table inside the tent, alongside the most recent photos of Ann with her grandparents. The cosy pictures of his nearest and dearest, safe at home, contrasted starkly with the destruction he'd witnessed in Italy. Bill prayed that his family would never have to witness such devastation.

By 2nd April 1944, it was six and a half years since the start of Bill's courtship with Lisbeth, but for the last four years — two thirds of that time — he had been in the army. It seemed incredible. He recalled the journey from Cullen to Stirling in April 1941 when he and Lisbeth were so down in the mouth. If only they'd known what was to come! April 42 in Cairo, April 43 *en route* to Tripoli, April 44 in Italy. April 45...?

But for all the difficulties and hardship the war had caused, Bill felt he had gained an enormous amount through the people he'd met, the places he'd been and the work he had done. He communicated the same in writing to Lisbeth:

> So, while I enter the fifth year of army life with the inevitable wish uppermost in my mind i.e. that this year will see the end of the war and that I shall then be able to return to you and Ann, at the same time I do not feel that I am entirely wasting my time.

Bill was in reflective mood as he completed his letter and retired for the night. He thought he would prefer to stay overseas for the duration of the

European war, then go home and *stay* home, rather than going home sooner only to find himself *en route* to Burma in six months' time. Lying on his bed he stared up into the dark apex of the tent and thought about where he and Lisbeth would make their home. He would love to return to Scotland, but it would all depend on where he could find a teaching position. He wondered how Lisbeth may feel about living in the Dominions. Over the past three years he'd met people from all parts of the globe, comparing notes on life in the UK and abroad. Leaving Scotland would be a wrench, but something to discuss if it would benefit the family. New Zealand was at the top of Bill's list. In Cairo and now in Italy, he'd met many Kiwis and considered them amongst the finest chaps on earth. He wrote to Lisbeth on the subject, but her feelings were clear. She couldn't contemplate leaving her mother and Scotland. Bill quelled her fears in his letter of 3rd May, confirming Scotland was his preference and he was sure he would find work there. Decision made.

Bill was not the only one considering his future. Lisbeth sent word that her brother and his intended would announce their engagement on 22nd April. This did not surprise Bill. Jack had written to him just a few weeks earlier giving Bill the distinct impression that Jack was very serious about his future with Vickie. Bill smiled to himself as he remembered posing the question to Lisbeth. Upon hearing 'yes' he had dashed off to play football! Now he was wondering if Jack would do the same. In his letter to Lisbeth he requested she pass on his 'very, very best wishes.' He would be as happy to have Vickie as a sister-in-law as he'd been to have Jack as a brother-in-law. 'There will always be an open door for them at oor wee hoose,' he offered.

The 22nd April would stick in Bill's mind for another reason; England once again beat Scotland at football. This time it was a 2–3 defeat at Hampden, making the loss even more difficult to swallow. Bill had listened to the latter part of the game and been unimpressed. At the end of the match he turned the wireless off and returned to his desk to be greeted by his superior.

'Did you catch the game this evening Scotty?' chirped Tilley. 'I heard from one of the chaps that you Jocks lost again.'

Bill was prepared. He picked up a sheaf of papers in front of him tapping them on the table and shaking the loose leaves into order.

'Aye sir,' he replied, rising from his seat. 'But surely one can't expect the Scots to single-handedly win the war *and* football matches at the same time?' Bill stood up and collected his papers. 'If you'll excuse me Sir, I believe there's a war to be won.' Bill marched out of the tent whistling *Cock O' the North* as he went.

Two days later on 24th April, Bill turned from football fan to player in a Branch vs Workshops game. The workshop lads won 5–2 which was no surprise to Bill as they were always kicking a ball about. Like most of the branch players, Bill was out of condition, but as winter receded, temperatures rose, and games began to be played in the evening. At the same time, mosquitoes began to appear. Bill had never had malaria but knew quite a few that had. It was *not* recommended. To combat the pests, he sprayed the inside of his tent with an awful smelling concoction one hour before sunset and closed the flaps for half an hour before anyone entered. Long trousers and anklets were mandatory and Bill rolled down his sleeves for further protection. Any skin remaining exposed was smeared with another queer liquid (a solvent for plastics).

The warm weather continued, but it didn't remain dry for long. Towards the end of April, the rain was incessant. One afternoon as Bill sat working at his table, a wee stream appeared in his tent, despite a channel being dug all around it. He perched there all day, looking out at the pouring rain. Much the same as Bill's workload, it had not stopped, but for once there was no noise, save for the chattering of birds. It put Bill in mind of the day he and

Lisbeth got soaked to the skin at Costorphine Hill. They had laughed at the wee bubbles of moisture that clung to Lisbeth's coat like the mist on the Pentlands. If Bill could only see Lisbeth now, he would be as happy as a lark.

Bill had been working with a chap by the name of Carswell on a 'special job.' While on the blether he established that Carswell was the headmaster at Elgin Academy. Carswell had heard that as soon as the German fight was up, the British Government intended to ship all teachers back to Blighty. There was also rumour of a plan to raise the school leaving age to fifteen. This would require a host of additional teachers.

'The government can't hope to fulfil the requirement from training colleges and ex-retirement,' Carswell said with confidence. As he'd not long left Scotland and was still in touch with people in education back home, Bill thought the information was credible and relayed it to Lisbeth.

On 6th May, HQ played their second match against an anti-aircraft regiment team and won 5–3. Bill got on the scoresheet once. The following day was a Sunday and work was not excessive. Bill longed to attend a good Scots Kirk, but there was not even a good Presbyterian Minister in his location. The English Padres were fine chaps outside the pulpit, but didn't much appeal to Bill inside it.

On Monday the colonel was down with a touch of sandfly fever, so Bill was doubling-up on duties, as well as running the Army Unit Cup. Bill's side played their first-round game that night, beating the Royal Army Service Corps 8–2. We are 'now on the lookout for our next victims,' he scribbled to Lisbeth in delight.

By this time, the AAG Edward Tilley, had a caravan. Bill inherited Tilley's old table, which was in significantly better shape than his. That evening, Bill placed the radio on his new table next to the photos of his family. He and his colleagues listened to the news, hoping to hear of the much-hyped, second-front starting. They would have to wait a further month before any such snippets trickled through. In fact, before that, Bill himself was on the move again as he confirmed to Lisbeth in his letter of 12th May.

'You will know by now that after all our planning in the past few months we're off again ... you won't be surprised when I tell you that I can't give you much information on what I do in the way of work! It's awful wondering what to tell you!'

Bill wouldn't have told Lisbeth the truth about the past five months even if he had been able to. What he made out to be a quiet period of planning before a definite offensive had in fact included three of the bloodiest, most devastating, close-quarter battles of the Second World War. The fourth and final at Cassino was just about to start. Over time, these four brutal encounters would become somewhat eclipsed by the massive invasion further north. But the men in Italy during the first half of 1944 would never forget. On 15th May, Bill updated Lisbeth as best he could.

'The battle is well underway now and we are as busy as coots. If I don't write so often in the near future as I have been doing, you will know the reason.... Let's hope we don't stop now until we reach Berlin!'

In fact, Bill did manage to write. His letters of 17th and 19th May, contained the following:

> The jolly old work proceeds apace, and I am quite enjoying it. Force of circumstances makes it necessary to do some quite high-pressure stuff from about 9pm to midnight and we have just finished.
>
> The AAG has a caravan now — quite a decent affair too — and this sort of 'evening shift' has to be done by both of us. It is very handy for me nowadays, as while there were objections — too lengthy to explain — to having two tents together, we have the

caravan right beside my tent, and can say anything we want to each other without having to walk up hill and down dale.

These caravans which the 'bigger boys' have are really quite excellent houses in the field. They have a bed, wardrobe, wash basin, table and shelves – all roughly speaking, in a thing the size of a three-tonner. They are actually built on a three-tonner chassis.

You remark that we appear to have been doing a spot of silent moving. 'Spot' is the funny word — if you only knew what it was like to move an army across the Apennines in winter-time I should think you would have chosen a different word my sweet one!

I've been as usual as busy as a coot but we had this show all taped and measured off from our point of view and it has been like clockwork. At the time of writing we are doing fairly well on the whole, so here's hoping the old Hun starts thinking he has had enough.

Bill stolidly ground away at his job and was constantly on the telephone. His colleagues reckoned after the war he would be lost if he was not able to stretch out his hand and pick up a phone. During the war it was an indispensable tool. Bill had made some long-distance calls during his time in the Middle-East, but reckoned on Sousse to Cairo being the farthest.

'That of course only proves what magnificent Signallers we have in the Eighth Army,' he wrote to Lisbeth.

Bill had learned a lot during his time in the army and he'd met people from all walks of life and all corners of the globe. Among them were Oxford dons, schoolmasters, farmers and barristers. He'd once met a young second lieutenant in the New Zealand forces who corresponded with Einstein on mathematical matters – even in wartime! A New Zealand DAAG told Bill the young chap was one of the foremost mathematicians in Australia and New Zealand and he was only twenty-five. There were artists, journalists and even international football players (Alex Jackson of Aberdeen and Scotland was the sports officer)[42] a motley assembly of every profession and trade one could think of. It was a wonderful education.

On 25th May, Bill wrote to Lisbeth:

> My deeds have been of the wandering type in the last few days and I have been scouting up front two or three times. Cassino is an absolute shambles and equal to any description or photograph I have seen of trench villages in the last show [First World War].
>
> There is literally not one building which is not either completely flat or badly knocked about and the whole place is covered in shell holes, filled with stagnant water and blackened tree stumps.

Bill was now spending considerable time on the road in the ever-capable hands of Donnelly and the not so helpful paws of Mick. The retreating Germans had blown up just about everything and the tracks Donnelly was following were difficult and deeply rutted. The Germans had also left mines, which were a further aggravation. Any thought of departing from the tracks was a definite no-no and while Audrey the Jeep may have had no roof, she handled the terrain. And so, the trek north continued. At long last, Eighth Army had broken through at Cassino and were heading for Rome.

---

[42] Alex Jackson was killed in a road traffic accident in late 1946. He was still serving for the British Army (in Egypt) at the time of his death

'The elephant in the foreground is me!
Below Cassino, March 1944'

'The same elephant!'
(far right, as marked)

'Highway 6 going into Cassino. Monastery Hill in background, May 1944'

'Cassino, May 1944'

FAREWELL TO DEAR FRIENDS

H aving broken out at Anzio, Clark's Fifth Army made haste to Rome. In an unplanned move, they made for Highway 7, the shorter route to the capital, rather than joining Highway 6. This enabled the German Tenth Army to continue fighting in retreat. The American Fifth entered Rome on 4th June 1944 just before the Normandy landings which overshadowed Clark's grab for glory.

Eighth Army were further east and continued to head north up the backbone of Italy. Subiaco and Perugia were amongst the towns that fell as the Eighth pressed on towards the Arno and Gothic Lines. Tactical (TAC) HQ was positioned at Lake Trasimene. The Allies entered Arezzo and crossed the River Arno in mid-July, a week before King George VI toured Italy. Oliver Leese journeyed with him to Castiglione airfield on 26th July. Brigadiers and a select few were presented to the King. Oliver Leese was knighted at TAC HQ.

The long-awaited second front assault began on 6th June 1944, with the amphibious landings in Northern France: D-Day. Facing them was Rommel, assigned to defend the Atlantic Coast against invasion. Allied forces fought their way off the beaches at Normandy at the start of the long campaign to liberate Nazi occupied France. Soon after, Allied aircraft began operating from French airstrips and Normandy landing sites linked up. As they did so, German V1 bombs were targeting London.[43]

On the Eastern Front, Russia was still ploughing west. Majdanek in Poland was the first concentration camp to be discovered by Allied forces. By

---

[43] London would go on to feel the impact of the first V2s in early September 1944

the end of July, the Red Army was closing in on Warsaw. Despite bitter fighting on all fronts, the Allies were slowly closing the pincers around a stoic, but retreating, German Army.

By early August, Eighth Army had taken Florence and under Leese's initiative, headed up the Adriatic Coast. At the end of the month they launched a major offensive and later broke through the Gothic Line. Bitter fighting was again in evidence as Eighth Army forced a route through to Rimini. Further west, Fifth Army took Pisa on 2nd September before launching their main assault on the Gothic Line. By the end of the month they were through, but both Eighth and Fifth Armies were grinding to a standstill against the resolute German defenders and mountainous terrain.

In Northern France, the breakout from Normandy was underway. By the end of August, Allied forces had liberated Paris and air superiority was paying dividends. Hitler was becoming desperate and isolated. In Southern France, Allied landings secured the Mediterranean Coast and Allied troops made progress, attempting to link up with those further north. In early September the Allies liberated Antwerp and Brussels. Less than ten days later, the US First Army entered Germany and they reached the Siegfried Line on 15th September. Montgomery — now a Field Marshal — then initiated Operation Market Garden, a plan to bypass the Siegfried Line and secure a route along which the Allies could advance further. However, enemy resistance was strong and the Germans successfully counter-attacked. Progress east would have to wait.

During the same period, the Russians had reached the East Prussian border and by the end of August had taken Bucharest. The Germans abandoned Bulgaria, and Russia entered the country in early September. By the end of the month, they had reached the Gulf of Riga and occupied Estonia.

*****

On 5th June 1944 Bill wrote to Lisbeth:

> I have had quite a few hectic days since my last letter to you as you will have no doubt gathered from the news. Rome is just one more big city on the way home. We have now covered about seventy-five percent of the way from Cairo to Berlin — but the last quarter will probably be the most difficult.
>
> I haven't been in Rome yet as we have all the work and no play this time! I believe the Yanks put up a very good show though and this success will help them to find their feet still more. We ourselves are still hopping along and I have been seeing a lot more villages and small towns.
>
> I was terribly sorry to hear about Duncan Mackay — he was another good chap. I didn't know he had gone to Burma. I was interested to hear of Alan Stewart's doings, too, particularly his Croix de Guerre.
>
> Next time I write I suppose it will be another twenty or thirty miles nearer home — soon I'll be able to smell the good clean fresh air of dear auld Scotland.

For the following five days, Bill flogged Donnelly and the Jeep hard, driving during the day and sleeping where they could at night.

'It has been a hectic week and a very eventful one,' he wrote to Lisbeth. 'I am glad to note that the second front has started[44] — what they urgently require of course is the Eighth Army beside them. If that happened, old Rommel would immediately and automatically start to retreat.'

In mid-June, Bill received word that Lisbeth's brother was in France and that her father had suffered a heart attack, though it was hoped he would make a full recovery.

---

[44] Normandy Landings (D-Day): 6th June 1944

'You will no doubt be thinking that your cup of misery is overflowing,' he replied, with sympathy. 'There is a bright side Lisbeth, and that is I'm sure the war in Europe won't last much longer. I'm giving it to the end of October now — but keep your gas-mask in working order. He'll use that as a last resort after his rocket guns and self-propelled aircraft.'

Since joining Eighth Army Rear HQ in April 1943, Bill had ventured up to the front most days in support of his opposite numbers. He formed a great many friendships with those men at the sharp end, and none more so than Charlie Rainford of the Royal Artillery.

On 18th June 1944, Charlie Rainford and three other men were out in a Jeep on a recce, when they drove over a mine.

'The kindest chap I have ever known was killed outright,' said Bill. The other men were taken to the Casualty Clearing Station. One died on the way there – and the other two men died later.

'I still can't believe that old Charlie's gone,' Bill wrote. 'He and I had some grand times together and we both came to HQ at the same time. He was an only child and his father and mother had built up a builder's business which he took over from them before the war. I should think it would just about break their hearts.'

Nothing hit Bill so hard as the death of his dear friend Charlie Rainford.[45] A Memorial Service was held for Charlie and his comrades on 22nd June. It ended with a lone piper playing *Ae Fond Kiss*, as he walked away from those gathered. It was the most poignant tribute Bill had ever experienced.

The AAG knew how close Bill was to Charlie and seeing he was

---

[45] Major Charles Rainford, Service Number 248873, Royal Artillery, died 18th June 1944 aged 37. Buried in Bolsena War Cemetery, Italy. Location I C 3 'He too loved life, he gave what he loved' (Commonwealth War Graves Commission)

struggling to cope with his friend's death, he insisted Bill take a day off and go to Rome.

Other lads were buying scents and lipsticks for their wives back home, but Bill couldn't muster any enthusiasm for shopping. In the afternoon, he and a few others made their way to St. Peter's Basilica and secured a guide. What appeared to be magnificent paintings inside the Basilica, were in fact the most intricately worked mosaics. The statues were something to behold, including that created by Michelangelo, depicting the Virgin Mary holding the body of Jesus in her lap. Bill also made a point of seeing the Jacobite monument to the Royal Stuarts. From there they visited St. Paul's Basilica and the Catacombs before heading to the Colosseum. The party left their guide at the Colosseum to continue exploring under their own steam.

As Bill settled down in his tent that evening, he remained soulful, but better for having had the trip to Rome. Tilley had been right to insist on it.

On 28th June, Bill received a note and package from 'Freddie the print.' The two men had been good friends since their Cairo days; Freddie was the one who squirrelled away Auchinleck's memo for Bill. He was now working in Number 5 Mobile Printing Section of Eighth Army Rear HQ. Bill read Freddie's note with interest.

'I thought you would like the magnum opus enclosed. Just a small token of my regards for the lads with the hairy knees.' Bill laughed out loud. Freddie had given him a bound collection of General Montgomery's personal messages to Eighth Army spanning the period from El Alamein (October 1942) to the capture of Ortona and Monty's farewell message (January 1944). Bill scribbled a note of gratitude in reply and secreted the volume away in his trunk.

In the last week of June, Bill wrote to Lisbeth:

'The Russians have started again, so perhaps the Huns will take a thought to themselves shortly. I certainly hope so darling for I am longing to see you again and to hold you tightly in my arms.'

It was 30th June before Bill found time to put pen to paper again. He asked after Lisbeth's father and in his war observations noted:

'the Russians seem to be belting along in good style and we are still getting nearer every day, albeit a bit slower than just recently. The second front too will soon be launching forth after the build-up, and altogether I take a very rosy view of things as they are now.'

Lisbeth wrote with news of John Wilson's death. John had been a foundationer at Heriot's with Bill, and they had known each other well. It was another bitter blow; another valuable life lost. Bill put it out of his mind and tried to think about Lisbeth and Ann. He remained convinced that the war would be over by the end of the year. Bill reminded himself that it wasn't the individual difficulties and troubles themselves that counted in life, but the way one dealt with them. He had developed a strong sense of what was important, and he was less inclined to worry about trivial things than he once was. However, occasionally events conspired to overwhelm him and became too much to bear. The day before his birthday was just such an occasion. Challenges at work, a desire to be at home with Lisbeth and thoughts of fallen friends pulled Bill into a deep depression. The death and destruction of the Second World War forced those involved to face their own fragile mortality head-on and this heavy burden could strike a man down psychologically, with the same brutality as bullets from a machine gun.

Three weeks on and Bill was still struggling with the loss of Charlie Rainford. Lisbeth had written about some difficultly with Auntie Meg, which seemed utterly inconsequential to Bill. He replied:

From my angle, many of the things you people worry about seem not worth tuppence. Not that I blame you — I used to worry and get annoyed because of the weather — or an unkind word said by someone — and probably in due course I shall do so again; but at present, in these circumstances, such incidents just don't affect me in the slightest.

I'm afraid I was not a little unthinking when I wrote to Mother about Charlie Rainford and the other chaps who were snubbed out. I was of course so cut up about it that I wasn't capable of doing much thinking of any kind.

Bill's twenty-eighth birthday held little to celebrate and largely passed him by. He was simply grateful that he had seen in another birthday. Charlie Rainford would not.

Before long, Bill, Donnelly and Mick were on the road again with Eighth Army, forcing the Germans back to the Northern Apennines. They were on the move from early morning till midnight or the *wee sma hours*. Bill didn't despatch his next letter until 21st July. In it, he told Lisbeth to expect a visitor. Major Derek Aldridge of the Royal Tank Corps was a regular soldier and returning home after eight years overseas. He had become a close friend and Bill asked Lisbeth to make him welcome.

'You deserve a damn good holiday,' Bill quipped to Derek, 'and in something with more room in it than that tank!'

Bill had not had a holiday since the two-day trip to Transjordan with John Robertson, and the subsequent four days in Alexandria. He'd returned from that trip on 22nd October 1942, for the start of the Alamein offensive. General Oliver Leese had led XXX Corps in Operation Lightfoot, part of the wider offensive under the control of Montgomery, and little more than a year later, Leese had taken over command of the Eighth Army. Now, Bill was travelling in the same convoy as Leese — only two vehicles behind him — as they made their way to Main HQ, based at Arezzo.

On 25th July Bill wrote:

'The last few days have been even more hectic than ever, Lisbeth, owing to the presence of a VIP as you will no doubt have gathered from the news.'

The VIP was King George VI. Bill witnessed parts of the visit first-hand. He hadn't been present for the knighting of General Sir Oliver Leese, but he was there on 26th July to see Leese introduce his boss and good friend Edward Tilley to the King on the shores of Lake Trasimene. General Harold Alexander, Commander of the Allied Armies in Italy, was also present and Bill was as pleased as punch for his superior. He saw the King again at Arezzo and the men of 'A' took snaps of themselves to mark the visit — proud mementos for all those involved. The visit had served its purpose in raising morale.

The brig ordered Bill to take two days leave from 2nd August. He spent the time on Polvese Island, the largest of three islands located in the Umbrian lake. It was absolute bliss. His enforced break was unexpected, as he explained to Lisbeth.

'I was away on the road for about two-three days and when I got back night before last, the AAG told me the news i.e. that the brig had said I was to go away for a clear two days where I wouldn't hear or see anything connected with the war.'

Bill reckoned the lake island was equivalent in size to Cramond Isle in the Firth of Forth. The rest house was a beautiful mansion, luxuriously furnished and decorated. The only other buildings on Polvese were a farm and the ruins of a castle and a church. Bill thought the isle must have been self-sufficient with the farm having pigs, chickens and all kinds of vegetables. There were a few bathing boxes and sundry items down at a sandy cove, including a raft out in the lake for sunbathing and diving. Bill spent most of his break there, lying back on the raft and feeling the sun's warmth penetrating his skin. 'It is, as one might say, just the job,' he wrote.

He also referred to the 'recent disturbances within Germany.' Lisbeth was pinning much hope on the Allied aerial bombing campaign, but he minded her not to do so.

The quickest way — and best way — to finish this war is to beat them on the ground and get to Berlin with our armies. I still think Hitler won't last much longer. It's fairly obvious that he hopes to keep us out of Germany until winter comes.

I still think that the Russians at any rate will be there before winter comes, even if we aren't.

According to the latest news, the second front seems to be making better progress.

Bill felt heaps better for his short spell in the sun, but wondered what awaited in camp. Would he be able to see his tent for the files and papers that would have accumulated? Tilley would do his best to contain matters, but Bill couldn't expect the AAG to deal with everything in his absence. He would cross that bridge when he came to it. In the meantime, he took full advantage of the remaining hours and rest on offer. If there was one thing the war had given Bill, it was the right slant on life. 'Common sense, a bit of nous and lots of hard work. That's all there is to it, darling,' he wrote.

When Bill scribbled a quick letter to Lisbeth on 6th August, he'd been back at the grindstone for two days. Tilley had dealt with a stack of files and paperwork during his leave and by the time of writing, Bill had pretty much caught up.

There had been no word from John Robertson for around three months and Bill was relying on John's wife for news, via Lisbeth. She had become good friends with Mrs Robertson back in Edinburgh and told Bill that John was hoping to get home soon. Bill still thought the better option was to stick it out in Europe and get home for good at some point rather than going home prematurely and risk further postings, but he hoped to see John before he left, whenever that may be. Lisbeth also mentioned that Vickie's family in London were suffering because of the German V1 flying bombs, otherwise known as Doodlebugs.

'I'm sorry that Vickie's people are having such a rough time of it,' Bill replied. 'It would appear that the only way to stop these flying bombs is to stop Germany altogether, and the way they are being manhandled all round seems to indicate that that shouldn't be so far away.'

Thinking of home, Bill's mind turned to the daughter he had never seen in person. It was easy to feel sorry for himself, but as long as Lisbeth and Ann were alive and well, there was everything to live for.

> Never since I joined GHQ MEF [Middle East Forces] has time hung heavily on my hands for which I should be thankful. It has been a great pity, dearest, that we should have had to spend these past three years of our life apart, but things could certainly have been a great deal worse and we have much to be thankful for.

Bill thought of the friends he'd lost, whose families were so terribly affected by their passing. For the sake of those still left, one could only hope for a swift end to the war. On 14th August, Bill wrote:

> Monty has pulled his finger out again — he's a great little man. In fact, he's almost as good as Oliver Leese, for whom I have a great admiration. He is every bit as good as Monty on the tactical side and is an extremely decent chap into the bargain. You may well remember I was pretty broken hearted when Monty left us, but I am certainly not now. I might as well warn you now that I am a fearful bore on the subject of military leaders, so I'd better shut up! You might note this for future reference and steer me clear of the subject in after life.

In Bill's mind, the war in the second half of August 1944 was going very well and he was sure German capitulation was close.

'A few more big cracks such as the one they have just had in Northern France and Southern France and the Hun simply must give up or be killed off,' he penned to Lisbeth. It was after midnight. Bill was consumed by work again and writing to Lisbeth was almost always restricted to the *wee sma hours*.

'Now that we have bust up the good old Gothic Line, I suppose we shall have another chase and accordingly the next few weeks will be as busy as the last ones,' he wrote.

Lisbeth's father, John Verth, was up and about again, though taking it easy with no prospect of a return to work in the offing. Bill told Lisbeth to do as she needed regarding the financial support of her parents. It behoves us to do our best to make their old age as happy as possible he thought, so why not? Bill spent virtually nothing whilst engaged in operational duties. If spare funds could be put to good use in helping to support the family, then so it should be. He was also pleased to hear that Jack's fiancée, Vickie, had not returned to London to avoid the atrocious bombing campaign.

As September arrived, the news from the BBC was that the Doodlebugs had pretty much finished, but it made sense for Vickie to remain in Edinburgh for a while longer.

Bill was as busy as ever and the war effort on all fronts appeared to be yielding results, but he began to fear another winter hold up.

'It will either end by the beginning of November or, I think, go on until next May/ June.'

Bill was writing from the shoreline of the Adriatic coast where he'd managed to get in a couple of swims on his trips up to the action. The travel was either very dusty or very muddy depending on what mood the weather was in, but either way, Bill was almost always messy. A swim provided a welcome interlude from work and an opportunity to get cleaned up. Donnelly continued to look after Bill's safety and security interests. Bill relied on him daily and didn't want to contemplate his not being there. However, Donnelly was due a home posting in the coming four months on account of his long service. Bill considered his own demobilisation. The Government had recently issued a white paper on an updated release scheme. Under Class A, Bill would be assigned a release group number based on criteria including age and length of service. Under Class B, Bill could request release if his civilian occupation was one that was required on civil reconstruction grounds. He'd heard a BBC broadcast confirming the three main occupations considered for Class B release were brick-builders, miners and teachers. Bill would slot in to the last of the three. He may get out earlier than he would otherwise, but wasn't aware of any additional benefits (or drawbacks) to taking the Class B option. The alternative was to wait a further two or three months and obtain his release under the standard Class A scheme.

Bill's thoughts on the most suitable release option were interrupted with the appearance of Donnelly and a welcome meal. Grub at that time was very good. Most rations came in tins and Donnelly supplemented them with locally acquired produce. Large quantities of fruit and vegetables were available, particularly oranges and apples, grapes, tomatoes, cabbage, beetroot, peas and turnips. Passing through an area which the Germans had left in a hurry also yielded a plentiful supply of eggs. The Padre (who was in Bill's mess) held the record of gathering three hundred in a single day, but even that number didn't go far when shared among twenty hungry officers. Bread came from local bakeries and the Main Army HQ cook, who was also a dab hand with pastry, producing sausage rolls and apple pies to everyone's delight.

During the first half of September, Eighth Army were busy and Bill did not find time to write again until the 20th. His endeavours in the war had already earned him an Africa Star but 19th September brought surprising news that Bill relayed to Lisbeth the following day.

'I don't suppose you know your husband has been mentioned in despatches; neither did I till last night![46] Don't ask me why – it just happened.'

Bill knew it was for services in Sicily and Italy up to December 1943, but more than that, he knew not. Whilst proud to don the bronze oak leaf, Bill's thoughts turned to the fallen. It was they who had made the ultimate sacrifice and it was they who deserved the highest of accolades. This belief would stay with Bill for the rest of his life.

---

[46] Published in the London Gazette, 24th August 1944

'Mick'
Italian Campaign, 1944

Granny Sinclair and Ann, 1944

'On H. M. The King's visit to the Eighth Army.
Oliver Leese, Lieutenant General Eighth Army: Arezzo, July 1944'

Bill Sinclair, DAAG Organisation: Arezzo, July 1944

*'King George VI meeting senior officers of the British Eighth Army. Here he is seen being introduced to **Lieutenant Colonel E.W. Tilley** by General Oliver Leese, Commander of the Eighth Army. Castiglione del Lago airfield, 26th July 1944.'*

© Imperial War Museum (Catalogue No. NA 17255)

'Lake Trasimene 1944
*Basil Clarke, Staff Captain 'A'... **Edward Tilley AAG**... 'Wee Mee' DAAG'*

Bill (left) and Donnelly (and Audrey the Jeep)
1944

By the KING'S Order the name of
Captain (T/Major) W. G. McR. Sinclair,
The Argyll and Sutherland Highlanders (Princess Louise's)
was published in the London Gazette on
24 August, 1944.
as mentioned in a Despatch for distinguished service.
I am charged to record
His Majesty's high appreciation.

Secretary of State for War

Mentioned in despatches: Italian Campaign
24th August 1944

RIMINI STADIUM

In July 1944, Rommel was badly injured when his car was ravaged by fire from a British fighter aircraft. An attempt on Hitler's life, and Rommel's association with some of the conspirators, led the Führer to connect Rommel with the failed assassination. As a result, while Rommel was convalescing at home, he was given an ultimatum and on 14th October 1944 he took his own life.

At the same time, the Moscow Conference was taking place with Churchill and Stalin trying to agree on how to split the Balkans. This included the division of Yugoslavia, which the Russians entered at the beginning of the month. By the end of October, the Red Army had entered East Prussia and by the end of December, they would surround Budapest, cutting off the remaining German and Hungarian forces. In typical fashion, Hitler demanded a fight to the death.

In Northern Italy, Eighth Army crossed the River Savio on 21st October, taking Cesena. Forli followed on 10th November. Further west in Italy, the American Fifth Army was building up to an assault on Bologna. Despite their best efforts, German resilience and the miserable Italian winter prevented any further advance. In addition, Allied troops and equipment continued to disperse for the fight in France and elsewhere in mainland Europe.

Towards the end of 1944, significant casualty numbers, extreme weather, and the loss of resources to priorities elsewhere, led to low morale amongst men in the Eighth and Fifth Armies. This almost certainly led to the arrival of Stan Cullis' touring football team as a means to placate the tetchy troops in Italy.

On the Western Front, the US Third Army crossed the River Moselle in early November. Within the month, the French First Army ploughed through the Belfort Gap, and Strasbourg was liberated on 24 November. The weather, as in Italy, was wreaking havoc on the Western Front. In what was their last major counter-offensive of the war, the German Army assaulted the Ardennes Forest in Belgium and Luxembourg, attempting to split Allied lines and disrupt the use of Antwerp as a key supply route for the Allies.[47] Despite the German advance, key positions were doggedly held by the Allies, including the municipality of Bastogne. The Germans were running out of supplies and with the resumption of Allied air attacks, their offensive was stalling. Under the command of General Patton, the US Third Army relieved Bastogne at the end of December 1944. Soon after, Allied forces would launch their own counter-offensive.

*****

Lieutenant General Sir Oliver Leese, issued his farewell message to Eighth Army on 1st October 1944, leaving for a role in India. Lieutenant General Sir Richard (Dick) McCreery took command. Bill had nothing against McCreery, but he admired Leese so much, he didn't want to see him go — nor any of the Eighth Army team that went with him. However, Bill had seen it all by the start of October 1944 and knew a wee ripple in command waters wouldn't push Eighth Army off course.

The Italian weather took a turn for the worse and this was more difficult to endure. Bill was no lover of the hot, arid dust bowl of the desert, but felt the Italian extremes of summer and winter were a curse. At least he had a fur coat, unlike the boys up front. They ate, slept and fought in the most terrible conditions. Lying on his bed, Bill longed for a mild, rainy day in Auld Reekie, though a couple of weeks of that would probably have him

[47] Commonly known as the Battle of the Bulge

complaining as well. It was often said that moaning was an Army privilege. As Bill tried to get warm, his thoughts turned to Lisbeth. On 6th October, she would turn twenty-nine.

'I must get home before you reach your thirties Lisbeth,' he whispered to himself.

John Robertson had arrived home to a large family gathering and celebration, which Lisbeth attended. Bill was envious of his friend, but happy for him nonetheless. One of the good guys had made it back, he thought, wondering if John's mouth had gotten him in trouble with his family yet. It was a subject they'd joked about more than once. After a time in the army, one's language became rather colourful and John was not particularly good at curbing it.

As the middle of October arrived, there was no let-up in the weather and it was now holding up progress. Would the war continue much further into 1945? It was looking more likely. Main HQ was awash with mud and water and Bill couldn't imagine how it must be for the boys up front. At least he had a pair of gum boots to keep his feet dry.

An improvement in the condition of Lisbeth's father was a relief to the family and lifted Bill's spirits. He had even been cleared to resume work, though restricted to light duties at the Post Office. In other family news, Bill was bucked to read that Ann had started kindergarten. Lisbeth had chosen St Serf's which was close to home and Ann had insisted, she walk herself home after the very first day. It was comforting to think that his darling daughter had taken to it like the proverbial duck to water.

On 17th October, Bill informed Lisbeth that he now had a caravan all to himself. Occasionally, he had been able to use one for work duties, but this was his own; four solid walls for eating and sleeping. Two days later the weather took another turn for the worse, making life that bit more difficult. The caravan was, Bill wrote, 'a decided improvement on a tent!'

Built on a fifteen-hundredweight chassis, the caravan had only two wheels. It was about ten feet long and seven feet wide with a standing height of about seven feet. The sides were constructed of plywood and there was carpeted planking to the floor. A table cum desk ran almost the full length of one side with drawers underneath at either end. Shelves above it acted as trays for the multitude of files, and attached to the wall was a single shelf on which Bill kept photos of Lisbeth and Ann. At the end of the caravan was a large box structure, complete with hinged lid that hooked up to the caravan wall at night. A spring frame sat in the box's top, on which Bill slept. His trunk and cases fitted in the lower part of the box. There was a wash basin complete with wooden frame. It swung back on a hinge and had storage space underneath, as well as a small toilet cabinet. A full-length cupboard contained Bill's clothes and boots. Overall, he considered his new home most comfortable — the best since Cairo.

The AAG was absent for a few days at the end of the month which increased Bill's workload and he struggled under the volume of paperwork. However, he would not allow 28th October to pass by without writing a few words to Lisbeth. Married for four years, they had never spent a wedding anniversary together. Love, marriage and a life together was what most people expected, but Mr and Mrs Sinclair had not yet begun theirs.

On 7th November, Bill wrote to Lisbeth telling her to expect a visitor. Peter 'Johnny' Johnstone was an old acquaintance of Bill and Staff Captain 'A' when he had arrived in Army HQ in Tripoli. A regular Royal Tank Regiment soldier, he'd returned to Cairo from Sicily and married a WAAF. She was now in Edinburgh expecting a baby. Peter (the great nephew of Rudyard Kipling) was returning on long service grounds and would go on to Staff School. Unable to impart detailed information about his work in letters home, Bill thought Peter could provide Lisbeth with all the griffin in person.

'If you want to find out exactly how I live and what I do for a living etc.
— and have done ever since Tripoli — Peter Johnstone will be able to give
you a better idea than anyone else I know as he lived and worked with me
for a long time.'

Peter was the fifth chap to disappear from the mess in little more than a
fortnight, including Peter Methven who was now fixed up as DAAG of a
division that Bill had once tried for. The mess was a lonelier place without
them, but there were plenty of good men left and replacements were coming
in all the while. Some were new faces, while others turned out to be old
acquaintances, last seen in Cairo, Cassino or elsewhere in-between.

On 9th November, all ears were pressed against the wireless for Churchill's speech[48] and Bill wrote the following appraisal:

> I heard Winston's speech relayed from the Lord Mayors banquet
> last night. I agree with him on most of the main items (kind of me,
> what!) and I do hope he is right in thinking we can finish it next
> year. We should be able to, but it will take a heck of a lot of hard
> work. One thing is for certain barring a miracle — it won't finish
> this year!
>
> I was also glad to see that he made an effort to put this Italian
> show in its proper perspective. It must be disheartening to the chaps
> here to find themselves — literally speaking, relegated to the back
> page. I think that when this year of the war appears in history books
> a much different story will be told, but of course by that time most
> people will have forgotten that there ever was a war!!
>
> I was interested to read the other day by a fairly responsible per-
> son, that it is a fact that this war will have changed everyone who
> took part in it — may be for better — may be for worse. I know my

---

[48] Speech at Mansion House, London, reviewing the progress made in 1944

outlook on life in general has certainly changed but I shall leave it to you — as the person best qualified to do so — to decide how I have altered. It must have done something to you too darling; the only reassuring item is that however we have changed we still love each other, so we can start from there, and I don't know of a better starting-point.

Bill was pining for home, not helped by the news from Lisbeth that Cousin Hamish had made it back to Blighty despite the injuries suffered in North Africa. He'd married in Edinburgh. Lisbeth attended the wedding. Hamish had gone five years without seeing his Fiancée.

'Five years is an awful long time,' Bill wrote, '[but] so is three and a half come to that!'

In the same letter of 12th November, he also confirmed his appointment as convenor of Eighth Army football. He'd buckled under pressure from colleagues who knew of his abilities and experience. In view of all the work to get through it would be a challenge, but Bill hadn't kicked a ball for quite a few months, and was looking forward to it. The first task was to get a Sinclair XI together to face a touring side comprising several international players — within a week!

Bill raced around and gathered some names, including George Hamilton (of Hearts and Aberdeen fame)[49] and Andy Beattie of Preston and Scotland. It was the start of a fruitful playing and managerial partnership between Bill and Andy.

'We shall get the boys together and fix up this international outfit,' Bill wrote. The outfit referred to was being managed by none other than Stan Cullis.

From the time he joined Wolves from Ellesmere Port

---

[49] Post-war, George Hamilton would go on to play for Scotland

Wednesday, it was clear Stan Cullis was not only a talented player but a born leader. He captained Wolves at nineteen and England when two days short of his twenty-third birthday. As a centre-half, he dominated and had excellent ball control which he often used to dribble clear from danger — a tactic he would later frown upon as a manager. When Wolves were the talk of English football in the late 1930s they twice finished First Division runners-up and also lost the 1939 FA Cup final to Portsmouth when hot favourites. In the first League season after the War, Wolves failed again to win the title, losing their final game to Liverpool, the eventual winners. It was Cullis' last game as a player but he would make up for all those near misses after he became manager in 1948, guiding Wolves twice to FA Cup final triumphs and three league titles as well as series of wins in prestige floodlit friendlies.[50]

The match in question took place on 18th November 1944. The venue was Rimini Stadium. Bill arrived early for a pitch inspection and general check of the playing area — a far more enjoyable form of reconnaissance than the norm. They'd need all the help they could get playing a team managed by Stan Cullis.

On a beautiful bright morning, Bill's team walked onto the pitch where a group of lads was already having a kick-about. 'Sorry Willie,' came the shout as the ball headed towards Bill. A young lad chased after it. As he approached, Bill thought he'd have some fun and crouched as though making ready to tackle. For a split second, he was back at Polkemmet Juniors. The lad running toward, trapped the ball and knocked it between his feet, maintaining his speedy path to the awaiting Bill. The attacker feigned a shift to the right by dropping his shoulder but then went left, deftly taking the

---

[50] Wolverhampton Wanderers Football Club, *Hall of Fame: Stan Cullis*

ball with him before Bill could re-adjust. He turned to see the lad run off into the distance — ball still attached to his feet. 'Nice one Willie!' called out one of the group. Bill turned to face them replying tongue in cheek, but acknowledging the lad's obvious skill. 'Willie bloody who... Thornton?'

The lad returned, ball in hand, placed it at the feet of Bill and extended the hand of friendship as he rose.

'Aye, Willie Thornton at your service Sir.' A smile came over his face. Bill took a moment to take in the chap who'd just run a ball around him as though he didn't exist. Then came the realisation.

'Oh conscience, we really are in trouble!'

[Willie Thornton] played like a classic centre forward and had a classic sense of sportsmanship. He had all the tools needed to be a quality goal scorer, including an excellent head for the game. This made his partnership with friend and right wing, Willie Waddell, devastating and it was no surprise Thornton became the first post-war Ranger to break the one hundred-goal barrier.

He joined, aged sixteen, in March 1936 on the princely wage of £1 a week and his debut against Partick Thistle less than ten months later made him one of the youngest ever Light Blues. Twenty appearances in the following season was just the precursor to him being a regular in the side of 38/39 which brought him his first of four Championship medals.

The war interrupted and found Willie serving in the British Army's only existent private regiment, the Duke of Atholl's Scottish Horse and ended with the player honoured for gallantry in the Sicilian Campaign.

Football returned and normal service was hastily resumed by the two Willies. In 47/48 they were involved in another record. The Scottish Cup semi-final against Hibernian was played in front of a staggering 143,570 people who saw the tie decided by a solitary Thornton header from a Waddell cross. They duly went on to win the final as well — a success in which Thornton's thirty-six goals played a major part.

Success continued for club and player alike culminating for Thornton in 1952 when he was voted Player Of The Year. Two years later he hung up his boots and went into management initially at Dundee and Partick Thistle, before returning to Ibrox as assistant manager to Davie White.[51]

The ice had been broken on the Rimini pitch; everyone shared a laugh and looked forward to the game ahead. On reflection, perhaps what upset Bill most, was not that Willie Thornton made a monkey out of him, but that Hearts once looked at him. How much better could life at the Edinburgh club have been if only they had signed Willie Thornton?

It was not the first or last time Bill heard of Willie's name in the context of great football matches, but in Bill's own mind, none was so great as the match played in Rimini stadium on that bright November morning in 1944, watched by a crowd of twenty thousand.[52]

In other matters, the war had tipped into its fifth year and the British Government were making more of an effort regarding home leave. Lisbeth enquired about Bill's prospects, but he remained focused on going home only when he could stay at home — for good! As he explained, he also considered there were others more deserving of a trip to Blighty.

As I suspected, you raise the vexed topic of home leave. I'm afraid there is a pretty slim chance of my appearing on the roster....The main reason for that is that the vacancies as far as possible are going forward to the infantry, gunners and chaps in the

---

[51] Rangers Football Club, *Hall of Fame: Willie Thornton*
[52] The Bill Sinclair XI lost 4–1 to the Stan Cullis XI

tanks, with long service counting among them.

It is funny to think that now we have obtained this home leave — after agitating for it for years — the original grounds on which it was first made i.e. that three and four years was too long to keep anyone away from his home and family etc., have gone by the board. Not that I disagree with the present method of allotting the vacancies.

Anyone further back from the Germans than a few miles can complain about his long service overseas until he is blue in the face, but the poor old infantryman never gets a chance to have long service overseas — unless he has lain on both feet and both hands.

I have however, seen today an order requesting all qualified teachers to submit the relevant details to the usual 'higher authority' so perhaps I may not have to wait so long after all. [53]

In not making home leave, Bill would miss the marriage of Lisbeth's brother Jack to his Fiancée Vickie. On 1st December, Bill wrote:

'I'm awfully sorry I won't be able to be at Jack and Vickie's wedding… I have never met Vickie but from what I have heard I think no one should have any fears about their future happiness.'

In December 1944, Bill was asked to run the HQ football committee in addition to the Eighth Army one. As such, football was at the heart of a week's leave in December. The trip took in Florence, Leghorn (Livorno) and Pisa. Bill set off on 15th December with a workshops officer, another chap and a truck 'complete with about £50,000 worth of football players.' Bill had turned manager and Willie Thornton now played for Bill's HQ XI. Jock Galloway (Rangers) also joined along with George Hamilton, Tom

---

[53] Bill's understanding at the time was the government would require something in the order of fifty thousand additional teaching staff post-war

Finney (Preston)[54] and others. Bill was feverishly excited about their chances for the game that evening and half-wished he was playing. On 18th December he wrote to Lisbeth recalling the big match against the American Fifth Army.

> I was keeping all of my fingers crossed last Friday night as my life would be unbearable if the Fifth Army beat us. Well darling, they didn't and the Eighth won 3–1, all of our goals being scored by George Hamilton of the Hearts.
>
> They had a terrific crowd there — about forty-fifty thousand and the excitement was extremely great. There was a crowd of guardsmen not far from where I was sitting. Judging by their accents they all hailed from Glasgow and every time Willie Thornton of the Rangers touched the ball, they announced the merits and deeds of the 'Glesca Rangers' to anyone within one hundred yards of them including quite a few Yanks. It does the old heart good to hear them!

After the game Bill joked with Willie:

'Not a bad display of fitness Willie considering you've been on the guns for a good few months. Still, ye cuid dae wi' a wee bit mair more game-time, me thinks,' he scoffed.

'Aye, weel ye coudnae keep up wi' me,' Willie replied in jest. 'Remember Rimini?'

In Florence, Bill visited the Church of Santa Croce. Florence, Bill observed, was like Edinburgh, with its open parks and squares. He also met up with a chap he had not seen in over five and a half years. Regimental Quartermaster Sergeant George Watson was with a gunner regiment, fighting with Allied forces in Clark's Fifth Army. The two blethered and

---

[54] Tom Finney went on to earn seventy-six caps for England

joked about George's brother, Alex, who was a dear friend of Bill's back in the day. George also told Bill that he wouldn't have recognised him — principally on account of his lack of hair!

The last match of the tour was a game against a Navy XI but it wasn't much of a contest with Bill's side winning 12–2.

'It was dead easy,' he said, 'but our chaps excelled themselves.' Sergeants of a local unit invited the team back to their mess and put themselves out to give the lads a good time. They sang all the old favourites and had terrific footballing arguments about the winners of previous Cups.

The team also visited Pisa during the tour. While there, an old acquaintance invited Bill out and the two had a glorious meal. They passed off a pleasant evening listening to an orchestra, a respectable tenor and soprano, rendering all the well-known pieces.

The following afternoon would have seen Bill taking in *La Bohème*, which was being performed in the Verdi Opera Theatre, had it not been for a pre-arranged game of football. Bill had agreed to play for the unit of another old friend on the promise of a good feed after. Bill thought he would have plenty of goodies, as the chap was still in charge of a reinforcement and transit camp. They won the match 6–1 and the food afterwards lived up to expectation — Bill did not regret missing the opera. His friend, George Watson, turned up and the three men blethered till the early hours.

By 24th December, Bill was back from leave and attended a midnight service — not because he felt he ought to — but because he wanted to.

> I also want just to wish you and Ann all the very best wishes for tomorrow and every other day until I can come home to try and make my wishes and hopes come true. I do honestly think that this time next year we shall be together and shall be able to look back on the end of the war in Europe, and forward to a life of peace and happiness together.

All we ask tonight, darling is that some of the spirit which one feels all around at this time, shall be instilled into the hearts and souls and minds of all mankind, so that we can all work for a better and a happier world.

I feel sure that the majority of people are fundamentally good and wish nothing but good for their neighbours. I can never understand why this majority cannot, by the sheer force of their example, turn all the wrong doers and evil thinkers from their present ways into the ways of all decent thinking people. However, perhaps if we keep up the struggle, we shall all be the same one day and there will be peace on earth and goodwill among all men.

I at least, have the opportunity now, and will continue to do so after the war, to influence considerable numbers of lives and I only hope that I am doing and always shall do it, in a proper manner.

Bill had a pleasant Christmas under the circumstances. On Christmas morning he played in a football match against a touring RAF XI which resulted in a 1–1 draw. The NAAFI served an excellent lunch with an orchestra playing, and there were more celebrations at night. Dinner finished around 10pm and then everyone sang songs (which only remained clean for a short while). Bill worked on Boxing Day, but set aside the evening for more celebrations and yet another Christmas dinner.

The period between Boxing Day and New Year was fairly quiet with one exception; Eighth Army organised a party for four hundred local children. The show lasted three hours and involved a good feed (sandwiches, cakes and buns), then five cartoon films, after which Santa Claus appeared and distributed oranges and bars of chocolate. Recalling the frivolity and racket, Bill remarked, 'I never knew there were so few required to make such a noise!'

Bill wished he could have been at the Sunday School party in Edinburgh with Lisbeth and Ann. Maybe next year. Even if the war continued well into the following year, Bill would be *Pythonised*[55] and back home by the middle of December 1945.

---

[55] Python was the codename given to the points-based system concerned with British troop repatriation from overseas

Personal Message from the Army Commander

This message is to say good-bye to you all. My orders to take over an Army Group came at short notice; this makes it impossible for me to see you and thank you personally.

You have fought your way in nine months from Cassino to Florence, from Ortona to Rimini. Now you have smashed the Gothic Line and broken out into the Plains.

The name of the Eighth Army, with its Desert Air Force, has never stood higher than today.   Together, you have a decisive part to play until Germany is finally overthrown.

To Lieutenant-General Sir Richard McCreery, who assumes command today, I hand over with complete confidence.   His long connection with this Army is known to many of you.

I leave our great Eighth Army, and my many friends among its formations, with real regret.   This Army has, and always will have, a spirit of comradeship all its own.   I shall always remember with pride your friendliness and cheerfulness in good times and bad, and the confidence you have placed in me throughout our battles.

I thank you all and wish you Good Luck.

Oliver Leese.

Lieutenant-General.

Tac H.Q., Eighth Army.
1st October, 1944.

Lieutenant General Oliver Leese, farewell message to Eighth Army
1st October 1944

'Rimini stadium November 1944 — self & Willie Thornton'
Bill Sinclair (left)

Team photo prior to Rimini match, 18th November 1944
Bill Sinclair, back row, far right
Andy Beattie, back row, next to Bill
George Hamilton, front row, centre

Award ceremony, Rimini match. Bill Sinclair receiving handshake
18th November 1944

Bill Sinclair: Pisa, December 1944

END IN SIGHT

Throughout the dismal winter of 1944–45, Allied and German troops watched each other vigilantly across the lines of the forgotten front — Italy. The Allies were now planning a spring offensive, necessitating the re-supply of equipment and munitions and the training of troops. The battle started on 2nd April 1945 in the east with Eighth Army. In the west, Fifth Army's assault began in earnest on the 14th. On the 20th they broke out of the Apennine mountains onto the plain. On the 21st, troops of the Fifth and Eighth Armies entered Bologna simultaneously. Phase I was complete. With Eighth Army having crossed the Argenta and the Fifth being in the Po valley, Phase II got underway. The Allies advanced quickly and the Germans retreated across the Po River, abandoning large quantities of supplies and equipment. The Allied breakthrough was soon complete and the enemy was surrounded. On 23rd April, the start of Phase III saw the Allies cross the river; Ferrara and Modena fell twenty-four hours later. Twenty-three days after starting Phase I, the remnants of the Hun surrendered south of the Po River, Verona was captured and Phase III was complete. Both armies continued their push with the Eighth entering Padua in the early hours of 29th April, Venice later the same day and Udine on 1st May.[56]

Eighth and Fifth Armies edged towards their Allied colleagues further north, who themselves had made progress, albeit slowly, during the harshest of winter conditions. In a bitterly cold January, the Germans were withdrawing in the Ardennes. Two weeks after the US First Army attacked

---

[56] Headquarters, 15th Army, *Finito! The Po Valley Campaign*, pp. 5–19

the Ardennes Salient, it was eliminated. By 1st February, the US Seventh Army had reached the Siegfried Line along the German western frontier. A week later they were through. The slog east continued and by early March the US First and Ninth Armies had reached the Rhine. Further south, Third Army took Coblenz and by the end of March had themselves crossed the Rhine. First and Third Armies now linked up and on the southern edge, Third and Seventh Armies did the same. On 27th March, Allied Supreme Commander Dwight D. Eisenhower proclaimed that 'the German Army as a military force on the Western Front is a whipped army.'

Hitler was slowly but surely being boxed in, and the end — at least in Europe — was in sight. Churchill and Roosevelt met in Malta to discuss the final throws of the campaign, which preceded the Yalta Conference in February. Yalta, included Stalin and was the second meeting of the so-called *big three*. The post-war division of Europe and approach for reconstruction was agreed, as was the pursuit of Nazi war criminals. Auschwitz had recently been liberated. Belsen, Buchenwald and Dachau would follow in April. The Yalta Conference was President Roosevelt's last. He passed away on 12th April 1945 and was replaced by Truman.

At the time of the Yalta Conference, the Red Army was closing in on Berlin from the east. Intense urban fighting continued as the Russians assaulted German defensive positions along the way. Hard fought battles from the beginning of 1945 resulted in Hungary and Poland being overcome, as German troops evacuated *en masse*. Meanwhile, the US First and Ninth Armies encircled German Army group B in Rhur. On 10th April, the US Ninth took Hanover.

By the middle of April, the war in mainland Europe was nearing its conclusion. Soviet forces occupied Vienna and prepared for their final offensive on Berlin. They made it there on 23rd April. The game was up.

In Northern Italy, Mussolini was captured by Partisans. He was executed and his body taken to Milan where he was strung up for all to see. Hitler would not suffer the same fate. He committed suicide in his Berlin bunker on 30th April 1945.

*****

Bill was sorry to see Donnelly go. He'd been at his side for almost two years and taken care of Bill's every need since arriving at Rear Army HQ. But Donnelly had completed four and half year's overseas service and deserved his passage home. Would Mick accompany him? Bill thought so, but Donnelly wanted the dog to stay.

'You'll nae cope wi'oot th' baith o' us, Bill.' There were tears in his eyes as he knelt and took Mick's head in his hands. And so, Mick stayed on to assist with the remainder of the Italian Campaign. Donnelly headed off, promising he'd look in on Mrs Sinclair. Bill warned his wife.

I assure you darling he has a heart of gold. You won't need to ask him any questions. He will never stop talking once he has started!!!

You already know a lot about him and what he has done for me, but I should like to remind you he has done a great deal — even more than you may realise, Lisbeth….He can tell you of our adventurous trips together to Tunis, Tripoli, in Sicily, Naples, Taranto, Rome, Florence and even Cairo when he used to come down with James McBrien [Mac], my predecessor in GHQ MEF [Middle East Forces] and also here. He can also tell you what my football ability is like these days, but don't believe him — he doesn't know one football player from another and you can tell him that from me.

Peter Johnstone had already made it back to Edinburgh and presented Lisbeth with flowers on account of Bill's service to him. She asked him to elaborate but Peter referred her to Bill, who wrote: 'Someday when we are all nicely cuddled up together, I'll tell you how that came about.'

Bill's MBE for conspicuous gallantry and distinguished service in Italy, was announced in the London Gazette on Thursday 21st December.[57] On 1st January 1945, he referred to it in a letter home.

'I see you have heard about my MBE.....I was fairly pleased about it myself as it should help after the war.'

Bill Sinclair MBE was struggling with the New Year of 1945. He missed Donnelly, not just because of everything that his batman and driver had done to ease everyday burdens, Bill missed his companionship and this made him long for home.

'When will we find ourselves positioned without the necessity to write to each other?' he penned to Lisbeth.

A letter from Peter Johnstone did nothing to lift his spirits. He complained about some of the civilians at home being rather complacent. Apart from those who had someone dear to them serving in the forces, the overseas soldier was not much thought of. Bill hoped Peter's impression was not representative.

In his letter of 7th January, Bill mentioned he'd 'heard old Monty's talk to correspondents about the recent German counter-attack, which appeared to be well in hand. I shouldn't think anything much will go wrong if he is left in charge of it — he was too well trained in the Eighth Army.'

Bill also expressed dismay at Lisbeth's cousin, Adam Moncur, being posted to India. He supposed Adam's wife, Ida, would not see him again for four years or until the end of the Japanese war, whichever came sooner. 'Not a very inviting prospect,' Bill wrote, 'which makes me glad in this year of 1945 that I left the UK in 1941.'

---

[57] Page 5848, supplement to the London Gazette: Captain (temporary Major) William George McKenzie Sinclair (15883), The Argyll and Sutherland Highlanders (Princess Louise's) (Edinburgh)

Mid-January in the northern wastes of Italy was cold, wet and dismal. Everything had ground to a halt. There seemed to be more going on with the Russian advance into Western Europe. Bill wrote:

'I have a funny feeling that the Russians will come pretty near to finishing it in their latest attack.'

Lisbeth sought Bill's advice on what to buy for Jack and Vickie's wedding present. He had few ideas other than a bedside rug or a standard lamp. As for the cost, he wrote, 'I'll close one eyelid if you go over £20 all told,' followed with, 'Jack is your only brother, and you have no sisters and I have neither brothers nor sisters, so why not do the chap as well as we can.'

The weather was looking up by the end of the month and Bill had secured the full-time services of Andy Beattie. As a result, football business was booming. Andy had a great deal of experience having played with the likes of Bill Shankly at Preston. Bill referred to Andy as a 'true footballing man.'[58] As regards team and match arrangements, the two cracked on with it, though army business regularly interrupted. 'If the war would only finish, we could really go big in this football business,' he wrote in his letter of 31st January.

That same day, Bill and Andy played for Army HQ. Staring out at the playing surface before the game, Andy sighed with disbelief. 'Never in your life could you imagine a pitch as bad as that Bill.' Hard concrete was covered with mud, ice, slush, snow and big pools of water, depending on where you stood. After the game it took an age for Bill to get the feeling back into his feet. He couldn't decide which was worse, this pitch, or a Cairo dust bowl.

At the same time, Bill was still expecting a conclusion to the war.

'I have great hopes still for this Russian offensive but, even if it doesn't

---

[58] Andy Beattie would go on to manage Huddersfield Town and Nottingham Forest. He was also the first ever manager of the Scottish national team

finish the whole thing off this time, it shouldn't take a combined East, West and South offensive in the early summer to see the end.'

Using intelligence summaries, Bill marked Russian progress onto his maps. In his mind, enemy continuation of the fight was futile; Bill wished the Germans would realise that they had had it, so that no more lives would be lost. Such thoughts remained at the fore as news came in of another friend, killed in action. When Bill was in Peterhead, he'd met a lovely chap named Donaldson, who had played for the Hearts 'A' team before the war. He was a gunner in an anti-tank regiment. Donaldson was killed in the battle for the Gothic Line. Bill later communicated to Lisbeth, 'I never even knew he was here.'

Attempting to shift his mind to more positive events, Bill considered the wedding taking place at home. 'Vickie and Jack are now, I hope, safely and happily married,' Bill wrote. 'Give them my very best. I had a note from Jack (air graph) thanking us for our present.'

Bill contemplated his own return home. After completing four and half year's overseas service, on 29th January 1946, he would qualify for return to the UK under the Python system. However, at the time of consideration the process was running one to two months ahead and he was hoping to be home in time for Christmas 1945.

A week later and Bill was cracking on with arrangements of a different kind — Eighth Army football matches. He and Andy Beattie now had a clerk to lend a hand and the Inter-branch Cup was underway. Bill played in a first-round match and, against form and expectation, his side won 3–1. He was struggling to recruit players as quite a few chaps had already qualified for Python and returned home at the end of January. This left a dwindling number of men with an Eighth Army clasp on their Africa Star. However, as difficult as it was, Bill and Andy always managed to scrape a side together from those that remained.

As planned, Donnelly visited Lisbeth in Edinburgh. Five and a half hours after knocking the door, Donnelly was still talking and Lisbeth was still listening. He brought her up to speed with Eighth Army progress and tales of his adventures with Bill. This helped Lisbeth feel closer to her husband, though she was less enamoured to hear of his volunteering for a Burma posting. Bill clarified matters in his letter of 15th March.

His former brigadier had accompanied Oliver Leese to India. Before leaving, the brig asked Tilley and Bill to join him. Bill considered the idea, because it could (in theory) have moved him a little further from danger and the long journey would give him an opportunity to rest. He'd asked Donnelly to join him, should the posting arise. Initially, Donnelly was positive, but as Python drew nearer, he had changed his mind. The transfer was eventually bounced on the grounds that Tilley and Bill would both be in India for too short a period before repatriation to the UK under Python.

With his mind back on football, despite his reservations, Bill's side made it to the final of the Inter-branch Cup. Army HQ XI were also in the fourth-round of the Inter-unit Cup and were becoming invincible under the management of Sinclair and Beattie. Other matches played since the middle of February had resulted in six victories from six fixtures: Desert Air Force, RAF Touring XI, adjacent 'Area' team (and a return fixture), Eighth Army Corps team and another from Fifth Army had all been beaten.

Each match required a huge amount of work to organise. Bill and Andy would have to get the pitch ready and marked, as well as making arrangements for the police, car-parking, accommodation and dinners. Then there was team preparation, kit, training and associated activities required to create and maintain the side. There were six internationals in the team, though they were not always available at the same time owing to operations. The impending spring offensive would make the task more difficult still.

To prepare for what was to come, Eighth Army moved again. It mystified Bill how the Germans kept going. He still thought the Russians would finally end it by striding into Berlin, even if the 'hunting down of the last fanatics may drag out for some time.'

A government minister was heard on the radio talking about reducing Python down to three years.

'Now that would be something to behold,' someone shouted back at the wireless.

'Fat chance,' came the call from another.

By 22nd March, Bill was living in a more 'wild open space.' Camp life varied according to the weather, but the previous five weeks had seen warm sunshine bathing Northern Italy and the wee caravan was still holding its own, keeping him and Mick in relative comfort.

The final of the Inter-branch Cup resulted in a 3–2 defeat with the opposition scoring all three goals in the first ten minutes. Bill was playing left-half where the committee thought he'd be most useful. Whilst his team pulled one back early in the second half, the score remained unchanged until ten minutes before the final whistle. To get back into the match, Bill moved up to inside-left and scored with five minutes left to play. It wasn't enough. They would have to try again in the Inter-unit Cup.

In preparation for the April offensive, the last days of March were the most hectic Bill had had for a while. Despite the difficulties, it appeared that the Allied forces were succeeding — at least according to Eisenhower. Bill mentioned this to Lisbeth.

'I shouldn't think old Ike would say the German Army is whipped without good reason and if it is, it can only be a matter of weeks before the end comes.'

In the same letter of 27th March, Bill referred to a dinner taking place that evening with Army Commander, McCreery.

'He is a very quiet chap but very efficient, although he will never make himself as popular a figure as Monty or Oliver Leese — he is too retiring and shy.'

By 5th April, Bill gained another footballing medal. Main HQ had reached the Inter-unit Cup final and won against an Area side. There was a decent crowd of around ten thousand who produced rattles and bells to watch Main HQ beat the Air Formation Signals XI. Andy Beattie played just behind Bill at left-back and George Hamilton took up his usual spot as centre forward. After the 6–2 victory, Bill's former AAG presented the Cup and winners' medals. Receiving the trophy from Brigadier M J Richards made the occasion even more special and the Irish Pipe Band rounded off a fantastic afternoon's entertainment.

By 9th April, Bill was shifting north again. His boss, Edward Tilley, had attended McCreery's address at Cesena five days earlier where he spelt out operational plans. After the operation proper began, Bill wrote to Lisbeth in the early hours of the following morning.

> As you will now know darling, we too, are on the move again and I trust this time we will not stop until the war is over. I have in some small way helped the Eighth Army through several battles now — Alamein, Mareth, Wadi Akarit, Enfidaville, Sicily, Italy, the Sangro, Cassino, the Gothic Line and now this one. It's been a long time darling, but it shouldn't be very much longer, and I am completely certain of our ability to stay the course and see this thing through.

> I should very much like to come home knowing that this war in Europe was finished and that there was no need for me to travel further abroad than that which I had by then completed.

> The great trouble, as I see it, is that unless the war finishes in the next four or five weeks, I cannot see myself coming home before my Python arrives.

Through the rest of April, the Allies continued to push on and Bill hankered after the long-awaited message that German resistance was over. There were rumours of great things on all fronts and the excitement in Main Army HQ was palpable. Bill was busy, owing to the success of the Allied advance in Northern Italy and German troops rolled into his PW camps.

Towards the end of April, Allied forces gave chase up to the Alps and Bill reckoned they had torn up and destroyed the best part of twenty-five German divisions in the process. With rumours of German surrenders and rapid advances on the Northern European front, Bill and his men were now hopeful of a full surrender within days. He concluded it was 'fairly good going, and a fitting climax to the career of the Eighth Army.'

These German Divs [Divisions] included some of the finest, best equipped, best trained and most experienced in the whole German Army, but even the Para Divs have been well and truly sorted this time.

The next few weeks promise to be very interesting as we shall be getting up in amongst the Alps soon. Apart from the scenery which should be grand, we shall thereby escape spending a decent part of the summer down in this Po Valley, which is striking hot and when the old mosquitoes have resumed their unfriendly antics! Gosh, I'll be glad when I can do away with my mosquito net, oils and creams and mepacrine tablets. They are an awful nuisance but a necessary one.

Padua and Venice should be interesting and I am looking forward to seeing them. I think we should have Venice tonight [29th April]. I haven't seen Bologna yet — we bypassed it in too great a hurry, but sometime I might get a minute to nip back there.

I see that Mussolini has had it — fair enough! I was disinclined to believe it but one of the US Divs confirmed the glad news today.

With all the furore around the impending end to the war, many men began to think about their futures. Bill's thoughts turned to the options related to Class A and Class B release. As a teacher, he'd likely be offered Class B if he requested it. At first glance, this appeared favourable due to an earlier release, but in the cold light of day, perhaps not. Class B offered fewer days initial leave than Class A. Class B also offered nothing in the way of additional leave for overseas service and cash grants under Class B would be withheld until general demobilisation. There were two further issues with a Class B release. First, if an occupation ceased to be of national importance, one could be recalled, though this was not likely in Bill's case given the need for teachers. Second, those in Class B must undertake employment wherever the Ministry of Labour determined. Bill would probably be placed in Scotland, but it wasn't certain. If Class A meant another three months in the field followed by the certainty of a home posting, then it would be better to wait. On balance, Bill though Class A was preferable and decided to sit tight.

ALLIED FORCE HEADQUARTERS

April, 1945

SPECIAL ORDER OF THE DAY

Soldiers, Sailors and Airmen of the Allied Forces in the Mediterranean Theatre

Final victory is near. The German Forces are now very groggy and only need one mighty punch to knock them out for good. The moment has now come for us to take the field for the last battle which will end the war in Europe. You know what our comrades in the West and in the East are doing on the battlefields. It is now our turn to play our decisive part. It will not be a walk-over; a mortally wounded beast can still be very dangerous. You must be prepared for a hard and bitter fight; but the end is quite certain — there is not the slightest shadow of doubt about that. You, who have won every battle you have fought, are going to win this last one.

Forward then into battle with confidence, faith and determination to see it through to the end. Godspeed and good luck to you all.

H. R. Alexander

Field-Marshal,
Supreme Allied Commander,
Mediterranean Theatre.

Field-Marshal Harold Alexander, Supreme Allied Commander,
Mediterranean Theatre: Message to Allied forces, April 1945

The Eighth Army, which started the great tide of Allied victory at El Alamein, is about to strike a knock-out blow against the Germans in Italy.

Our Armies in Germany, and those of our Allies, have, sent the enemy staggering back towards Berlin, but he is still fighting and he must not be allowed to use his Armies in Italy to form a garrison for a Southern German stronghold.

With the powerful aid of the Desert Air Force, which has been our partner in every victory, we will destroy or capture the enemy South of the River Po.

The American Fifth Army will be assaulting at our side, and the American Air Forces in Italy will bring their full weight to bear in support of our attack.

We have a unique opportunity to destroy the enemy in his present positions because, owing to lack of fuel, he is incapable of large-scale and rapid movement. As in every battle, there will be hard fighting, and difficulties will have to be overcome, but I know that Eighth Army will show how the job can be finished off quickly.

We must take every advantage of our overwhelming air superiority, our tanks and our artillery, and drive hard and deep with speed.

From Tobruk to the Po Plains the brave soldiers of Poland have been fighting with us, and it is a matter of especial pride to our Empire Army that in this battle our gallant Polish Allies will be striking a decisive blow.

The Eighth Army recognises and appreciates the part that gallant Italian forces are taking in the struggle.

Together we will all go forward to final victory.

Good Luck to you all.

R. L. McCreery

Main H.Q.,
Eighth Army.
April, 1945.

Lieut.-General,
G.O.C., Eighth Army.

Lieutenant General Dick McCreery, message to Eighth Army
April 1945

VICTORY, LEAVE, RETURN

The first German surrender came in Italy on 2nd May 1945. Fought in the shadow of the higher profile Normandy Landings and the Russian advance on the Eastern Front, the Italian Campaign was crucial in bringing the war in Europe to an end. It included some of the most intense, close-quarters fighting of the war and claimed the lives of almost fifty thousand Commonwealth troops alone.[59]

Two days later, German forces in Holland, Denmark and the north west of Germany surrendered. It was all over in Europe and on 7th May, General Jodl — with approval from Hitler's successor, Admiral Dönitz — signed an unconditional surrender. VE day followed on 8th May, with huge celebrations and throngs of people daring to believe that a peaceful existence had at last dawned. The German surrender was ratified in Berlin, which was held by the Russians, and discussions on partitioning the city followed.

Though the war in Europe was at an end, the Japanese fought on. In a chilling trial of what was to come, on 16th July an atomic bomb was tested at Alamogordo in the Mexican Desert, as part of the long-running Manhattan Project.

In the second half of July, the third and final conference between the *big three* took place in Potsdam, near Berlin. Truman had replaced Roosevelt, and part way through the conference, Atlee replaced Churchill. The atmosphere had changed, though the desire to bring Nazi war criminals to justice remained. Matters of geographical and political borders came to the fore and reparation and peace treaties were discussed.

---

[59] Commonwealth War Graves Commission, *The Italian Campaign*

Now that the war in Europe was over, the common purpose of defeating Nazi Germany was replaced by the division of mainland Europe. There were four resulting zones of occupation in Germany (American, British, French and Soviet) and Polish borders were agreed, which included areas that hitherto had been part of Germany. Reparations were agreed, begrudgingly, and whilst there were to be free and democratic elections in post-war nations, the American, British and French felt that Communist rule in Eastern Europe would not necessarily facilitate a democratic election outcome. Suspicions on all sides were growing in what would become a clear dividing line between East and West.

The Potsdam conference also resulted in a declaration on Japan, demanding unconditional surrender. Japan rejected the Allied demands and on 6th August 1945, the first atomic bomb used in warfare was dropped on Hiroshima. Three days later, a second atomic bomb was dropped on Nagasaki. Japan agreed to an unconditional surrender on 15th August and Victory over Japan (VJ) Day followed. The fighting was over.

*****

As you will no doubt have heard — and I daresay with a considerable amount of relief — our war has ended. That this whole thing will be over in a matter of hours I have no doubt, but I was naturally glad that we had the pleasure of receiving the first surrender, and that Monty got the second one. I should imagine there will be a lot of happy homes in the UK tonight at the thought of the British Army in Europe having fired its last shot in anger.

The mere fact I haven't written for a week, should however give you an indication, darling, that the problems of 'A' Branch do not ease with the end of hostilities — in fact, if these few days can be taken as average, life promises to be pretty full. I do not think they can be, though, as a large part of my time has been taken up by the disposal of some forty thousand PW we took before the war finished, and the fact that the army is now strung out over a very great distance has multiplied the usual daily problems through difficulties of communication. All that should cease when we are nicely settled down somewhere as an army of occupation.

Bill's letter of 6th May 1945 had been five years in the making. How many times had he prayed for hostilities to end and uttered the words, ruddy war? He could barely believe what he was writing. The sense of relief was palpable. For the first time since April 1940, Bill allowed himself to plan instead of dream. He would make enquiries to various Education Councils as soon as a general cessation of hostilities was announced, and asked Lisbeth to provide the addresses. Now, he could map out a future without wondering whether his plans would actually come to fruition. The sense of empowerment was overwhelming.

Victory in Europe (VE) day came forty-eight hours later on 8th May. If only he could have been at home to experience the atmosphere. At least Lisbeth's brother Jack had got back in time to celebrate. The following day the whole family joined a mass of Edinburgh residents in Princes Street Gardens. Folks were packed in tighter than a herring barrel and a renewed sense of optimism carried the crowd along. Ann was all dressed up for the grand occasion.

Bill celebrated with a day's leave and a trip to Venice. He and his friends floated peacefully around the remarkable city in a gondola before visiting St Mark's Square. Exploring the shops in a relaxed environment, Bill purchased some silk stockings and a silk scarf for Lisbeth. As tempting as it was, he stopped short of buying a piece of Venetian glassware for fear of breaking it on the journey home.

The next day, Eighth Army were on the move again, enabling HQ to break free from the heat rising in the plains. By 14th May, Bill was in the foothills of the Alps where conditions were more bearable. Mick was happier too. Despite being a Tunisian native, the young dog seemed more suited to cooler climes.

'Nothing can beat that view Mick, eh?' On hearing his name, Mick rose to his feet and looked at his master. Sitting on the caravan steps, Bill gazed upwards at the lush green hills and valleys, framed by snow-capped mountains, sitting atop the fertile fields below. This beautiful view coupled with the sense of relief at the end of the war, made this a special moment. He now had no scruples about going home on LIAP (Leave In Addition to Python).

For those who had completed more than three years' service, LIAP presented an opportunity to go home for a period of leave before returning and further serving until Python was due. Bill reckoned he had a fair chance of qualifying in July.

At each Alpine location the scenery improved. By this time, Bill had seen a fair bit of Southern Austria and this beautiful country made a lasting impression on him. The freshness and greenery were the very antithesis of the North African desert. He marvelled at the glass-like surface of lakes, reflecting a background of tree-lined hills and mountains with craggy, snow-covered peaks. The natural varying shades of green, brown, white and blue seemed infinite. It surpassed anything he had seen in pictures or books. On the Wörthersee Lake, between Villach and Klagenfurt, Bill lay back in a rowing boat, feelings of freedom and relief washing over him. It was over. How fortunate he was to be alive to witness it all. Bill believed that survival was simply a matter of good luck and he was one of the fortunate ones. As he lay back in the boat, he gave thanks to all those in North Africa, Sicily and Italy who were buried where they lay. Good friends lost forever.

Despite the cessation of hostilities in Europe, political uncertainty remained and the ongoing conflict elsewhere could not be ignored, but the relative peace brought the slackening of censorship regulations. Bill wrote to Lisbeth, 'We left Cesena and moved up to Forli just before the battle started.[60] We then moved to Imola on the road to Bologna, and then to Ferrara, Venice, and now we are about a dozen miles north of Udine on the way to the Austrian frontier from Venice.'

As mid-June arrived, so did the most wonderful news. Bill was granted LIAP, which comprised of six weeks: four weeks at home and one week's travel either way. Bill was ecstatic. In his letter of 17th June, he confirmed to Lisbeth that he would soon see her for the first time in four years.

Bill started planning. He would depart on 21st and expect to be in London on the 27th or 28th. If he got back in time, he could take the night Scotsman train up to Edinburgh — if it still ran. If not, he would stay overnight in London and catch the 10am train the following day.

Having spent days on the road, Bill arrived in London on 27th June, but not in time for the night Scotsman. Instead, he stayed overnight in a hotel arranged by a HQ colleague who was already there. The following morning, the 10am train from London left on time with Bill on board. He'd wired Lisbeth to let her know when he'd arrive at Waverley Station; she and Ann were to meet him there. The journey passed quickly as his face was glued to the window, his eyes wide taking in British scenery for the first time in almost four years.

As the train drew into Edinburgh, Bill felt a sense of trepidation. For four years, all the things he wanted to express had to be written down; now he could speak to Lisbeth in person and meet his daughter for the very first time. Bill breathed hard and slow as he gathered his belongings and made for the carriage door. Stepping off the train onto the platform was

---

[60] Po Valley Campaign

momentous. He'd dreamed of this for so long and now it was here. The smell of home pervaded the air as he made his way to the exit.

The first thing Bill noticed was Lisbeth's Auburn hair; the next was the wee girl beside her. Hand in hand, Ann and her mother made their way towards Bill. He'd played this scene over in his mind so many times. There was an embrace and bright smiles. Bill was desperate to escape from the masses and Lisbeth had ordered a taxi to take them home — unheard of under normal circumstances, but the occasion merited it. Unfortunately, Ann had a tantrum and screamed most of the way home, so Lisbeth's attention was diverted. This was not the homecoming Bill had imagined.

Making their way up to the second floor at Northumberland Place, the tread of the steps didn't seem so deep and wide as Bill remembered. It was so long since he'd been there, reality had been replaced by memories that had changed the form and feel of structures and surfaces. Bill touched walls and doors as he passed them as though trying to re-establish the reality he once knew. He quickly came to realise things would not fall back into place immediately. It would take time — for everyone.

Bill and Lisbeth had lived separate lives for four years. Now, it felt like he was peering through a window into another world. Physically and mentally tired, Bill needed time to settle down and learn to put one civilian foot in front of the other.

The Verth's and Bill's mother had been saving coupons to provide a celebratory meal for his first day back. It didn't disappoint. But Bill tired quickly of questions that seemed to come at him as though fired from a Bren gun. Lisbeth's father, John, understood that Bill was overwhelmed. He'd felt the same returning from the First World War and had taken time to adapt and re-engage with civilian life.

'Stop pestering the lad,' he snapped as another question came from Lisbeth's mother. 'Bill will tell us all about it when he's had chance to settle in. Leave him be for now.'

After a few days of re-familiarisation, things started to calm down and Bill found the routine of family life more of a comfort. Ann took up a large part of Lisbeth's day, which Bill had not anticipated, but the couple eventually found time for themselves. Slowly and purposefully, they began to talk and their worries faded to nought as they held each other for the first time in four years.

Being confident of his final return before the year's end, Bill thought he would manage the next parting well enough, but a lump came to his throat when saying goodbye. Four weeks previously, he'd arrived at Waverley Station; it now played host to a tearful farewell. The train jolted forward and eased away from the platform. Bill craned his neck to take the last glimpse of his loved ones and saw Lisbeth and Ann waving, frantically. As they disappeared from view, he thought about the last walk he'd taken with Lisbeth. Granny Sinclair had looked after Ann to give the couple some time together and they'd made the most of it.

Once back on French soil, Bill travelled by road. It would be an arduous journey and he was in low spirits after leaving Lisbeth and Ann. Main Army HQ was now split between Vienna and Udine where Bill had left it. He assumed Mick was still there and was looking forward to being reunited with his four-legged mate, when he heard news of Eighth Army being disbanded. He knew this was coming and now it was official. Who would he work for? Perhaps the 'Allied Commission, Austria' or something similar. He would find out soon enough. The following morning, he posted a birthday card to Ann with best fourth birthday wishes.

Bill travelled with others by road from Calais to Sedan and then to Mainz in Germany. The towns he passed hadn't been cleaned up much, but the countryside still looked prosperous enough. Mainz itself had a clean main street, but the rest was badly knocked about. Many buildings were nothing more than heaps of rubble. After a night in Mainz, Bill travelled through Mannheim and Pforzheim before stopping in Ulm on the Danube. He estimated that about eighty percent of the town was in bits, but he'd seen worse. Nothing he witnessed, came close to the devastation of Cassino; a pitted landscape in the same vein as the moon, was how he described it.

From Ulm, the route back to HQ took in Innsbruck and the Brenner Pass. He arrived at Villach on 2nd August where Basil Clark was waiting with the jeep and a certain four-legged friend. Mick was whimpering with excitement and bouncing on the spot with tail wagging like an RSM's finger. Basil drove the jeep back into camp where Bill spent the early evening talking to Edward Tilley and the rest of the boys. Tilley said the workload had been as bad as ever, only relenting just before Bill's return. With the arrival of two new subalterns (junior officers) any upturn in work could at least now be shared out.

Bill met Tom Agnew for dinner that evening. During his leave, Bill had written to the Perthshire Education Committee. As Tom was from Dundee, Bill sought his opinion on the schools there. Tom mentioned, Dollar, Morgan, High School of Dundee, Harris Academy, Perth Academy and Morrison Academy at Crieff, all of which he felt would be suitable academic institutions for a returning teacher.

The following day brought confirmation of Bill's new posting. He was not too enamoured at losing his Eighth Army badge, but there it was. Perhaps it was fitting for the Eighth to have come to an end in line with the war in Europe. He'd just have to get used to British Troops in Austria (BTA).

Bill's work for the new BTA outfit, was eased slightly, by the two new staff members. They had taken a considerable weight of detail off Donald and Basil, who did likewise for Bill. As a result, he accumulated some spare time and sought approval to take a trip to Venice with Tom Agnew. Permission was granted. It was part sightseeing, part shopping and part work

— if taking Brig Richards out for a farewell dinner counted. He was leaving their command, and would soon be some three hundred miles away.

On arrival in Venice, they made their way to the '86 Area' to borrow the old brig's boat. He was more than pleased to see them and the three set sail for the Lido, an island in the lagoon of Venice. They arrived in good time for lunch. The island itself was about ten miles long and a mile wide with a large promenade and beautiful beach. The hotel there catered for all needs and the three gents dined there in the evening.

They discussed all things military and civilian and Bill learned a good deal about houses from the brig who owned a few in the Dorset area. On a military front, they spoke at length about the new atomic weapon deployed in Japan. The first bomb had been dropped on Hiroshima three days earlier on 6th August. The second, at Nagasaki, was dropped on 9th August, the very day the three were sitting in Venice enjoying a meal. Bill referred to this in his letter home that evening:

'I have no official reason for stating so, but I have a shrewd idea that these remarkable bombs might induce Japan to pack up much more quickly than she might otherwise have done.'

On Tuesday 14th August, Bill shifted north east to the estate of a large mansion near Treibach, a pleasant spot about thirty miles north of Klagenfurt. Their route took in a rest camp belonging to Donald's old division and they spent a relaxing few hours on the water at Ossiacher See. Bill again thought the scenery was glorious with the mountainsides sliding steeply down to the water. It reminded him of the Norwegian Fiords he'd visited on a school trip. Afterwards, Bill and Donald took the funicular railway to experience a fantastic vista across the Alpine mountain tops, before picking up the rest of the lads back at the lakeside and continuing their journey to Treibach.

Shifting to the new camp meant Bill's Mediterranean allowance was replaced by Field allowance, meaning a drop of 1 shilling per day. Subalterns had it worse with a drop from 4 shillings and 6 pence to 2 shillings. There was also an increase in the numbers of men leaving. The chief welfare officer went, followed by Johnny Bland from Army Medical Services. Edward Tilley was also in line to go and anticipated being around for no longer than a month.

Bill was naturally inquisitive about his superior's replacement, but he had one eye on his own repatriation. Tilley's replacement would be a regular from the 'R Tanks' who was currently on leave.

The departure of colleagues always saddened Bill, but it did mean there were plenty of farewell parties. The peninsula of Maria Wörth on the banks of Wörthersee was a favourite destination. Parties were raucous affairs with a lot of drinking and singing. They were however, something of a double-edged sword as they reflected the dwindling numbers of men working in camp. Processing LIAP requests and handling a multitude of Germans and Hungarians was consuming much of Bill's time. Tilley promised to speak to the brig about securing some help.

'Even if it were only to deal with the surrendered and displaced,' Bill remarked.

'I'll do my best Bill, but with LIAP, Python, releases, local leave and courses, it's difficult.'

With no warning, Tilley informed Bill that he had to visit England as his mother had been taken ill. At the same time, Dick McCreery was planning a trip back to Blighty and invited Tilley to join him. By this time, Bill was pleading for additional resources and McCreery assured him that he would find a solution. Within the space of thirty-six hours, Bill acquired five new staff officers. McCreery had seconded Basil back from Army Medical Services (where he'd shifted after Johnny Bland's departure) and provided two more subalterns, a staff captain and another chap from 'G' Branch. As a result, Bill, who was acting AAG in Tilley's absence, distributed all work related to surrendered and displaced persons, recalcitrants and Allied PWs. After three days of chaos, Bill drew breath.

Tilley returned earlier than expected on 8th September, just in time for the shift of 'A' Branch into winter quarters in Klagenfurt. His return also enabled Bill to take two days off which he spent down in Trieste. He had never been there and he wanted to see the Aldershot Tattoo that 13 Corps was running.

The Tattoo took place on the evening of his arrival, starting at eight and finishing just before midnight. There were some seven or eight bands and a further three pipe bands: 1st Scots Guards, 1st London Scottish and 1st London Irish. There were detachments of British, American, Indian, Italian and Yugoslav Armies, plus the Royal Navy and Royal Marines. In a show of power, there were parades, guns and tanks firing and crocodiles spouting flame while bombers roared overhead. There were several drill parades followed by Indian stick and fire dances. The Divisional Signals demonstrated their trick riding skills and one of the armoured brigades put on a magnificent show of horsemanship. The set from the Yugoslav Army choir brought proceedings down to a slower pace and softer tone before the finale and a grand march past. All nations that had participated in the Italian Campaign were represented. Despite the late finish, Bill and colleagues were invited back to the brigs mess at 13 Corps where they were served drinks and sandwiches.

With a thick head for his trouble, Bill enjoyed a long lie in before taking breakfast and starting a day's sightseeing and shopping. He made just one purchase — a transparent mackintosh for Lisbeth. The trip to Trieste had been a tremendous success on all counts, although on returning to Klagenfurt, Bill still had a headache! He was glad of the relaxed atmosphere at Army HQ, Klagenfurt. This remained even with the arrival of the new brig.

Brig Thurburn[61] was a Cameronian and Bill's first impression was good, though the new brig knew nothing of 'A,' having only been involved with 'Q' previously. Regardless, he was rumoured to be off to Vienna to be near the commander in chief.

The winter quarters in Klagenfurt were a step up from the caravan. Bill had a large office room to himself with a respectable view. Sleeping quarters were in a shared house in the suburbs. His bedroom contained the obligatory bed, wardrobe, table and two chairs. The only other residents were Tilley, one staff captain and a subaltern. With the fire lit, Bill was comfortable and well dug in for the winter, although he would be eligible for repatriation under the Python scheme on 10th December. It just needed another brig's signature. When told who it was Bill's eyes widened in surprise, quickly followed by a smile. 'Brig Woods!'

> Brigadier Woods, the 02E King in CMF [Central Mediterranean Forces] is coming up to see me in the middle of October, and I shall get him to ensure that I am called forward on the 10th or thereabouts. He and I used to be mortal enemies because he was First Army and I was Eighth, and we were both very involved in the subject of Rfts, regarding which we had very different policies. Terrific arguments went on between us from Sicily up to Vasto, when at last we hit a compromise.

> Subsequently, we both admitted that there was a lot to be said in favour of each other's system and now we are in the best of relationships. In fact, he now writes to me as 'My dear Scotty,' and signs himself, 'Yours very sincerely, John Henry.'

---

[61] Cameronians, *Brigadier Roy Gilbert Thurburn,* OBE CB CBE, saw active service in North Africa and Italy and was twice mentioned in despatches. By the end of the war he was chief of staff in Austria. He was also ADC to the Queen from 1952 to 1953 and was a member of the American Legion of Merit.

So, I don't think there will be much trouble in arranging my departure for the 10th!!!

If Bill got a signature from Brig Woods, he reckoned on being at home around 15th December. There would be a month's leave which would have him reporting to the depot in Perth around 15th January. After a further two months he would be due for final release. If he could find out from the Perthshire Education Committee where they might want him, then all would be looking good. 'Careful Sinclair,' Bill muttered, 'you're in danger of being conned into thinking plans will work out.' He would take one step at a time and first see if Brig Woods signed his ticket for the 10th.

Lieutenant Colonel A.P.C. Crossley OBE, of the Kings Dragoon Guards, arrived in Vienna on 22nd September. The man he was to replace, Edward Tilley, was in hospital due to a problem with his throat, so Bill stepped into the role of welcoming party and travelled to Vienna to pick up his new superior. Bill and his driver left at 12.30pm and arrived in Vienna around 6pm — a reasonable trip considering it was almost two hundred miles away. Bill thought they may get held up crossing the Russian zone of Austria, but the frontier guards waved them through with nothing more than a cursory glance.

Bill took the new AAG out for dinner at one of the HQ messes in Vienna, before retiring for the night in the Park Hotel, opposite Schönbrunn Palace. He would like to have seen something of Vienna, but duty called, and the group set off early for the journey back to Klagenfurt. The Russians weren't quite as accommodating as they had been on the outward leg of the trip and held the party up twice, scrutinising Bill's United Nations pass before letting them through.

Bill used the six-hours jeep time to bring the AAG up to speed with all he could expect from 'A' Branch. Having mentioned the likelihood of departing for Blighty on 10th December, he also enquired about the possibility of getting away slightly ahead of time. One of his colleagues, Nobby Clark, was also due for demob, but before heading for Calais was to attend to a last bit of business in Milan. Nobby was scheduled to leave Klagenfurt on 1st December and Bill asked the AAG if he could join.

'I don't see why not,' Crossley replied. Bill thanked his new superior and smiled as they passed the snow-clad mountains. All he needed now was Brig Woods' signature on the paperwork to bring the plan together.

ALLIED FORCE HEADQUARTERS

2 May, 1945

SPECIAL ORDER OF THE DAY

Soldiers, Sailors and Airmen of the Allied Forces in the Mediterranean Theatre

After nearly two years of hard and continuous fighting which started in Sicily in the summer of 1943, you stand today as the victors of the Italian Campaign.

You have won a victory which has ended in the complete and utter rout of the German armed forces in the Mediterranean. By clearing Italy of the last Nazi aggressor, you have liberated a country of over 40,000,000 people.

Today the remnants of a once proud Army have laid down their arms to you—close on a million men with all their arms, equipment and impedimenta.

You may well be proud of this great and victorious campaign which will long live in history as one of the greatest and most successful ever waged.

No praise is high enough for you sailors, soldiers, airmen and workers of the United Forces in Italy for your magnificent triumph.

My gratitude to you and my admiration is unbounded and only equalled by the pride which is mine in being your Commander-in-Chief.

H. R. Alexander

Field-Marshal,
Supreme Allied Commander,
Mediterranean Theatre.

Field-Marshal Harold Alexander, Supreme Allied Commander, Mediterranean Theatre: Message to Allied forces, 2nd May 1945

On 9th April, the Eighth Army started the last great battle in Italy. Twenty-three days later, on 2nd May, the enemy surrendered unconditionally. We achieved our object of destroying the enemy South of the River Po. North of the Po a relentless pursuit prevented the remnants of the enemy from making any further stand. This final and decisive victory in the history of the Eighth Army was achieved only after hard and bitter fighting. In the first seventeen days the enemy's best troops were smashed and reduced to remnants. The enemy had great advantages of ground, strong defences on a succession of river obstacles, extensive flooding, and deep minefields, but all difficulties were overcome by the splendid fighting spirit, skill, determination, and endurance shown by All Ranks, and the excellent co-operation of all Arms. In this battle, as always, the decisive factors have been the magnificent fighting qualities of our soldiers and good junior leadership.

This battle has been a model of Army and Air co-operation, at every stage the gallant and daring pilots of the Desert Air Force have given us wonderful support. The destruction along the South bank of the Po is striking evidence of their work.

The unconditional surrender of the enemy brings the Eighth Army many new and urgent tasks. We have a big job to do in helping to win the peace. The reputation of our Eighth Army has always been high, and it has never stood higher than it stands today. There will be many changes in personnel, but wherever Eighth Army men go, in enemy or Allied territory, the civilian population must respect you. Your conduct must always be worthy of those men who made the historic march from El Alamein to the Alps.

Above all let us thank God, and may we always remember and honour those gallant soldiers of the Eighth Army who, from the early days in the Western Desert through the long years right up to this final battle, have given their lives for their country and to make this last victory possible.

R. L. McCreery

H.Q., Eighth Army.   Lieut.-General,
3rd May, 1945.   G.O.C., Eighth Army.

Lieutenant General Dick McCreery, message to Eighth Army
3rd May 1945

ОФИЦИАЛЬНЫЙ ПРОПУСК
СОЮЗНЫХ ВОЙСК

Номер *4968*   Действителен только по *24 Sep 45*

настоящий Пропуск разрешает проезд пассажиров и автомашины
№ *М.5633126* в город Вена и обратно через Линц или Юденбург

H.Q. EIGHTH ARMY
"G" (Operations)

Офицер контроля пропусков

OFFICIAL PASS
ALLIED MILITARY FORCES.

Number *4968*   Valid for date *24 Sep 45*

This Pass is authority for the passengers and vehicle

Number *M.5633126* _____ to proceed to or from
VIENNA via LINZ or JUDENBURG.

H.Q. EIGHTH ARMY
"G" (Operations)

Control Officer.

LAISSEZ-PASSER
DES FORCES ALLIÉES.

Numéro *4968*   Valable le *24 Sep 45*

Le présent laissez-passer autorise le(s) passager(s) et

le(s) vehicule(s) No. *M.5 633126*

à se rendre dans la ville de VIENNE et retour via
LINZ ou JUDENBURG ou inversement.

H.Q. EIGHTH ARMY
"G" (Operations)

L'officier de service

Military pass for travel to Vienna
24th September 1945

OPERATION FROSTY FRIDAY

N uremberg is a name that will always be inextricably linked with the trials of Nazi war criminals. It was also the site of Hitler's annual Nazi propaganda rallies, and therefore, deemed an appropriate place for the trials which marked the end of the Third Reich. Hitler, Himmler and Goebbels had already committed suicide, leaving others to face prosecution for war crimes. The most high-profile defendant was Hermann Göring, who remained defiant to the end, committing suicide the day before his planned execution. Half of those put on trial were sentenced to death and the rest were imprisoned. Three defendants were eventually acquitted.

The Nuremberg Trials were arguably the most famous trials in history. They not only played a pivotal role in shaping the rules governing the conduct of war, but also the entire body of international human rights law.[62]

By the time the trials started, the United Nations Charter was in force, which stated that the purpose of the United Nations was:

To maintain international peace and security, and to that end: to take effective collective measures for the prevention and removal of threats to the peace, and for the suppression of acts of aggression or other breaches of the peace, and to bring about by peaceful means, and in conformity with the principles of justice and international law, adjustment or settlement of international disputes or situations which might lead to a breach of the peace;

---

[62] Imperial War Museum, 2018, *The legacy of the Nuremberg Trials*

To develop friendly relations among nations based on respect for the principle of equal rights and self-determination of peoples, and to take other appropriate measures to strengthen universal peace;

To achieve international co-operation in solving international problems of an economic, social, cultural, or humanitarian character, and in promoting and encouraging respect for human rights and for fundamental freedoms for all without distinction as to race, sex, language, or religion; and

To be a centre for harmonizing the actions of nations in the attainment of these common ends.

Subsequent trials followed and went on until 1949. Though not without controversy, most saw them as serving their purpose in bringing about criminal justice. Trials of Japanese war criminals were held in Tokyo from 1946 to 1948.

*****

After several farewell parties spanning some three days (and nights), Edward Tilley left Klagenfurt on 3rd October 1945. The final bash had been held the night before in the mess and it was quite a rowdy affair. Someone had lifted a considerable amount of champagne in France on return from LIAP. It had the desired effect. As the evening ticked by, the volume increased in accordance with the level of alcohol consumed, culminating in the usual songs; each man trying to sing louder than the next.

The previous night, Bill had been at another party. One of the sub-area commanders had invited some of the men over to his place at Graz. Getting there had involved a long, but picturesque journey over the mountains. A colossal mansion housing the mess stood in the grounds of a large estate about seven miles outside of town. There was a grand meal from 8pm followed by drinks. What started as a dignified evening in keeping with the surroundings, evolved into a raucous, drunken poker night. Having pushed through till 3am, Bill folded his cards, got up and made for the door, tiptoeing around those who had long since flopped. With no knowledge of the mansion's layout, he staggered around the baronial halls in search of a more comfortable resting place. He vaguely recalled having a meaningful conversation with a stuffed bear and awoke just a few hours later opposite his new furry pal. Slouched in an oversized armchair, Bill opened his eyes to see Edward Tilley standing over him.

'Christ Bill, you look like the Wreck of the Hesperus. What time did you quit?'

'About 3am.' Bill shifted and rose to his feet, gingerly. 'I thought in this chair I'd found a half decent place to sleep, but my back is suggesting otherwise. That guy snoring didn't help!'

Tilley turned to look at the stuffed bear, standing nine feet tall, and burst into laughter. Feeling more than a little worse for wear, the two men found the rest of the gang — in varying degrees of stupor — and sometime later made their way to the jeep and back through the freezing cold day to Klagenfurt.

Lisbeth turned thirty years old on 6th October 1945 and Bill penned best wishes in his letter of the day. For the first time in five years he was confident this would be the last birthday they would spend apart. There would be another four or five weeks' work before starting the handover process to Donald, who would assume Bill's role. It would then need about a week clear of any duties and responsibilities to pack up and say goodbye to old pals. In the meantime, towards the end of October, Bill made his way to Vienna for three days as part of a War Establishment Committee, investigating the reorganisation of HQ. The committee only needed Bill for five hours per day so he would have an opportunity for a look around. It was only his second visit to Vienna, the first being to collect his new AAG, when he'd had no time for sightseeing.

After taking a sleeper train, he felt refreshed and able to start work on the morning of arrival. Before departing, Tilley had asked Bill to write the history of Eighth Army HQ war affairs from December 1944 to VE Day. Having contributed to the Eighth Army maintenance notes from late 1942 to early 1943, Bill knew not to underestimate the task. He started making notes on his first evening in Vienna.

On the second evening, Bill took some time away for a pre-arranged dinner with a dear old friend from Popski's Private Army (PPA). Bill described the army to Lisbeth as a 'gang of daredevil's who have been acting as super-commandos for the Eighth Army for years.' He met his old pal in a mess located in an ancient castle, filled with antique weapons and furniture, stuffed birds and animals. 'You again,' Bill said to the nine-foot bear guarding the entrance.

Dinner was an excellent affair with liberal quantities of food and drink. The two friends filled a few hours with stories of their time together, from backs against the wall in the Western Desert trapped under the heel of the German boot, to the subsequent push and relentless pursuit of the enemy. The two friends had very different roles to play during that time, but each just as important as the other.

'You have integrity Bill, my dear friend.'

'What do you mean?'

'Doing your job when nobody is watching. Few people except those of us involved, understood what you and the men of "A" did for us reprobates.'

'And reprobates you bloody well were,' replied Bill, with a smile. 'Now shut up and have another drink.'

The two friends blethered away, only breaking off to listen to the wireless as Churchill and Monty shared their thoughts on the Battle at Alamein three years earlier. Bill stumbled back to his hotel after midnight having enjoyed the most wonderful evening with a man he truly admired.

Reconnaissance and raiding units such as the LRDG, PPA and SAS (including Greek SAS) had made a significant impact on the war effort, contributing to success in the Western Desert and Italian campaigns. At various times, the lives of thousands depended on the courageous men from these elite fighting forces. Bill was proud to have played his part, providing them with suitable personnel and reinforcements.

Having finished at the War Establishment Committee a day early, Bill fulfilled a promise he'd made to Lisbeth's brother, Jack. He made his way to the address of a Corporal Weiss who had worked alongside Jack, having escaped from Vienna to join the British Army. Corporal Seige Weiss had last heard from his parents in 1942 and was desperate for news of their circumstances and whereabouts. Bill was accompanied by an Austrian waiter from the Advanced HQ mess who would translate. A very nervous and almost deaf woman was found at the address. She informed Bill that Corporal Weiss' mother spent two years in Auschwitz before being murdered there in 1944. The young man's father had survived and was still living in the house, although he wasn't there at that moment and wouldn't return until late. Bill met him the following morning, and he confirmed the old woman's account. He handed over two letters which Bill forwarded to Corporal Weiss via Jack. It was a tragic story.

Later that afternoon, Bill met up with an old mess pal and three of his engineer mates. They made their way to an officer's hotel called Sacher before heading off to a big horse race meet in Vienna. Dick McCreery also joined. Sacher, was reputed to be one of the six best hotels on the continent and it didn't disappoint. The horse race meet was the first Bill had attended and after losing all the cash he had set aside to gamble, he concluded it may well be his last. The group then went down market to Le Cafe Bohème. It was crowded, full of Russians and smooth-looking civilian types, many of whom Bill suspected, were armed to the teeth. However, the music was good, so the lads got stuck into it before finishing off the evening in Jimmie's mess, discussing the personal characteristics of Eighth Army commanders — a subject Bill was happy to indulge.

During his time with Eighth Army, Bill had been near three commanders: Montgomery, Leese and McCreery. Montgomery had arrived in mid-August 1942, yet it was the end of October before the offensive at Alamein. For all the rhetoric, Montgomery was a stickler for detail. Like his predecessor, Auchinleck, he sought to ensure the requisite troops, equipment and armour were available before attempting to push the Germans back. Unlike Auchinleck, Montgomery had the support of Alexander who replaced *The Auk* as commander in chief. Alexander provided an effective buffer between Churchill and Montgomery, securing more time for Monty to prepare his offensive. Like Churchill, Bill thought Montgomery was the right person for that role at that time. A complex man, he had the skill and self-confidence to tackle the situation and he inspired confidence in his men. He was an outstanding orator; few others could rally and hold the attention of a crowd like Montgomery. He also had temerity and a penchant for rubbing people up the wrong way — his American counterparts being a case in point — but his men loved him.

Before the war, Montgomery had instructed Oliver Leese at Camberley Staff College. In May 1940, Leese joined the British Expeditionary Force in France as deputy chief of staff. As the Germans forged west and north, they forced the Allies to retreat to Dunkirk and back to Blighty, Leese among them. In September 1942, Leese shifted to North Africa at the request of Montgomery. Leese was acting lieutenant general of XXX Corps. He remained with Eighth Army throughout the North African Campaign and further to the Italian invasion. When Montgomery was called back to assist with the Normandy Landings, Leese took command of the Eighth. Bill's experience of Leese in the Italian Campaign reinforced his view that he was a formidable officer; a tough, forceful, old-school disciplinarian, but one who was tuned into his men and who listened. He was tactically astute with a keen eye for detail and built credibility with those under his command. Leese's posting to South East Asia at the end of September 1944 disappointed Bill. The war in Europe was being won but there was still much to do in Italy.

Leese was replaced by McCreery, who was an expert in the use of armoured vehicles. McCreery helped plan the Alamein offensive and later held key roles in the Tunisian and Italian campaigns before succeeding Leese as commander of Eighth Army. While Montgomery was a showman, McCreery was quiet in comparison and engaged with his men differently. Some may have considered McCreery to be slightly aloof, but Bill respected him and thought of him as being reserved rather than detached.

Putting the relative merits of Eighth Army commanders aside, the following morning, Bill was back at Klagenfurt. He got to kick a ball for the first time in an age when his 'A' Branch team played against a side scraped together from those in the punishment and detention barracks. Bill scored one goal but 'A' Branch lost 3–2. Two days later Bill's side played a workshop company team. It was a first-round match in the HQ Branch Cup, and Bill was thrilled to bits with the 4–1 win.

As November arrived, Bill realised that he had forgotten his wedding anniversary — again! Or was it Lisbeth's birthday that had bypassed him once before? He couldn't remember. He acknowledged the mistake and was honest enough to remark that the special day had not occurred to him until he read her letter of 28th October. When he saw the words, 'on our memorable anniversary,' he'd tilted his head to the sky and mouthed, 'idiot!'

In the second round of the HQ Cup, a team from the motorised transport department knocked 'A' Branch out. The score was 3–0, but if nothing else, the game was good practise for another match played two days later. The Officers vs Sergeants game on the Sunday was part of a wider set of activities that included darts and tombola, before a dinner and dance in the evening. Bill picked a suitable officer's team including one major general (the chief of staff) and one brigadier. This should be fun, he thought, looking at the draft team sheet.

The match provided many laughs; the chief of staff's attempts at keeping goal were the source of most. To provide a semblance of control, Bill put himself in at centre-half, but to no avail. They lost 4–1. High-tea in the sergeant's mess afterwards was a scene of much banter and bravado, with something in the order of two hundred attending. Bill selected his darts team from the footballing XI, including the chief of staff, whose darts skills outshone his footballing ability. The team played eight or nine matches and won them all.

While everyone was together, Bill conducted a straw poll of those who could attend the farewell party for himself, Tom Agnew, Bob Speller and Freddie Hanwell — codename, Operation Frosty Friday. Planning for the party had swung into action a few days earlier when Brig Woods finally signed the paperwork. All four were confirmed for a 10th December departure. He'd also approved Nobby Clark's trip to Milan and Bill would be joining him. The two of them would depart from Klagenfurt on 1st December and take in some Austrian sights before embarking on a tour of Northern Italy, to include Milan, Trieste, Florence, Venice, Padua and Bologne.

The Post Hotel at Maria Worth was chosen as the venue for the farewell party of the *Thirsty Four*. Invitations went out well in advance and plenty of humorous replies came flooding in with the total attending somewhere near eighty.

The party started at 7pm on Friday 16th November 1944 and within ten minutes, nobody could move at the bar. Savouries and pastries were served first and the eighty-strong rabble sat down to dinner at 8.15pm to the sound of a band playing. Speeches followed that sparkled with wit. With only six women and over seventy men, the competition for dance partners was keen, with the women trying to take turns with everyone.

As the night progressed and more alcohol was consumed, the attendees reminisced about good times — and bad. There was many a toast to those who hadn't made it through to *Frosty Friday*. The majority of partygoers stayed until the end, which came in about 2am. Bill had a room at the hotel so didn't have far to stumble. In fact, he was up and in the office for 8.30am, though he was flagging by lunchtime, and needed a few hours in bed that afternoon. Writing to Lisbeth about the farewell party, Bill said he was 'as happy as a wee pig at the thought of hitting the trail in exactly a fortnight's time.'

On 19th November, he received the following:

'Authority is given for the evacuation to the UK of the above-named Major W.G.M. Sinclair on grounds of long service overseas.'

It confirmed his despatch by 30th November for onward routing via Milan on *Medloc B*.[63] The letter had only been in Bill's pocket for three hours when he wrote to Lisbeth with the good news. He'd read it multiple times to ensure his eyes were not deceiving him and kept patting his trouser pocket just to be sure the letter was still there.

Whilst not wanting to tempt fate, Bill overhauled his kit in preparation for his departure and came across the original orders from July 1941 to report to '1st Reserve 70 Regiment Royal Artillery for draft conducting overseas.' Bill stared intently at the instruction and was overcome. It had been a long slog, he'd endured personal heartache, and now he was realising

---

[63] Train journey that departed from Milan and ran through Simplon in Switzerland with destination Calais

the enormity of it. There was also a sense of relief and thanks that he'd survived.

'Come on boy,' he said as he rose to his feet, 'let's finish this job off and I'll tell you again all about bonnie Scotland.' Mick cocked his head to one side and awaited his master's next instruction.

For the homeward journey, Bill travelled light with just a small suitcase and valise. His heavy kit would be shipped back via the military forwarding office. He took his trunk down to, 70 punishment and detention barracks, who kindly riveted it with a hasp and staple for added security.

Bill thought about Ann as he ventured back to the mess. He wondered about expanding the family to include another wee red wrinklie and a brother for Ann, but he and Lisbeth had decided to wait a while after his return, to settle into normal life again.

In his letter of 21st November, Bill asked Lisbeth not to reply as he'd not fixed up a travelling address and wouldn't be able to before departing. It was a strange and rather uncomfortable feeling to think he would receive nothing further in writing from his wife having depended on it, so much, for so long. He considered how many times since being posted overseas he'd felt despair and how he had relied on Lisbeth's written word to give him strength and support his spirit. On 1st December 1945, Bill sent his last communication to Lisbeth before arriving back in Blighty for good. He whispered the words to himself as he put pen to paper.

'My darlingest wife. The next time you hear those words, or rather the next time they pass from me to you, they will be verbal, I hope, and not written. I should be home about same time as this letter, or a day or so later and I shall not write anymore.' He pictured his wife and daughter as he closed off the letter with his usual love and best wishes.

'Look well after yourself,' he wrote. 'Give my love to Ann and tell her that I am longing to see her again too.'

Farewell Performance

BTA presents

SPELLER - SINCLAIR
AGNEW - HANWELL

(through a haze of alcohol) in

"THE THIRSTY FOUR'S
FINAL FAREWELL"

on

The Frosty Friday,

16th November, 1945, at 1900 hrs, at

THE POST HOTEL, MARIA WORTH

Bring your own
ambulance   RSVP   *Feeding arrangements*
                                         for drivers

PTO

The Frosty Friday, farewell performance programme (front)
16th November 1945

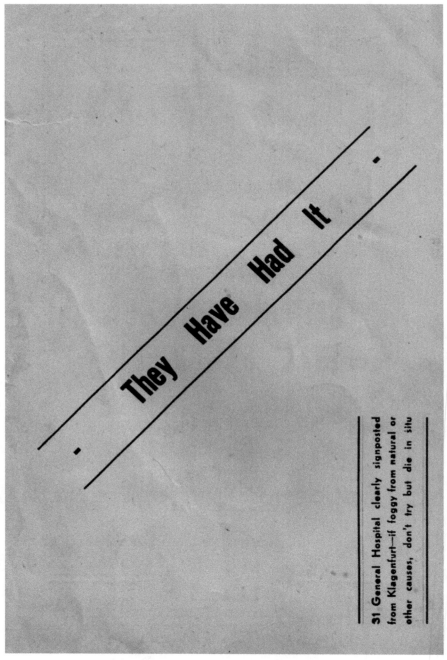

The Frosty Friday, farewell performance programme (rear)
16th November 1945

Lt. Col. C. L. Harrison thanks the "Thirsty Four" for this most generous gesture and regrets to inform them that he WILL HAVE MUCH PLEASURE in viewing them through a haze of alcohol on Frosty Friday 16th November 1945 at 1900 Hrs.

He has no intention of bringing his own ambulance for the simple reason that WELFARE BEGINS AT HOME, therefore he will if necessary remain AT THE POST all NIGHT.

'Lt. Col. C. L. Harrison thanks the "Thirsty Four" for this most generous gesture and regrets to inform them that he WILL HAVE MUCH PLEASURE in viewing them through a haze of alcohol on Frosty Friday 16th November 1945 at 1900 Hrs.
He has no intention of bringing his own ambulance for the simple reason that WELFARE BEGINS AT HOME, therefore he will if necessary remain AT THE POST ALL NIGHT.'

Response to The Frosty Friday invitation: November 1945

FROM   :   A NTICIPATION
            (P) OSITIVELY
            (S) TUPENDOUS
             S TUPENDOUS
            C, ONGRATULATIONS

TO   :   S.A.S.H. FORCE

A XXX/XXX/X   UNCLASSIFIED (.) OPERATION FROSTY FRIDAY APPROVED (.)
               INFORMATION CONCISE AND INTENTION PRAISEWORTHY (.)
               METHOD OBVIOUS (.) WHOLEHEARTED SUPPORT ASSURED (.)

'UNCLASSIFIED (.) OPERATION FROST FRIDAY APPROVED (.)
INFORMATION CONCISE AND INTENTION PRAISEWORTHY (.)
METHOD OBVIOUS (.) WHOLEHEARTED SUPPORT ASSURED (.)'

Response to The Frosty Friday invitation: November 1945

NEW BEGINNINGS

Like so many families across the world, the Sinclairs lost part of their lives to the Second World War. Bill arrived back at Waverley Station on 15th December 1945. He was twenty-nine years old. Four months later, on 11th April, the army released Major W.G.M. Sinclair from military service.

Bill was ready to resume his teaching career and both the Perthshire Education Committee and the Edinburgh Education Authority expressed an interest in securing his services. Bill had attained his Teachers General Certificate in 1939 and it was six years since his last (and first) teaching role at Invergowrie. He would be rusty, but the intervening years had seen him evolve into a mature and wise man, who would bring substantial life experience to the job. He also had an impressive list of commendations including one from Lieutenant General Sir Oliver Leese, with whom Bill felt a great affinity.

Bill took up a temporary teaching position at the Royal High School (RHS) Edinburgh on 7th June 1946. Employed as 'Unattached Staff' in the service of Edinburgh Corporation, the starting salary was £420 per annum. Joining in June meant he could ease himself in, over what little remained of the summer term before the long school holiday began. It was a gentle reintroduction to teaching and civilian working life that suited him well.

In the main, teachers were hard-nosed, disciplinarians who used corporal punishment, such as the Lochgelly Special,[64] to keep pupils in line. Bill was a disciplinarian but decided on a different way to garner attention

---

[64] The Lochgelly Special or *Tawse* was a leather strap with forked end used to administer corporal punishment

from his pupils. It seemed to Bill that the most effective leaders, set clear boundaries and expectations, while engaging with those in their charge to share their vision. His aim was to motivate and to encourage commitment and loyalty. Oliver Leese had taught him this.

Sport was a perfect basis on which to practise his teaching philosophy. Bill was always keen for children to develop an interest in sport and thought it important in any child's life. One could learn self-reliance from playing solo sports such as golf or tennis, whereas team games such as football and hockey were invaluable in teaching cooperation and interdependence. Through sport, pupils learned these values without even realising it. He also believed that age was no barrier. The earlier children were introduced to sport the better. If they showed no interest, he would gently encourage and coach them.

An enjoyable summer term at RHS reinforced Bill's commitment to his teaching career. As a teacher, he would be serving not just his own family, but a whole generation of children. He was therefore thrilled to be offered a permanent position at Murrayburn Primary School in Edinburgh, and took it without hesitation. The role at Murrayburn saw Bill establish himself as a teacher under the experienced eye of Headmaster, Tom Butcher. Murrayburn was a relatively new primary school in the south west of Edinburgh and Bill began in the autumn of 1946. He considered children to be ingenious — even the wee ones — as they found their feet. Nothing gave him greater satisfaction than encouraging and steering them in the right direction, watching them blossom like spring flowers.

Bill looked forward to using the subjects he'd studied at varsity in his teaching: psychology, philosophy, zoology, botany and geology. A knowledge of botany and zoology would enable him to educate the young children at Murrayburn whilst doing the most ordinary of things, like taking a nature walk. And he would use sport as a way to build character. Bill considered himself fortunate to be in such an influential position.

Autumn 1946 was a happy time for Bill and Lisbeth. At five years old, Ann was accepted into George Watson's Ladies' College (GWLC), an all-girl fee-paying school. Lisbeth became pregnant and Sinclair number two was scheduled to appear the following May. In September 1946, Bill received the MBE awarded for his part in the Italian Campaign. And lastly, the family moved into their own home in Juniper Green. Lisbeth's brother Jack and wife Vickie moved in with them soon after.

Living at 599 Lanark Road was closer to work for Bill, and the family had their first real home together. The house was at the end of the village and five miles from the centre of Edinburgh. Close by was the Co-op, though the Sinclairs tended to use Miss Martin's grocery shop further down the street. The property at Lanark Road was a good size. Off the hall was a living room and scullery as well as a bedroom and a large unfurnished room. On the first floor was the good room, which overlooked the area to the front of the house. Opposite was Ann's bedroom, a bathroom and Bill and Lisbeth's bedroom. Going downstairs from the main hall to garden level, there was a washroom with huge sinks for the weekly wash. There was also another large unfurnished room where Ann could play and Bill hung a swing for his daughter in the doorway. A passage led to the back garden from the washroom and Ann would sit by the door blowing bubbles with a clay pipe. In the back garden was a wooden coop where the family kept hens for a while. Beyond the garden wall, the ground sloped away down an embankment, covered with brambles, to the railway line which joined the villages from Edinburgh to Balerno. Beyond that lay the Water of Leith. There was a large garden to the side of the house with little paths winding their way through bushes of gooseberries, blackcurrants and raspberries. On the wall sat a black cauldron filled with sweet peas.

Bill and Lisbeth's second child, William Craig Sinclair, was born on 14th

May 1947 at Elsie Ingles Hospital, Edinburgh. Bill had phoned the night before, just around midnight, but the matron told him that nothing much would happen for a while. She encouraged him to rest at home and wait for news. Easier said than done. An anxious Bill woke virtually every hour and at 5.15am could stand it no longer. Phoning the hospital for an update, he was told his wife had given birth to a son. Bill wrote:

> Thank you, my sweet, for this terrific effort of a son — you are still marvellous!...Poor Ann — she is still asleep, but she is going to be peeved — she told Kathleen [Tait] yesterday afternoon that she was going to call her baby Muriel!!!...I'll be seeing you a couple of hours after you get this...PS Reminds me of the army days writing a letter to you...PPS Gave J&V [Jack and Vickie] a cup of tea in their bed this morning. The poor souls were awakened by yours truly rather early!!

The family stayed in Juniper Green for a further year, during which time, Bill continued teaching at Murrayburn, travelling in by train to Longstone Station. Lisbeth played piano once a week for country dancing classes in Gogarburn Hospital (then a mental institution) to supplement the family income. The Sinclairs did a lot of walking at weekends, usually down by the Water of Leith or through Muir Wood. Whilst playing football largely gave way to watching, Bill played golf whenever time allowed, smacking many a long drive off the 14th at Lothianburn, and watching the ball bounce and roll away down the hill. His schoolfriend's Dougie McVey and Billy Tait often joined him — the Taits living near by in Juniper Green.

In 1948 the family moved back into Edinburgh as travelling into school for Bill and Ann had become inconvenient and expensive. Number 70, Comiston Road, Morningside, was a top-floor corner flat in a tenement building. If carrying bags, one would be peching (out of breath) by the time one reached the door. The flat was bright, spacious and airy. There was a large dining kitchen with a Raeburn stove and the usual cupboard for coal. This room faced north over the communal backgreens of the other tenements, towards the town. Ann and Craig's bedrooms faced south to the tenements on the other side of Comiston Gardens, as did the bathroom. The lounge provided a view up and down Comiston Road. There was an Esse Dura stove and a large mahogany dining table sat in the bay window. Using a pencil, Ann indented (vandalised) the table with the words 'BIG PIG.'[65] Her mother was unimpressed.

The lady in the flat below was a Mrs Menzies and she kept an Irish Wolfhound, the size of a small pony. A dog less suitable for a flat one couldn't find, but he was a real love and Craig and Ann enjoyed stroking him.

Before the war, Bill had been a member of George Heriot's School Former Pupils Golf Club and he re-established this association on returning to Edinburgh. He took the role of Treasurer in 1948, the same year he won the Couche Trophy for the Hole and Hole contest. The club also achieved its first major success in 1948, winning the Dispatch Trophy with Bill's childhood pal, Dougie McVey, being in the team of four that won. Three years later in 1951, Bill won the Lothianburn Championship being the third Herioter to win the title in three successive years.[66]

Most Sundays, the family walked from Comiston Road to Granny Sinclair's at Cowan Road. She was a dab hand at cooking and baking and encouraged Ann to do the same. Making toffee was a favourite pastime and Ann would stand on a chair in the wee scullery over the gas cooker stirring the mixture, all on her own. When the toffee cooled, she hammered it into chunks with a small metal hammer, put the pieces into a glass jar and passed it around. When the family left to go home, Ann and Craig would turn

---

[65] The words remained on the table until it was disposed of in 1959
[66] George Heriot's School Former Pupils Golf Club, 1961

around at intervals and wave all the way until reaching the canal, when Granny disappeared behind the high sides of the bridge. In the autumn, the smell of moist, fallen leaves was prominent, and Ann and Craig would kick them up in all directions as they scuffed along.

There were Halloween parties at Northumberland Place where the kids dooked for apples and tried to take a bite out of a tattie scone hanging from a pully. The scone was smeared with treacle to entice the kids in for a bite and there would be at least three yanks of the pulley before Grandad Verth finally held it still, allowing the lucky player to take a mouthful. Grandad Verth also made ginger wine. It tasted delicious but left a heat in the throat like a hot coal.

Christmas was a simple festival. The family put up the tree a few days before and hung it with lots of hand-made decorations. Some of these went on from year to year, including the paper lanterns that Bill used to make with Ann and Craig, using materials lifted from school. They strung up colourful paper chains around the room and decorations hung from the ceiling and walls in all directions. On Christmas Eve, Bill left Ann and Craig a stocking (one of his socks) outside their bedroom door. This contained a tangerine, a penny and several small items. In the morning they rushed into their parents' bedroom to find a pillowcase each, containing larger presents. 'Santa's been!'

Bill's mother and Lisbeth's mother and father would descend on Comiston Road for their meal. Jack, Vickie and their two sons Brian and Alastair also joined. Scotch Broth was followed by chicken (a rare treat) and for dessert, Lisbeth served trifle or tinned strawberries with Carnation evaporated milk. Granny Sinclair brought homemade advocaat and Grandad Verth brought ample supplies of his ginger wine. Lisbeth took requests and played tunes on the piano, accompanied by Ann who also loved to play. Ann started learning at eight years old, and like her mother before her, took lessons with Miss Watson at 25 Gayfield Square, off Leith Walk. Initially, because Ann was so small, she had a brightly-coloured knitted cushion that boosted her height just enough to reach the keys. Miss Watson's mother would bring her daughter a cup of tea mid-lesson and pass a sweetie to Ann at the same time. Not long after Ann started playing, Miss Watson took a period off teaching when her mother died, at which point she asked Lisbeth to take over her lessons at St Denis' private school.

On Hogmanay, there were parties with the Taits, McVeys and other family friends. On New Year's Day the Sinclairs went over to Jack and Vickie who were now living at 13 Mordun Park Avenue. A meal was served after Jack and Bill returned from the traditional Hearts vs Hibs football match. Granny Verth would say that she could hear them coming home before she could see them.

Oor Bill's Awa'

O Billie's gone to Fernieside
With books and strap an' a'
To teach the kids their A,B,C
And clear their doubts awa'
O Billie's young and Billie's bonnie
Loe'd by ane and a'
O what will Murrayburnie do
With Billie gone awa'

Chorus
O Billie's gone to Fernieside
Promotion's been our bane
We wish him a' the very best
Our loss has been their gain

In Edinburgh toon there's soccer fans
And Bill is one o' them
He follows the fortunes o' the teams
The Hearts — the Hibs — ahem
The Hearts were led by Wullie Bauld
The results were really silly
The Cup, the League would both been theirs
If they played oor baldy Billie

Chorus

O Billie's sure a deil for work
He makes things fairly rip
The tickets he's produced for shows
Would sink a battleship
He is a master at his job
The guillotine he sets
The French would welcome his employ
At chopping off their tetes

Chorus

O Billie's suit is getting loose
He's beginning now to wilt
He won't be happy till he gets
Right in his Army kilt
He now has stopped his school dinners
And brings his lunch all wrapped
The Dining Centre feels the breeze
And half the staff are sacked

Chorus

The School was once not on the map
And only known to few
But now with trophies, flags and cups
To ignore us is to rue
So much of this is due to Bill
His zeal has been unending
His soccer teams have fought their way
And caught the others bending

From the staff at Murrayburn Primary School

After almost eight years at Murrayburn, Bill was tempted away with promotion to deputy headmaster at Fernieside Primary School. There, he employed the same approach with regards to teaching, sport and concerts, but now he was able to influence the overall direction of the school.

Bill and his family made the most of the long summer holidays that came with being a teacher. During the Murrayburn years, they ventured to North Berwick, Montrose and St. Monance. Grannies, Sinclair and Verth visited for odd days coming over by train. Dougie McVey and his father joined them in North Berwick on two occasions. There, Ann and Craig would go to the High Street bakery with their father each morning for rolls, standing outside and waiting for the shop to open at 8am. The aroma of warm bread brought immediate feelings of contentment. Later in the day they would visit the chip shop around the corner. A 6 penny poke of chips hit the spot. Down the road towards the harbour was the Victoria café where they served the most wonderful ice-cream. Bill would get Ann and Craig cones while he always had a slider (ice cream wafer).

For three years from 1954, the family broadened their holiday horizons and travelled up to Boat of Garten in the Cairngorms. The first year they did so by train, sending the trunks on in advance. At Boat of Garten station, the porter met the expectant holidaymakers complete with trunks, and pushed them up the road on a hand cart to Apple Grove on the main street. The house belonged to a Miss Libby Duncan and her father. They decamped for the summer into a wooden shack at the bottom of the substantial garden. Ann was sent down each day with a couple of pennies to get fresh vegetables from Miss Duncan. There was a plentiful supply of raspberries down by the Spey and they were picked by the dozen; Lisbeth brought Kilner jars with her from Edinburgh to make jam.

One day, the family set out to find Loch Garten but got lost, eventually stumbling out of the trees at Loch Mallachie. Bill strode off on his own to find Loch Garten, asking the others not to move an inch until he returned. 'Hooray!' shouted Craig when his father arrived back. Bill's mind flashed back to the war.

'I've never been lost; temporarily displaced a few times, but never lost.' He winked at Lisbeth. Ann and Craig were oblivious.

As they rounded Loch Garten, a boat was being rowed across with a piper standing in it, practising. The tunes reverberated around the loch and the trees echoed the evocative sound back over the water.

During holidays to Boat of Garten, there were other trips out to Nethy Bridge, Grantown on Spey, Aviemore, Loch an Eilein and up to the Moray Firth coast to Nairn and Roseisle beach. One day the family took a runabout ticket on the railway and went to Dava Moor. The guard thought they were mad. 'Nobody gets off at the Dava.' But the Sinclairs did, and the intrepid walkers found their way to Lochindorb with its ruined castle – yet another stronghold of the Wolf of Badenoch, just like Loch an Eilein.

If the weather was bad and rain set in for the day, Bill lit the fire in the parlour and fetched the cards. Competitions were drawn up to include all the usual favourites; knock-out-whist, rummy and stop-the-bus, to name a few.

By 1957, Lisbeth's father John (Grandad Verth) and Bill's mother Elizabeth (Granny Sinclair) had passed away. 48 Cowan Road was sold but Granny Verth continued to live at 4 Northumberland Place. Around that time, Bill acquired his first car, a Triumph Standard Vanguard, registration LWS 219. Holiday horizons could now be broadened even further. In 1958, the Sinclairs set off, along with Granny Verth, to visit Cornwall – a mammoth undertaking. An overnight stop preceded the journey to Mawgan Porth, but they still didn't arrive at the B&B until midnight. Even then, the landlady provided cold meat, salad and trifle for the weary travellers. There were days out to Torquay and Land's End, and a visit to Cheddar Gorge on the way home.

As the first full decade since the end of the war neared its conclusion, Bill continued at Fernieside and maintained more than a passing interest in Edinburgh Schools sports events. Having been assistant secretary and treasurer of the Edinburgh Primary Schools' Athletic Association since 1954, he took on the role of secretary in 1958. By that time, he had forged winning teams in athletics and football across both Murrayburn and Fernieside, helping them to attain the following:

Football:

Inspectors Cup:	1950, 1953 1957, 1958
School Board Cup:	1953, 1954, 1958
League Pennant:	1950, 1952, 1953, 1957, 1958

Athletics:

Shennan Banner:	1951, 1952, 1955
Pretsell Shield (girls):	1951, 1955
M.P.'s cup:	1952, 1953, 1954

Bill was happy with his lot. How the lives of his family developed over the 1950s left him feeling proud and comfortable. Lisbeth continued to teach music, Craig was following in his father's footsteps as a young schoolboy at Heriot's, while Ann's time at GWLC was coming to an end and her thoughts turned to university.

See next page for transcription

TO WHOM IT MAY CONCERN

No 158883 Major WGM Sinclair, A & SH, joined Headquarters Eighth Army on 4th April 1943 as DAAG.   From then until I left on 6th December 1943, he was working directly under me.   Since then, I have seen a great deal of his work as I commanded the Eighth Army Area until the final break up.

I have always found Major Sinclair a most loyal and cheerful friend.   He never spared himself for a moment, and did excellent work.   He has a very good clear brain.   He was popular with all ranks, and a footballer of considerable ability.

I rate his organising ability as above the average, and his honour and integrity as beyond all question.

He was successful in everything he undertook, whether it were controlling the operational side of "A" or raising Eighty Army football to great heights.

He was awarded a mention in despatches, and subsequently the M.B.E.   I feel certain that he will make a success in civilian life.

M. J. Richards, C.B.E.

19 January 1946.

Brigadier
Commander
212 Area

Commendation from Brigadier Malcolm Richards
19th January 1946

TO WHOM IT MAY CONCERN

No 158883 Major WGM Sinclair, A&SH [Argyll & Sutherland Highlanders], joined Headquarters Eighth Army on 4th April 1943 as DAAG. From then until I left on 6th December 1943, he was working directly under me. Since then, I have seen a great deal of his work as I commanded the Eighth Army Area until the final break up.

I have always found Major Sinclair a most loyal and cheerful friend. He never spared himself for a moment, and did excellent work. He has a very good clear brain. He was popular with all ranks, and a footballer of considerable ability.

I rate his organising ability as above average, and his honour and integrity as beyond all question.

He was successful in everything he undertook, whether it were controlling the operational side of "A" or raising Eighty Army football to great heights.

He was awarded a mention in despatches, and subsequently the M.B.E. I feel certain that he will make a success in civilian life.

M. J. Richards C.B.E.

19th January 1946   Brigadier

Commander

212 Area

From:- Lt. Col. E.W. Tilley, O.B.E.

TO WHOM IT MAY CONCERN

    For two years I was intimately acquainted with Major
W.G.M. Sinclair, M.B.E., and for nearly the whole of that
time he worked under me as D.A.A.G. of 8th Army and B.T.A. -
an appointment which he held from 4th April 1943 to 1st
December 1945.

    He was a most loyal, efficient and energetic officer
with a very quick brain and an ability to assume responsibility
and take decisions. He has a pleasing personality and gets
on well with his associates. He is keenly interested in sport
and a good organiser of sporting events.

    He was awarded an M.B.E., and a mention in despatches.

    I am not familiar with his academic qualifications but
I consider that his intelligence and initiative are of a very
high order and his character excellent.

Commendation from Lieutenant Colonel Edward Tilley
January 1946

From:-   Lt.-General Sir Oliver Leese, Bt., KCB, CBE, DSO.

Headquarters, Eastern Command,

Hounslow,

Middlesex

17th January, 1946.

While I was commanding the Eighth Army from December, 1943, to October, 1944, Major W.G.M. Sinclair, MBE, was my D.A.A.G. (Org.).

During this time he did extremely good work. He was very hard-working and most reliable; and everyone who came in contact with him had great faith in his judgment and ability.

He got on well with everyone, and I hope very much that he will in peace-time find an appointment worthy of his excellent record during the war.

Oliver Leese.

Lieutenant-General.

Commendation from Lieutenant General Sir Oliver Leese
17th January 1946

CENTRAL CHANCERY OF
THE ORDERS OF KNIGHTHOOD,
ST. JAMES'S PALACE, S.W.I.

Sir,

I have the honour to send to you herewith the
Warrant under The King's Sign Manual granting you the
dignity of a Member of the Military Division
of the Most Excellent Order of the British Empire, and
to inform you that the Insignia has been sent to you
under separate registered cover.

Would you please be good enough to acknowledge
the receipt of these on the attached form.

I have the honour to be, Sir,

Your obedient Servant,

[signature]
Brigadier

Registrar of the
Order of the British Empire.

Major William G.M.Sinclair,
                              M.B.E..
11th September 1946.

Notification of MBE award
11th September 1946

Royal High School, Summer Term 1946: Bill Sinclair, second from right

Ann (left) and Lisbeth Sinclair

Craig Sinclair

(from left to right) Bill Sinclair, Billy Tait, Dougie McVey

'Inspectors' Cup 1949 – 1950: Murrayburn School'
(Back row left to right) Tom Butcher, Bill Sinclair, Hector McLeod
D. Craven, G. Hall, J. Brown, J. Proudfoot, D. Black, W. Lamb, W. Henderson, I. Walker
J. Whitelow, B. Gilhooley, J. Dow, I. Robertson, J. Marren

LATER YEARS

In 1959, the Sinclairs moved again though not far. Number 8, Bramdean Rise was a dormer bungalow, newly built by property developer, William Hunter. It had a single bedroom upstairs facing north towards Edinburgh City. Downstairs there was a good room (rarely used) and three further rooms: a bedroom each for Ann and Craig and a lounge to the front. The kitchen overlooked the back garden which was accessed via some steps constructed from granite sets. It was a good-sized corner plot with space to the side and a garage to the rear of the property, accessed via Bramdean Place.

Neighbours soon became friends; the Chappells, Wights, Lindleys all on the same street with Jimmy and Sheila over the back, next to the Burrows. Next door at number 6 were Margo and Leslie Mitchell, close friends in no-time at all and an association that lasted decades. The house was a short walk from the Braid Hills Approach road and golf course where Bill had played as a member of the Thistle Club.

The move to Bramdean Rise also brought a change of church to Fairmilehead. This was as much about the Minister, Rev Ross — who Bill and Lisbeth liked a great deal — as it was about the location, and they started to attend more regularly.

Interest in school sports continued and in 1960–61, Bill helped lead an Edinburgh Primary School's XI to the Wilson Trophy. This was a national football competition of repute, won by Edinburgh Primary Schoolboys, six years in a row. Bill helped guide the team through a series of matches without defeat and the boys retained the trophy, beating Dundee 4–1 in the two-leg final.

Several lads that went on to greater footballing achievements passed through the school system under Bill's tenure including Ralph Brand (Rangers), Alan Gordon (Hearts, Hibs, Dundee, Dundee Utd) and John Proudfoot (Hibs).

Bill continued playing golf with the Heriot's Former Pupils Golf Club, including the 1961 Dispatch Trophy. The team of Bill, H.C. Brownlee, I.M. Watt and old pal Dougie McVey appeared to have been selected in variance with the club's youth policy at the time (on account of their ages), but proved very effective in reaching the semi-finals where they lost by one hole to the Ministry of Labour.[67]

Bill left Fernieside to become deputy headmaster at Sciennes Primary School in December 1960. Craig was still at Heriot's and Ann had gone on to the University of Edinburgh to study German, French and Geography.

Ann wanted to teach primary school children just like her father. In her third year she took Scottish History and Moral Philosophy and earned her degree in July 1962. She moved down the Royal Mile to do a year's post-graduate teaching course at Moray House Teacher Training College, just as her father had done. During her time at university, Ann met her husband, Bob Robbie. He was working at Cowan's Paper Mill in Penicuik and the pair first met at the Edinburgh Palais on the eve of a rugby dance; Bob was playing for Lismore at the time. In November 1962, Bob moved back to Dundee to work for Valentine's, the card company, which meant shunting back and forth at weekends. Bill told his daughter he'd done the same at the beginning of 1940, whilst teaching in Invergowrie. If it was meant to be, it would be.

Ann and Bob were engaged on 13th July 1963. A year later, on 18th July 1964, Elizabeth Ann Sinclair married Robert Henry Robbie at Fairmilehead

---

[67] George Heriot's School Former Pupils Golf Club, 1961

Parish Church, Edinburgh, holding their reception at the Roxburghe Hotel in Charlotte Square. As father of the bride, Bill gave Ann away and, in his speech, recalled the day he first clapped eyes on his daughter at Waverley Station in 1945. She'd screamed blue murder all the way home in the taxi because of 'this strange man.'

By the time of Ann's wedding, Bill was on the Edinburgh Corporation list for promotion to headmaster and in August 1966, he became headmaster at Preston Street Primary School, Edinburgh. He spent two years there before becoming headmaster at Dumbryden Primary School in 1968. It was a brand new school which opened with three teachers but no pupils! The school was the first of four primary schools to be opened in the new Wester Hailes development of five thousand houses, but at the time, only twenty houses were occupied and none contained any children of primary school age. The long-term plan was for six hundred and thirty children to attend the school.

The first pupil to attend Dumbryden in 1968 was Audrey McCartney. Clutching her mother's hand, she arrived at the gates and was ushered into the school building by Bill, introduced to her teachers and shown her classroom. Audrey was then sent home and told to 'wait until there are a few more pupils for the school.' They would arrive soon enough.

Despite the demands of his headmaster's role, Bill always found time to play golf. He joined the Heriot's Former Pupils Committee in 1961 and took the captain's role for two years in 1964 and 1965. By that time, he was a member of the prestigious Mortonhall Golf Club, the oldest course in the City of Edinburgh, which was also just around the corner from home. Bill played at several other courses across the city, teaming up with old friends and work colleagues. It was during one such outing that tragedy struck.

Just one month after starting at Dumbryden, Bill was playing at Ratho Golf Club with three friends from the Edinburgh school system. Donald

Mathieson was Bill's successor at Preston Street, Finlay Munro was the deputy headmaster at Broomhouse Primary, and Hector McLeod was the headmaster at Tollcross Primary. Bill and Hector were partnering against Donald and Finlay. They had reached the eighth green when heavy rain started to fall. It became too intense for them to continue and so the four men took shelter under a nearby belt of trees.

When Bill came around, he was lying flat on his back staring up at the sky. He rose to his feet as Donald was regaining consciousness. Finlay and Hector were lifeless. Bill raced to the clubhouse and raised the alarm, passing other golfers who said they had seen an almighty flash of lightning in the trees where the four were standing. Donald and Finlay suffered burns, from the lightning strike, but Hector was killed.[68]

Hector McLeod had been a dear friend and colleague since the Murrayburn School days. The two teachers had stood proudly behind the boys in the photograph of 1950 having just won the Inspectors Cup. Hector had been deputy headmaster at Gracemount Primary School before taking the position at Tollcross. He'd been there a matter of weeks when the tragedy struck. Bill would never forget it.

Lisbeth's mother, Granny Verth, passed away on 10th March 1967. She had continued to live at 4 Northumberland Place right up to her death. It was a pivotal moment for Bill and Lisbeth, serving as a reminder of their own mortality. Determined to enjoy life to the full, vacations were taken across Scotland and south of the border into England during school holidays. Bill took up lapidary and spent hours in the garden shed, cutting, grinding and polishing gem stones into items of jewellery and household ornaments. On more than one occasion, the hobby took Bill and Lisbeth abroad to the gemstone mining and lapidary centre of Idar-Oberstein in

---

[68] Edinburgh Evening News, 1968, *Golfer tells how best friend died*

Rhineland-Palatinate, Germany.

There were regular trips to Germany for another reason too. In 1954, Ann had taken a penfriend, Margret Wasenitz,[69] whose family lived in Kiel, Northern Germany. There were several exchange visits in the early days and later, both sets of parents became friends, taking it in turns to visit each other. Margret's father had been a U-boat commander in the war. He and Bill talked at length about those difficult years, giving each other a different perspective on the war.

Craig graduated from the University of Edinburgh on 6th July 1968. The young Civil Engineer married Margaret (Maggie) McDowell on 26th June 1971 at St. Mary's Church, Biggar.

There would be two further family weddings in the 1970s. Jack and Vickie's two sons, Alastair and Brian, also married: Alastair Verth and Jennifer (Jenny) Banks in 1973, and Brian Verth and Fiona Miller, the same year. Whilst the Verths remained in the Edinburgh locale, Craig and Maggie Sinclair emigrated to Vancouver, Canada. Ann and Bob Robbie moved first to Manchester and then to Kingstone, a small village outside Uttoxeter, Staffordshire.

During one visit to Kingstone, Bill made good on his promise of July 1941; if he survived the war, he would call in to Abbots Bromley and see the village for himself.

'I'm going over,' chirped Ann. 'Just need to drop something into a friend so why don't you come?'

'How long will you be?'

'I'll stop for a coffee with Jill, so around thirty minutes. You can take a wander.'

Ann drove the seven miles from Kingstone and dropped her father off

---

[69] Ann and Margret remained firm friends for over 50 years

in the middle of Abbots Bromley. Having walked along the main road and one or two side streets he arrived back at the village centre; the agreed meeting place. He paid his respects at the war memorial.

Bill didn't generally share his memories of the war, unless he was in the company of other men who had been there; men who could empathise. Veterans were better able to open up and re-live their unique experiences in each other's company. The experiences they shared bound them together.

Bill walked the short distance from the war memorial to the Butter Cross and placed his hand on the central timber column. It was a moment of solitary reflection. Images of Tripoli three decades earlier were conjured up as though it was yesterday. Bill vividly recalled Cock O' the North blasting out with vigour as the Highland Division concluded their fourteen hundred mile slog from Alamein to Tripoli, and the pride he'd felt at the effort and sacrifice the troops had made.

Bill closed his eyes, but that did not prevent tears from rolling down his cheeks at the memory of fallen colleagues. Charlie Rainford, John Craig, Bill Brechin, Freddie Sills, Cliff Barham, Reg Wiskin, Charlie Hallet, Duncan Mackay and John Wilson were just some of the friends that had lain down, by the end of the war. It was a moment of solemnity, but Bill soon vanquished dark thoughts from his mind and tried to remember the good times he'd had with those courageous men who had given their lives.

The moment was interrupted with the short blast of a car horn.

'You day dreaming over there, Dad? Ready to go?'

Bill opened his eyes; Ann was shouting at him from the car. She was far enough away not to see the emotion on her father's face. A wave of acknowledgement told her he was ready. He gently patted the Butter Cross as a final gesture of respect and walked away.

Bill spent the rest of his working life at Dumbryden Primary, taking the school from its beginnings, building it into a thriving seat of learning, and doing what he could to encourage and positively influence the children of Wester Hailes. He also fought strongly for budgets and improvements across the Edinburgh school system when circumstances demanded it. In 1974 he wrote to his MP, raising key points on the crisis in the Scottish teaching profession as he saw them. A young Malcolm Rifkind MP responded. Bill continued to do what he could for the benefit of colleagues and pupils alike, right up until his retirement in June 1977. He was sixty years old.

Best wishes and fond tributes came in from teachers, parents, former pupils, other Edinburgh schools and Lothian Regional Council members. The sentiment was consistent, referring to Bill's support, encouragement and sheer common-sense. There was also a bit of leg-pulling as demonstrated in a letter from the Lothian Regional Council Divisional Education Officer, G.E. Ferguson.

Dear Mr Sinclair,

I should be grateful if you would attend a meeting in my office on Thursday, 30th June, at 12 noon to discuss the following topics:

1) The relation of Internalization to the Development of Conscience.
2) Socio-emotional, Perceptual-motor, Cognitive Development.
3) Testing for Conceptualization of a Value.

This is a very special meeting and the first of its kind to be held in the Division. I do hope therefore you will make a special effort to be present.

Yours sincerely
G. E. Ferguson

Bill replied accordingly.

Dear Mr Ferguson,

Thank you for your letter requesting my attendance at the meeting in your office on Thursday 30th June at 12 noon, and I am pleased to inform you that I shall be able to be present. As the subjects under discussion have been studied by me at various times — indeed I have Honours Degrees in all three of them — I feel sure that I shall have a worthwhile contribution to make. I was most relieved to observe there was no indication of any Bacchanalian connotations, although as this is the first meeting of its kind to be held in the Division, I shall be pleased to assist in the baptismal ceremony.

Yours sincerely

W.G.M.S

Bill was not the only one to be leaving work for the last time at the end of that academic year. Jack McKenzie had been a pal of Bill's for over forty years. First pictured together at varsity OTC camp, their life journeys had been remarkably similar. They went through varsity, North Africa, Italy and the Edinburgh school system in parallel, culminating in headmaster roles for both. Jack had helped Bill drag his newly purchased trunk through the streets of Cairo in July 1942 before disappearing up into the blue. Now, thirty-five years later, they were both heading off into retirement.

To Jack and Bill

When the Khamsin wind was blowing by Benghazi and Matru
And Sinclair and McKenzie were drinking Stella Brew
There in the Western Desert as the sun shot down at night
They planned for Dave and Douglas a world where all was right
By Maadi and Almaza and Abassia too
They did their bit for Britain like that other youngster — Drew
Bardin, back in Blighty, they battled on once more
Frizell, George Keith and Catterly, directors by the score
But now they're going to leave us and this we'd like to say
Thank you for your company and help in every way!

June 1977, Allah Keyfik

Lisbeth retired at the same time as Bill and the two began to enjoy their freedom. They took holidays to their static caravan in Comrie and drove the VW Camper to Norfolk, Yorkshire and further afield to Germany. Family holidays to Kingstone continued and there were excursions to Vancouver to see Craig and Maggie in 1978 and 1981. Bill and Lisbeth celebrated their Ruby Wedding Anniversary on 28th October 1980 with families Sinclair,

Verth and Robbie all in attendance at Bramdean Rise.

For someone who had contributed so much to the Allied effort in the war and to his beloved Edinburgh and local community across subsequent years, Bill's diagnosis in 1982 was simply unfair. There was also nothing to be done; the pancreatic cancer had already advanced to the point of no return. As humble and stoic as ever, Bill recorded key events, people and moments in his life, and wrote letters to his grandchildren wishing them well and offering snippets of advice. As with everything in his life, he prepared well.

William George McKenzie Sinclair passed away peacefully at home at 8.30pm, on 10th November 1982. He was sixty-six years old. His funeral service was held at Mortonhall Crematorium, Edinburgh, on 15th November.

Lisbeth continued to live at Bramdean Rise until the size of the house and garden necessitated a move. Craiglea Place was a short distance away and offered familiarity and independence in the relative comfort of a retirement complex. She would later move up to Grantown on Spey to be near her daughter Ann, who retired with Bob to the nearby village of Nethy Bridge in 1998.

Elizabeth McGillivary Sinclair (née Verth) stayed in Grantown on Spey until her death on 7th February 2002, aged eighty-six. Her funeral service was held at Mortonhall Crematorium, Edinburgh, on 14th February. Lisbeth's eulogy contained the following words:

> Following the birth of Ann in 1941 and Craig in 1947, Lisbeth had devoted her energies to creating a happy and stable environment in which to raise her young family. Northumberland Place, Lanark Road, Comiston Road and Bramdean Rise were the source of many good memories for family and friends. Throughout her life, Lisbeth gave freely of her time and abilities, especially her

musical talent, playing the piano at church groups, hospitals and schools. As Ann and Craig grew older, she commenced work as a peripatetic music teacher in the Edinburgh school system, encouraging and inspiring her pupils in music making, ranging from choral singing to instrument playing. She later worked alongside Bill at Dumbryden until retirement in 1977.

Lisbeth was a lifelong churchgoer, being initially associated with St. Andrews and latterly Fairmilehead and Greenbank Parish churches. Her faith sustained her after Bill's untimely death. Thereafter, she was involved with various church activities, whether it be visiting the housebound and elderly, or volunteering assistance in the City Hospital tea room. Lisbeth was always quick to play the piano and regularly played for services at Craighouse Hospital. She was a gracious lady who gave of her time in a selfless manner.

*****

War shaped Bill's life. The Great War took his father's life before the two had chance to meet, leaving Bill an only child. The Second World War took Bill away from his family, his new wife and the daughter he'd never seen. These experiences shaped him mentally, teaching him to be stoic, practical, pragmatic — and to compartmentalise. Bill naturally felt a strong sense of public duty, but this was strengthened by the impact war had on him and the lives of those he held dearest.

Bill took this sense of duty forward into his teaching career. Determined to instil a sense of empathy, care and understanding in his pupils, he also encouraged them to strive to be the best they could be. He thought one of the most significant and positive impacts he could make was to empower his pupils. His approach and success were perhaps best summed up in the following letter of 1st July 1977, written by fellow teacher Hector Campbell on the occasion of Bill's retirement.

> I'd like to record my thanks to you not only for the beneficial influence you had on mine and the other kids who were in your care, but also for the overall effect you had on the development of the [Wester Hailes] scheme, particularly in its early days. I have not been in the scheme for some time, but I think that Wester Hailes would now be looking like a bomb site had it not been for the values you instilled in the kids with regard to care of trees, plants and things generally. The debt owed to you by the people of Wester Hailes may never be realised, but I was aware of it, and value my brief association with you. I hope that you and Mrs Sinclair have a long and happy retirement. You've certainly earned it.

Former pupils continued to send Bill letters and Christmas cards after his retirement. Lisbeth continued to receive these after her husband's death and after Lisbeth's passing in 2002, Ann became the recipient and the legacy continued.

Bill Sinclair lived his life doing his duty. He was a loving husband and father; a courageous soldier; a loyal friend and team mate; and a generous and committed teacher and headmaster. In 2016, on the day of Ann's funeral, some thirty-nine years after Bill left the Edinburgh school system, a Nethy Bridge resident approached the family outside the Old Kirk. She had been a pupil of Bill's and recalled a man that had been an inspiration to many.

8 Bramdean Rise, Edinburgh

'Wilson Cup Winners, 1961'
Bill Sinclair: back row, right hand side

Bill Sinclair

Lisbeth and Bill Sinclair

'Dispatch Trophy 1961'
Herriot's Former Pupils team
H. Brownlee (back left), I. Watt (back right)
Bill Sinclair (front left), Dougie McVey (front right)

*'Wedding of
E.A. Sinclair and R.H. Robbie'*

Fairmilehead Church, Edinburgh
18th July 1964

Back: left to right
Margaret Macdonald, Bertie Robbie (Bob's mother), Henry Robbie (Bob's father)
Bob Robbie, Ann Robbie, Bill Sinclair (Ann's father), Lisbeth Sinclair (Ann's mother),
Sandy Robbie (Bob's brother)

Front: left to right
Rona Mitchell, Karen McLeod

*'Wedding of
M.R. McDowall and W.C. Sinclair'*

St. Mary's Church, Biggar
26th June 1971

Bottom: left to right
John McDowall (Maggie's father),
Lisbeth Sinclair (Craig's mother),
Craig Sinclair, Maggie Sinclair,
Maisie McDowall (Maggie's mother),
Bill Sinclair (Craig's father)

Lisbeth and Bill Sinclair
1982
Back garden of 8 Bramdean Rise, Edinburgh

AUTHOR'S RECOLLECTION

As a young boy I remember lying awake in bed one evening listening to the sounds below my bedroom; people talking, dishes being put away in kitchen cupboards, drawers closing with a bump — contents rattling. The voices migrated from kitchen to lounge and became lost beneath the noise of the television. The telephone on the hall table rang. Mum (Ann) answered it in her usual manner.

'Dapple Heath 697.'

Silence.

'Oh no!' she cried.

The sound of shock in Mum's voice brought me out of my bedroom. I peered downstairs to see what was going on. My dad strode out of the lounge into the hall; an ashtray in one hand, a cigar in the other, smoke trailing behind him. Mum clutched the phone to her chest, she had tears in her eyes.

'Dad has been diagnosed with pancreatic cancer!' she said with difficulty.

I didn't fully understand, but knew by the state Mum was in that it was terrible news. Her tears were infectious. I wanted to go downstairs, but instinct told me this was not the time to be asking questions.

My parents retreated to the lounge, their muffled conversation replacing the sound of the television. Still sitting at the top of the stairs, I couldn't make out what was being said, so returned to my bedroom, climbed into bed and cried myself to sleep.

*****

Ann Robbie (née Sinclair) was my mum. Bill Sinclair was my grandad. I remember little about the immediate aftermath of that evening in 1982, when news broke of his cancer diagnosis.

From that evening until Grandad's passing, things — at least in my mind — happened quickly. The family travelled north and visited Grandad at home in Edinburgh. At the time I was unaware that his cancer was terminal. The quantity of get-well-soon cards suggested otherwise. However, looking back, there was a kind of finality that came with the family photographs taken that day in the back garden, and the letters Grandad wrote to nearest and dearest. He wrote mine on 10th October 1982 from the Edinburgh Royal Infirmary and passed away one month later.

If I had to produce a word to describe my grandad it would be: engaging. Although I was only ten years old when he died, I have very clear and fond memories of time spent with him visiting the National Museum in Edinburgh, standing on the Heart of Midlothian, watching games at Tynecastle and playing cards. He taught me so much, but made everything seem like fun — smart man.

One thing he taught me was how to hold a golf club and how to make slight shifts of grip and stance depending on the club, the lie of the ball, or the gradient of the slope. With those lessons came warnings to be careful playing golf, particularly with mates wielding golf clubs and trying to smash the ball away. How I wish I'd listened. In 1982, during a visit south to Kingstone in the February half-term holiday, Grandad brought some clubs for me to practise with. I told him I was going out to play with some mates.

'Who's going?' he asked.

'Dunno,' I replied. 'Probably Corbo, B, Charlie, Bode, Tithead, Boog and Bloory.

'A motley crew. Sounds like a bunch of lads I used to know. You make sure you're careful. No accidents,' he said.

His words were ringing in my ears when I ran back into the house thirty minutes later holding my chin. One of the lads had accidently hit me with a five-iron and there was blood everywhere.

Mum drove as fast as possible to Stafford old hospital with Grandad holding my chin with a dish cloth. I will always remember waiting in A&E and seeing a butcher being carried in by two friends with what must have been a twelve-inch knife embedded in his knee.

'I wonder if his grandad told him to be careful,' said Grandad as he put a comforting arm around my shoulder.

On another occasion, I remember Charlie (real name Mark) calling for me one morning. I answered the back door and invited Charlie in to the kitchen, where Grandad asked him if he wanted some toast.

'Yes please,' Charlie replied.

Grandad popped the toast on a plate and asked Charlie if he wanted butter on it. When Charlie said yes, Grandad unwrapped a new pat and dropped the entire thing on top of the toast. Handing it to Charlie he asked, 'Is that enough butter?' We burst out laughing.

That's the kind of thing I remember about Grandad. A childish, slapstick sense of humour with a dry wit to match. A charismatic man who engaged with all those around him.

Some years after Grandad's death, the house at Bramdean Rise became too much for Gran to manage and I helped her clear the place out in readiness for her move to Craiglea Place. In the attic, sifting through boxes that hadn't seen daylight for decades, I found a small suitcase and large trunk, tucked away in a corner. I dragged the trunk (purchased in Cairo) closer to the attic entrance to shed some light on it and lifted the lid. It contained a mass of printed documents, photographs, hand-written notes, souvenirs, maps and cypher messages marked 'TOP SECRET'. The small suitcase contained the letters Grandad wrote home between January 1940 and December 1945.

Fast forward twenty-five years and I resolved to build a structured archive and share Grandad's remarkable journey and inspiring story. I only hope I have done it justice.

Colin Robbie

THE JOURNEY

1. Edinburgh
2. Invergowrie
3. Aberdeen
4. Chester
5. Aldershot
6. Droitwich
7. Gosport
8. Stonehaven
9. Peterhead
10. Cullen
11. Stirling
12. Burton-on-Trent
13. Uttoxeter
14. Liverpool
15. Greenock
16. Freetown
17. Durban
18. Geneifa
19. Cairo
20. Tripoli
21. Mareth
22. Sfax
23. Sousse
24. Souk El Khemis
25. Tunis
26. Malta
27. Syracuse
28. Catania
29. Messina
30. Taranto
31. Vasto
32. Venafro
33. Arezzo
34. Cesena
35. Mestre
36. Udine
37. Klagenfurt
38. Milan
39. Calais
40. Edinburgh

BIBLIOGRAPHY

Bullen, Andrew. 1987. "Country dance and song." *Country dance and song society.* Accessed September 17th, 2018. https://www.cdss.org/images/cds_online/country_dance_and_song/v.17.pdf.

Cameronians. n.d. *Brigadier Roy Gilbert Thurburn.* Accessed June 30th, 2019. http://cameronians.siteiscentral.com/1901/people/thurburn.

Cheshire Regiment. 1939. *The Old 22nd.* Chester: Practical Press Ltd., London.

Commonwealth War Graves Commission. n.d. *The Italian Campaign.* Accessed October 3rd, 2019. https://www.cwgc.org/history-and-archives/second-world-war/campaigns/war-in-the-west/the-italian-campaign.

Edinburgh Evening News. 1968. "Golfer tells how best friend died." *Evening News*, September 3rd.

Everton Football Club. n.d. *Players: Jock Thomson.* Accessed February 12th, 2019. http://www.evertonfc.com/players/j/jt/jock-thomson.

George Heriot's School Former Pupils Golf Club. 1961. *https://www.heriotsfpgolfclub.co.uk/about/history/2/.* Accessed July 30th, 2019.

Headquarters, 15th Army Group - Italy. 1945. *Finito! The Po Valley Campaign.* Headquarters, 15th Army Group - Italy.

Holdoway, Mike. n.d. *Military Convoys WS.10.* Accessed February 12th, 2019. http://convoyweb.org.uk/ws/index.html.

Holocaust Encyclopedia. n.d. *Allied military operations in North Africa.* Accessed September 16th, 2019.

https://encyclopedia.ushmm.org/content/en/article/allied-military-operations-in-north-africa.

Imperial War Museum. 2018. *The legacy of the Nuremberg Trials.* December 13th. Accessed October 10th, 2019. https://www.iwm.org.uk/history/iwm-after-hours-the-legacy-of-the-nuremberg-trials.

Ministry of Information (for the War Office). 1944. *The Eighth Army (September 1941 to January 1943).* London: His Majesty's Stationery Office.

National Archives. n.d. "National Archives Collection of World War II War Crimes Records." *National Archives.* Accessed September 24th, 2019. https://www.archives.gov/research/guide-fed-records/groups/238.html.

Rangers Football Club. n.d. *Hall of fame: Willie Thornton.* Accessed February 13th, 2019. https://rangers.co.uk/club/history/hall-of-fame/willie-thornton/.

Ryder, Rowland. 1987. *Oliver Leese.* London: Hamish Hamilton Ltd.

Wolverhampton Wanderers Football Club. n.d. *Hall of Fame: Stan Cullis.* Accessed January 16th, 2019. https://www.wolves.co.uk/club/history/hall-of-fame/stan-cullis/.

INDEX

Page numbers in **bold** refer to illustrations.

Oor wee schouls a grate wee skool.
Its made o briks an plaster.
The only thing that's rong wi its'
The boldie heedid mastur.

Taken from the book *This is your life* presented to Bill Sinclair
on retiring from Dumbryden School, 1977